A History of Contraception

FAMILY;
SEXUALITY AND SOCIAL RELATIONS
IN PAST TIMES

GENERAL EDITORS:
Peter Laslett, Michael Anderson and Keith Wrightson

Western Sexuality: Practice and Precept in Past and Present Times
Edited by Philippe Ariès and André Béjin
Translated by Anthony Forster

The Explanation of Ideology: Family Structures and Social Systems
Emmanuel Todd
Translated by David Garrioch

The Causes of Progress: Culture, Authority and Change
Emmanuel Todd
Translated by Richard Boulind

The English Noble Household, 1250–1600
Kate Mertes

An Ordered Society: Gender and Class in Early Modern England
Susan Dwyer Amussen

Porneia: On Desire and the Body in Antiquity
Aline Rousselle
Translated by Felicia Pheasant

Medieval Prostitution
Jacques Rossiaud
Translated by Lydia G. Cochrane

Wet Nursing: A History from Antiquity to the Present
Valerie Fildes

Sexuality and Social Control, Scotland 1660–1780
Rosalind Mitchison and Leah Leneman

Highley 1550–1880: The Story of a Community
Gwyneth Nair

A History of Contraception:
From Antiquity to the Present Day
Angus McLaren

FORTHCOMING

Mobility and Marriage: The Family and Kinship in Early Modern London
Vivien Brodsky

The Country House Establishment
Jessica Gerard

The British Servant in the Twentieth Century
Kate Mertes

The Making of a Woman's World
Kate Mertes

Marriage and the English Reformation
Eric Carlson

The Children of the Poor, 1660–1914
Hugh Cunningham

A History of Contraception

From Antiquity to the Present Day

Angus McLaren

Basil Blackwell

Copyright © Angus McLaren 1990

First published 1990

Basil Blackwell Ltd
108 Cowley Road, Oxford, OX4 1JF, UK

Basil Blackwell, Inc.
3 Cambridge Center
Cambridge, Massachusetts 02142, USA

British Library Cataloguing in Publication Data
A CIP catalogue record for this book is available from the British Library.

Library of Congress Cataloging in Publication Data

McLaren, Angus.
A history of contraception: from antiquity to the present day/Angus McLaren.
p.   cm. — (Family, sexuality, and social relations in past times)
ISBN 0–631–16711–0
1. Birth control—History. 2. Contraception—History. I. Title. II. Series
HQ766.M35   1991
363.9'6'—dc20
90 34917
CIP

Typeset in 11 on 13 pt Garamond
by Hope Services (Abingdon) Ltd
Printed in Great Britain by T. J. Press Ltd., Padstow, Cornwall

Contents

Preface and Acknowledgements

The writing of this book was suggested to me by Virginia Murphy of Basil Blackwell. I was at first reluctant to embark on the ambitious and possibly foolhardy attempt to trace over the space of something like three thousand years the changing motivations of those seeking to control fertility. But once I began the research and writing, I found it a far more pleasurable project than I had anticipated. Readers with quite different backgrounds and perspectives will, I think, share the excitement I felt in discovering that the issues raised by even the most recent breakthroughs in reproductive technologies are firmly rooted in the cultural traditions of the west.

My work on the history of procreation was begun many years ago and has benefited from the generous assistance of many scholars. I owe special debts to Arlene Tigar, Lesley Biggs, Barbara Brookes, Catherine Crawford, Donna Dippie, Ellen Gee, Diana Gittins, John Gillis, Deborah Gorham, Ludmilla Jordanova, Jean L'Esperance, Ralph Houlbrouke, Andrée Lévesque, David Levine, Jane Lewis, James Mohr, Wendy Mitchinson, Geoffrey Quaife, James Reed, Ellen Ross, Joan Sangster, Chiara Saracemo, Veronica Strong-Boag, Judith Walkowitz and Adrian Wilson. In writing this book I had to venture into areas about which I knew very little. For critical readings of the manuscript and expert advice, I have to thank Keith Bradley, Brian Dippie, Tim Haskett, Michele Muchahey, Mary Lynn Stewart and Wally Seccombe. Peter Laslett kindly provided a critique of the final draft. They saved me from making many blunders; they all would have liked me to have made further changes. I am responsible for the mistakes that remain.

Friendly help was provided in the archives and libraries in which I worked in Canada, the United States, Britain and France. Especially useful sources are housed in the Sophia Smith Collection of Smith College, the Houghton Library of Harvard University, the

Countway Library of Medicine in Boston, Massachusetts, the British Library, the Wellcome Institute for the History of Medicine in London and the Library of Congress. The editors I have dealt with at Basil Blackwell made the publication process a pleasure.

I was able to carry out the work on this study because of a research time stipend grant provided by the Social Sciences and Humanities Research Council of Canada. I thank the Council for its generosity.

All unattributed translations are my own.

Introduction

A number of books have been written on the history of the regulation of reproduction and, in particular, the advance of birth control. Most serve the unintentional purpose not so much of providing an understanding of past cultures as of applauding our own. The first question their authors usually ask is *when* did restriction of fertility begin. Having established their benchmark in the eighteenth or nineteenth century and named their 'pioneers', they then proceed to chronicle 'advances' made in the production and distribution of birth-control devices. Women in the 'bad old days' of the pre-industrial world, such works commonly argue, were plagued by repeated unwanted pregnancies; in rational modern societies reliable contraceptives assure control of one's body.[1] Family size is smaller today, biological forces have been subdued by modern technologies, but are such changes best interpreted as a simple passage from subjection to freedom? A glance at two 'snapshots' of fertility control in action suggests otherwise. The first, taken in the fourth century, is of St Augustine, or rather of Augustine prior to his religious conversion. This upper-class North African, although cohabiting with two concubines in succession for over fifteen years, fathered only one child. Presumably such low fertility resulted from Augustine's and his partners' employing those 'execrable' methods 'against nature' which he was later to lead Christians in condemning.[2] Our second photo, provided by two medical sociologists, is a 1975 group portrait of 200 clients of an American inner city pre-natal clinic. On examining it closely we find that 21 per cent had aborted, 15 per cent had miscarried, 60 per cent had experienced an undesired pregnancy, 25 per cent did not know why they had become pregnant, 25 per cent did not understand the contraceptive methods they employed, 40 per cent said they and their partners did not agree on the method, and 14 per cent said they did not discuss it with their spouse.[3] What is one to do with this sort of evidence? It would be foolish to suggest that in the course of 1500 years little progress was made in fertility control, but such cases might make one a bit more cautious in following those social scientists who argue that the history of family planning is a tale of unalloyed advances.

Such researchers often speak of two 'contraceptive revolutions'. The first was the employment by men in the eighteenth and nineteenth centuries of coitus interruptus. 'Until then', asserts Martine Segalen, 'people had not even imagined the possibility of influencing the sexual act, which was an act of nature, and it was this change in attitude towards their bodies that constituted a revolution in mentalities.' The second of Segalen's revolutions took place in the 1960s with the advent of the pill and legalized abortion. 'The *real* difference between them [the two revolutions] is that modern contraception is a female matter. For the first time, the responsibility for creating life is given to those who bring it forth.'[4] Segalen – along with most scholars interested in the history of fertility – is understandably fascinated by the past century's dramatic decline in family size, which freed women from lifelong careers of bearing and rearing children. This plummeting of western fertility, so carefully documented by demographers, may well be the most important single change to have affected the mass of the population in the last hundred years. An argument can be made that the modern nuclear family is both a cause and effect of highly effective forms of contraception.

But historians, in sharply contrasting a world in which fertility is technologically restricted with one in which it was not, run the risk of ignoring important nuances. Those who ask *when* fertility first came to be 'controlled' consciously or unconsciously avoid contemplating the possibility that perhaps it was *always* controlled. Family planners of the 1950s, imbued with the view that the Third World's population crisis could only be solved if it adopted western contraceptive practices, popularized the idea of science's recent, sudden triumph over fertility. Western societies, they cheerfully conceded, were once as incapable as today's developing world in rationally restricting family size. The emergence of a 'modern mentality' was what saved us; the Third World's salvation similarly lay in embracing the solutions offered by modern medicine.

Most social scientists who advanced such claims were men. They based their arguments on the evidence of earlier generations of male doctors, demographers and politicians that 'revolutionary' changes in attitudes towards childbearing took place in the late nineteenth century. Such arguments had certain weaknesses. In the first place they were ethnocentric and narrowly focused on the recent past. Could not one describe as 'revolutionary' the Christian condemnation in the late Roman Empire of the resort to infanticide, abortion and contraception which had long been employed and condoned? And in the second place such theorists rarely considered the evidence offered by women. Would a woman in the early twentieth century faced with an undesired pregnancy feel much different, one wonders, from her eighteenth- or thirteenth-century counterpart?

Keeping in mind that childbearing has always necessarily meant different things to men and women, I set out to review the vast literature pertaining to fertility control, and from the very outset was struck by the fact that there were as many continuities as revolutions in the history of western attitudes towards childbearing. Changes obviously did occur, but in taking a long-range view I soon discovered that the history of fertility control was marked by both 'breakthroughs' and 'reactions'. I had to conclude that any account of its history that suggested that reproductive decision making was once impossible but now was 'easy', that implied that it had ceased to be a cause and consequence of conflict, was inadequate. There was always a concern to influence or shape fertility, to reduce or increase conceptions and births.

Such an hypothesis is not new. Carr-Saunders asserted in 1922 that even in prehistoric times attempts were made to control numbers. 'There is another class of factors the primary and not the incidental function of which is either to reduce fertility or cause elimination. These factors are prolonged abstention from intercourse, abortion and infanticide. The view put forward here is that normally in every primitive race one or more of these customs is in use.'[5] Norman Himes in his pioneering study, *A Medical History of Contraception*, went so far as to declare that 'the desire for control is neither time nor space bound. It is a universal characteristic of social life.'[6] But what Carr-Saunders and Himes failed to document were the ways in which changes in fertility-control ideas and practices influenced and were affected by changes in family forms and gender roles. Moreover, in his propagandizing defence of birth control Himes skirted the question of whether or not fertility control could be turned to contradictory purposes. Today it is easier to see that, though it can be liberating for women, a high rate of fertility control does not necessarily mean women enjoy greater freedom. To understand fully the purposes to which fertility controls are turned requires locating them in their cultural setting.

Research on the fertility of past societies has been carried out primarily by demographic historians and economists. Their deterministic models do go some way in accounting for long-term variations in fertility, but at a price. Although the more sensitive quantifiers acknowledge that 'culture' has to be somehow built into their equations, most are clearly ill at ease when dealing with such a slippery subject. A simple, linear history of the development of fertility control can, in short, be easily provided, but only at the cost of wrenching the issue of procreation out of its cultural context. I have chosen what some might take to be a maddeningly roundabout approach to the subject. I have drawn on demographic, medical, literary, religious, family and women's history to show the complex ways in which reproductive decision making was entangled in a web of social, cultural and gender relationships. Changes in attitudes towards limitation of number of children, I argue, can only be understood if placed in the context of both economic and social conditions and evolving religious, medical and philosophical preoccupations. Childbearing, I will seek to show, has always been weighed as much in emotional as in economic terms. In the modern west we tend to think that birth control is used simply to limit number of pregnancies. But such controls have been exercised in other times and cultures for a variety of purposes. In some periods the promotion rather than the limitation of fertility was sought. The changes in the fertility rate and the means employed to bring about such changes were always contingent. Fertility control, I suggest, is best understood not as somehow predetermined but as a contested outcome, one possibility amongst many.

This study is based on two key premises. The first is that there have always been societies, or at least important groups within them, who have for one reason or another, at some periods in their history, taken steps to limit their progeny. The methods employed depended on particular circumstances. The idea of fertility control was rarely absent, but the motivation to act on such ideas varied. The technological means necessary to restrict fertility could always be produced when necessary. There was accordingly no unilinear growth in fertility control practices; they emerged at times and disappeared at other times. I have carefully avoided the temptation to take the Whiggish line of argument that the movement was one from ignorance to knowledge, from 'primitive' to ever more effective forms of contraception; the point of this study is that each age gave its own meaning to effective family planning and invented its own methods of exerting control.

This is not to say changes did not occur. The awareness of what a couple or woman could do through deliberate action to influence procreation, the means available (availability being both a technical and a cultural matter) and the degree to which such actions allowed people to have the children they wanted when they wanted altered over time. Similarly what constituted a 'large' or 'small' family was a question of perception, with new norms often quickly internalized. The modern contraceptive 'revolution' is in some senses simply an increase in the degree of control available and the percentage of the population exercising such controls, though obviously it also marks a change in the mode of regulation, a shift from the spacing to the stopping of births. Fertility control has always been a culturally dependent category. Accordingly it is impossible to write 'the' history of the patterning of fertility, since the experience of each society has been unique.

Different cultures employed different methods of family limitation. It is presumptuous to make authoritative claims as to the effectiveness of many of the fertility-control strategies employed in past times. Doctors tell us that most of the purported abortifacients and herbal contraceptives that will be mentioned could not 'work'. What has to be noted, however, is that such concoctions had both a symbolic and a practical value. At the very least the exchange of such recipes by networks of women shored up a sense of female solidarity; at best some did provide a vital margin of protection. But why, if even such unreliable controls were available, is the evidence of their employment rarely noted in historical accounts? If the evidence has been slighted it is due in part to the fact that few researchers have asked the right questions or employed the right sources. I am reminded of Planned Parenthood's recent complaint that the American television networks dedicate tens of thousands of hours to depicting sexual encounters, but never make any mention of contraception. A future historian basing his or her account of twentieth-century sexual mores on such television scripts would reasonably conclude that North America was ignorant of birth control.

If by fertility restriction one means employment of modern contraceptives, obviously it is not going to be found in the past. But if the definition of control is broadened to include whatever methods were employed – including 'natural means' such as abstinence and extended nursing – to reduce overall family size, different conclusions can be reached. In fact there is abundant evidence of a vast variety of fertility-control practices having been employed in past times. Indeed the abstinence, abortion, withdrawal and extended nursing which were used by the ancient Greeks were to remain the basic forms of family limitation employed by the mass of the population until well into the twentieth century. Only in the 1960s with the arrival of the oral contraceptive and the plastic IUD did the public's complete faith in a fertility 'technological fix' fully blossom.

It was perhaps a momentary triumph. Middle-class North American women who had been the first to employ the pill were, from the 1970s, the first to give it up and swing back to barrier methods of contraception. These women also led the return to a postponement of marriage and an extension of breastfeeding.[7] Overseas family planners at about the same time began to realize that modern methods of birth control could not simply be imposed upon Third World countries. Such contraceptives, even when adopted, often only replaced traditional methods used to space births. More worrying was the finding that technological forms of family limitation could undermine the success of traditional fertility-controlling practices – the oral contraceptive, for example, put an early end to a woman's ability to space births by extended breastfeeding – and thus have the perverse effect of actually driving up the birth rate.[8] The most positivistic social scientists were forced to concede that even the modern contraceptive's 'effectiveness' is socially determined.

The second premise on which this book is based is that reproductive decisions are of greater significance to women than to men.[9] By asking who has sought to control reproduction one opens up the issue of the politics of human fertility. Such concerns have recently become common currency as a result of the moral and legal dilemmas posed by the debate over abortion and the surge in reproductive technologies. But this study argues that the question of gender relations – who controls fertility and for what purposes – is not a recent development. This debate can be traced back as far as we can see. There has never been a culture whose people have been indifferent to this question or who have been prepared to assign all causal influences to extra-volitional forces. Take the example of whether or not a mother breastfed her child. If she extended her lactation up to two years she not only assured the health of her child; she also provided herself with a margin of safety against a subsequent conception. In some societies a taboo against intercourse while a woman was nursing supplemented the protection offered by postpartum amenorrhoea. But if the husband insisted on enjoying his conjugal rights – a claim supported by some religions – the well-being of both mother and child could be jeopardized.

At an even more basic level it can be argued that procreative outcome is a result of conflicting gender objectives and prerogatives because of the particular nature of western sexuality. Uninterrupted heterosexual coitus is only one possible form of sexual activity, but this form was made paramount and all others repressed. Demographers simply avoid the idea that it could be any other way. But because sexual desire and a sense of conjugal rights are powerful drives and determinants of coital behaviour; sexuality must be treated not as a given but as an 'independent variable'. Evidence on sexual ideology is scarce, but its influence in a procreative regime must be considered.

The following pages provide an overview of the interaction of changing gender relations and various forms of fertility control. Such a history has both its critical and its compensatory aspects. Since in the western world gender relationships have been ones of domination, the study takes into account the ways in which the larger society sought to turn to its own purposes women's reproductive power. But because such power was in the first place held by women, the study also attempts to unearth and analyse the suppressed and unarticulated ways in which they sought to control, and often succeeded in controlling, their fertility.

Anthropologists have shown us that in fertility regulation the

process and *meaning* are often as important as the outcome.[10]
Women gained status through motherhood, but what was often
most important for previous generations was not so much the
question of how many children were born as who bore them, when
and why. Marriage played the most obvious role in the social
regulation of fertility. The married woman's fertility was sanctioned
as crowning the family's success in mate selection and assurance of
heirs. But the community sought to repress the unmarried
woman's fertility, challenging as it did the notion of procreation
serving not individual but family interests.

Having large families did not mean married couples viewed
fertility control as unthinkable. Nor did resort to what we take to
be ineffective methods imply irrational resignation. To understand
fully the reproductive experience, the element of agency has to be
recognized as central. To comprehend what reproduction *meant* to
women in past times it is necessary to take seriously the vast range
of taboos, potions and rituals which they employed to limit
pregnancies. Similarly, their various attempts at increasing fertility,
spacing children, determining the children's sex and protecting
their own health need to be analysed to round out the discussion.
The procreative practices of past generations become intelligible
once we understand both what they were striving to achieve and
what they were able to achieve.

Anthropologists have also alerted us to the dangers of attempting
to isolate the issue of contraception from other fertility-regulating
practices. Early twentieth-century birth controllers, partly for tactical
purposes, attempted to draw a clear line between contraception
and abortion. But much of the evidence suggests that women
traditionally viewed both as located on a continuum of fertility-
regulating strategies. Moreover, the twentieth-century western
notion that abortion is employed only after contraceptive methods
fail was not necessarily shared in previous periods. Induction of
miscarriage was often the first line of defence against unwanted
pregnancies. Women often preferred practices that they controlled,
that did not require the assistance of either husband or doctor. This
study accordingly reviews the entire range of fertility-regulating
stratagems.

It follows that the history of the family has to serve as a
backdrop for this study because specific family forms led to the
employment of different types of fertility-controlling practice. In

the twentieth-century western world in which the companionate family became the norm, it was expected that communicative couples could successfully agree on the use of 'coitus-dependent' contraceptives such as the condom or douche. In societies where separate male and female cultures impeded such discussions women looked, not to their spouses, but to their female friends and relatives for advice on stratagems to be employed well before or after intercourse.[11] Confrontations between partners over appropriate forms of fertility regulation, despite the best wishes of marriage counsellors and birth controllers, were, of course, not put to an end by either the invention of modern contraceptives or companionate marriages.

Implicit in the arguments of most demographic and family historians is the idea that both the decline in family size and the rise of companionate marriage were 'good things' that separated off today's rational world from the irrational past. That such accounts are inherently ahistorical in that they tend to judge the past by the standards of the present has been the burden of the argument of a new generation of family historians, who are providing a more sensitive portrayal of earlier family forms. Feminist scholars have been particularly critical of the notion that the struggle between the sexes over reproduction is any less significant today than it was in previous centuries. Radical dichotomizations – traditional versus modern, irrational versus rational – are clearly misleading when applied to the history of fertility control. It is probably true to say that infertility has always been viewed as a problem and that childbearing has always provided women with status. It is also the case that in modern times lack of birth control exacerbated inequalities, and the provision of reliable contraceptives was a *means* of improving women's conditions. But the idea that contraception can by itself overcome social and economic inequalities is no longer seriously entertained. Indeed the contradictions and complexities posed by high-tech forms of fertility control are beginning to be acknowledged. The warning first voiced by feminists, that the new reproductive technologies have the potential of usurping women's reproductive power, has served as a fresh reminder that fertility regulation is never a simple issue.

Sociologists and anthropologists can ask their subjects about the most intimate subjects. The historian has to rely on written evidence in which detailed accounts of the actual employment of contraceptives are, not surprisingly, rarely encountered. Usually what we are really studying is the reaction of contemporaries to their employment. The analysis of western ideas and conceptions regarding procreation provides often little more than inferences about actual practices. Whether or not such practices were condoned, each age defined and judged them differently. Fertility control has always been a symbol and symptom of changes in the relationships of men to women, and of the family to the community. Did men and women have the same motivations to regulate fertility? Did concepts of mothering and fathering change over time? Did the economic value of children alter? Did the church and larger community seek to influence reproductive decisions? We better understand a society when we comprehend the meanings it gives to fertility limitation, and appreciate why, even in ages when such practices were purportedly not widely employed, they still drew so much attention.

This study is the first comprehensive overview of the history of fertility control since Himes' classic 1936 account. My goal in drawing on much recent work in family, medical and women's history has been to provide an accessible, interpretative synthesis. There have been many books and articles published in the last decade on the history of birth control in the modern period; I have accordingly devoted particular attention to the less well-known discussions of fertility that took place in the ancient and medieval worlds. In each of the book's seven chapters – devoted to the Greek world, the Roman Empire, the Christian west, the Middle Ages, early modern Europe, the industrializing west and the twentieth century – the intent has been to flush out the intended and unintended consequences of fertility control and their relationship to changing family forms and gender roles. The question remains the same; the answers always differ.

Notes

1 Peter Fryer, *The Birth Controllers* (Stein and Day, New York, 1965); Edward Shorter, *The Making of the Modern Family* (Basic Books, London, 1976); John Knodel and Etienne van de Walle, 'Lessons from the Past: Policy Implications of Historical Fertility Studies', *Population and Development Review*, 5 (1979), p. 227.

2 Brent D. Shaw, 'The Family in Late Antiquity: The Experience of Augustine', *Past and Present*, 115 (1987), pp. 45–6.
3 Shirley M. Johnson and Loudell F. Snow, 'Assessment of Reproductive Knowledge in an Inner City Clinic', *Social Science and Medicine*, 16 (1982), pp. 1657–62.
4 Martine Segalen, *Historical Anthropology of the Family* (Cambridge University Press, Cambridge, 1986), pp. 164, 166.
5 A. M. Carr-Saunders, *The Population Problem: A Study in Human Evolution* (Clarendon Press, Oxford, 1922), p. 214.
6 Norman E. Himes, *A Medical History of Contraception* (Williams and Wilkins, Baltimore, 1936), p. xii. On other views see John Caldwell, Pat Caldwell and Bruce Caldwell, 'Anthropology and Demography: The Mutual Reinforcement of Speculation and Research', *Current Anthropology*, 28 (1987), pp. 25–43.
7 J. E. Goldthorpe, *Family Life in Western Societies* (Cambridge University Press, Cambridge, 1987), pp. 164–5.
8 Malcolm Potts and Pouru Bhiwandiwala, eds, *Birth Control: An International Assessment* (MTP, Lancaster, Mass., 1979), p. 51.
9 Riaz Hassan, *Ethnicity, Culture and Fertility: An Exploratory Study of Fertility Behavior and Sexual Beliefs* (Chopmen, Singapore, 1980).
10 Lucile F. Newman, ed., *Women's Medicine: A Cross Cultural Study of Indigenous Fertility Regulation* (Rutgers University Press, Brunswick, NJ, 1985); William G. Archer, *Songs for the Bride: Wedding Rites of Rural India* (Columbia University Press, New York, 1985).
11 C. H. Brewer and Sandra T. Perdue, 'Women's Secrets: Bases for Reproductive and Social Autonomy in a Mexican Community', *American Ethnologist*, 15 (1988), pp. 84–94.

1

The Patterning of Fertility in Ancient Greece

'As many women are always doing, doctoring themselves'
Hippocrates (*c.*400 BC), 'Illnesses of Women'

Polybius (*c.*150 BC), although strictly speaking not a product of the classical era, left what was to become the most famous depiction of the population problem of ancient Greece.

> In our own time the whole of Greece has been subject to a low birth-rate and a general decrease of the population, owing to which cities have become deserted and the land has ceased to yield fruit, although there have neither been continuous wars nor epidemics. If then any one had advised us to send and ask the gods about this, and find out what we ought to say or do, to increase in number and make our cities more populous, would it not seem absurd, the cause of the evil being evident and the remedy being in our own hands? For as men had fallen into such a state of pretentiousness, avarice, and indolence that they did not wish to marry, or if they married to rear children born to them, or at most as a rule one or two of them, so as to leave these in affluence and bring them up to waste their substance, the evil rapidly and insensibly grew.[1]

Polybius' pro-natalist lament has such a modern ring that it is difficult to avoid the notion that the Greeks in their concerns for over- or under-population were 'just like us'. But to provide a cultural history of fertility control it is necessary to do more than simply tot up every reference to what today we might interpret as contraceptive acts. Fertility and fertility-control tactics are cultural artifacts. The historian seeking to understand earlier societies has to make a conscious effort to avoid asking the anachronistic question of how close they came to sharing our values and practices. Certain acts employed by the Greeks no doubt either curbed or encouraged fertility, but to appreciate whether that was their prime purpose or an unintended consequence we have to determine how they were regarded at the time. What often mattered was not so much the act as the social construction of meanings given to it and the individual responses to such meanings. In order to place the issue of fertility control in its social setting, I begin this chapter with an analysis of men's and women's roles in the Greek family, then turn to ancient attitudes towards procreation and finally – in the light of what we know of the familial and cultural concepts of the age – review the available evidence on fertility control.

In the ancient world families were relatively small. A variety of causes played a role. Life expectancy was short, at birth probably no more than twenty or thirty. A study of skeletal remains in Greece has suggested an average life expectancy for those who survived childhood of 45.0 years for men and 36.2 for women, but even this sounds too high. Birth and death rates per year hovered between thirty-five and fifty per thousand of the population. In good times only modest population growth could be expected; in bad times the intermittent scourges of war and famine wiped out entire generations.[2]

Married life was not viewed by all as an unalloyed pleasure. Many men chose not to marry; those who did wed produced small broods. Given women's early age of marriage (between fourteen and seventeen) five to six births were possible, but it has been estimated that on average only about four children were born and only two to three survived. A number of reasons have been advanced to explain such reduced numbers. Even amongst the married the public tolerance and, in the Greek case, the lauding of male homosexuality could have played a part in limiting reproduction. In Crete homosexuality was, according to Aristotle, officially supported as a population control tactic.[3] Dedicated heterosexuals had their own options. Widespread resort to courtesans provided a sexual outlet to males who preferred not to impregnate their wives. And even if children were conceived, the malnutrition and diseases that mothers experienced no doubt resulted in high levels of fetal wastage.

Small family size resulted from both high mortality rates and restrictions on fertility that were often the unintended consequences of non-procreative social practices. But many consciously sought to limit births. The manipulation of fertility was clearly desired and believed to be possible.[4] Plato, for example, when responding to the question of how population stability could be assured, responded: 'There are many devices available: if too many children are being born, there are measures to check propagation; on the other hand, a high birth-rate can be encouraged and stimulated by conferring marks of distinction or disgrace.'[5] Abundant evidence indicates that many men and women in the ancient world concurred that fertility should and could be controlled. But given the nature of the ancient family, men and women might well have had different reasons for and employed different means in pursuing such a goal.

The position women enjoyed in the Greek family is still very much a subject of debate. Those who opt for the darker view of the Attic character stress the themes of male dominance and violence that permeated the ancient myths.[6] It is indeed difficult to ignore the countless references to patriarchy and misogyny in so much of Greek literature. Zeus had, according to Hesiod (c.700 BC) punished man for Prometheus' theft of fire by creating woman and endowing her with crafty speech, thievish habits and a licentious mind. Semonides, in what has been considered the earliest work in European literature devoted to women (c.640 BC), portrayed the female as rivalling in vice the sow, vixen, bitch, ass, ferret, mare and monkey.[7] Male mortals were, for their part, candidly outspoken defenders of a sexual double standard. 'We have', asserted an Athenian orator, 'courtesans for pleasure, concubines to look after the day-to-day needs of the body, wives that we may breed legitimate children and have a trusty warden of what we have in the house.'[8]

Optimistic scholars have argued that female status was not always as low as such rhetoric would imply. Fictional female characters like Penelope and Clytemnestra were represented in the Homeric poems as respected in the loosely structured family units of the eighth century BC. They were not restricted to childbearing and their procreative role was not as vital as it was to become in the fifth century, when the smaller family ethos emerged. Although the evidence is admittedly thin, one historian has concluded that,

'Since heirs were freely bred from concubines, or freely adopted, the child-bearing services of the wife were less critically essential than in an era when only the legitimate wife could produce a legitimate heir.'[9] This greater stress on the chastity and seclusion of women presumably emerged with the replacement of the older warrior aristocracies of the 'Dark Ages' by the urban oligarchies of the city states. Such a state was little more than a federation of the *oikoi* or households under the power of individual patriarchs. There was no Greek word for 'family' as we use the term today; the *oikos* included not only a man's wife and children but his slaves and property as well.

The domestication of females that took place in this particular family form, as spelled out in the laws, was obvious, respectable women in theory having no life outside the home. Determining the reality of the situation is more difficult. Women's position varied considerably according to class, time and place. Moreover, it must be remembered that our evidence is drawn primarily from documents pertaining to the lives of upper-class Athenians. The sort of female segregation envisaged would have been a luxury accessible only to an elite. Even within this segment of society female deference was so insisted upon that one has to suspect it was infrequently achieved. Certainly, Greek literature was peopled by powerful female characters. Depending on whether one looks at the portrayal of women in the law, theatre or medicine one comes away with distinctly different views of their status.[10] Perhaps the best that can be said is that for a variety of reasons men and women often lived quite separate lives. Males dominated the public world of the political forum, the gymnasium and the symposium. Women oversaw the domestic sphere. Sparta was famed for the liberties its women enjoyed, but elsewhere in Greece the ideal of female subservience and seclusion was pursued.[11]

The difference in the age of spouses presupposed quite different outlooks on life. Late age of marriage was eventually to become a major means by which Europeans maintained a fertility equilibrium. In the Greek cities men married at close to thirty (when their own fathers, if still alive, were preparing to make way for the next generation) whereas brides were often in their early teens. Aristotle regarded late marriage as healthy because 'to abstain from early marriage conduces to self-control; for women who have sexual intercourse too soon are apt to be wanton, and a man's body also is stunted if he exercises the reproductive faculty before the semen is full grown.'[12] An older husband presumably could more easily control a young wife, but Aristotle voiced the fear that she might prove sexually demanding. To dissuade men from entering into marriages in which there would be too great an age disparity the Athenian law held, claimed Plutarch, that the wife had a legal right to demand her husband be physically capable of fulfilling his conjugal duties at least three times a month.[13]

The arranged marriage was in effect a bargain struck by the father-in-law and the prospective son-in-law. The young bride entered a foreign household to obey a new patriarch and worship new gods. Love was expected to be a result rather than a cause of marriage; perhaps it was. The purpose of marriage, however, was to produce children. Anaxandridas, king of Sparta, according to Herodotus, at first refused to divorce his barren but 'much beloved' wife and only took a second spouse when forced by the magistrates.[14] Xenophon makes Socrates say: 'Surely you do not suppose that it is for sexual satisfaction that men and women breed children, since the streets are full of people who will satisfy that appetite, as are the brothels? No, it is clear that we enquire into which women we may beget the best children from, and we come together and breed children.'[15]

A male heir was essential. Only a man could be the owner or *kyrios* of his lands, children and spouse. A woman could not be a *kyria* because she was in effect a sort of 'guest' in the household. Daughters were never given up by their father, but only 'loaned' to other families. Should they divorce they returned with their dowries to the paternal home. Such was the concern in Athens that the family should not see its property alienated that Solon's law held that a daughter who had not yet produced a male heir, but who in losing her parents had become an 'heiress', was obliged to marry her father's next of kin, even if this required divorcing her husband.[16] The heiress in effect became part of the inheritance.

Since only males could be effective heirs a man might, if he had only daughters, adopt a young man for this purpose. The new heir in turn would be obliged to marry one of the daughters. Adoption was common in the ancient world, but those adopted were usually adults; the purpose was not to provide for the poor, but rather to obtain a suitable claimant to protect the family's property. As one's own children were often a disappointment adoption was, asserted the over-rational Democritus (c.400 BC), the most reasonable way in which to assure oneself of worthy inheritors.[17]

The ancient Greek familial system – which in its true form only applied to the property-owning elite – was motivated by the twin desires of making sure that no household was left without a male heir and no woman left unmarried. The ideal household was one which was self-sufficient and had children who maintained the family property and continued the worship of the family gods. The fertile wife was valued. She directed the domestic slaves, enjoyed temporary power while her husband was absent, and as a widow exerted considerable influence through her son. Indeed, the Greek myths were peopled with formidable female characters, argues Philip Slater, because Greek men never psychologically recovered from their impressionable childhood years of seclusion with terrorizing and doting mothers.[18]

The wife's fertility was honoured, but it was equally important – if the family's wealth were not to be divided up between too many claimants – that the number of children be limited. Hesiod summed up the view that one would 'hope for an only son to nourish his father's house, for this is how wealth waxes in the hall'.[19] The ideal was to have one son to maintain the family name and one daughter to cement a marriage alliance with another family. The goal was clear; the means employed to reach it – divorce, remarriage, adoption, contraception, abortion, exposure – depended on circumstance.

This notion that the Greek family, and in turn the city state, could only successfully function if procreation were controlled was a commonplace in public writings. The ancients did not view the arrival of every child simply as a blessing. Hesiod declared that one son was enough. Antiphon the Sophist (c.440 BC) warned, 'But in the very pleasure lies near at hand the pain; pleasures do not come alone, but are attended by griefs and troubles . . . Suppose children are born: then all is full of anxiety, and the youthful spring goes out of the mind, and the countenance is no longer the same.'[20] The critique of the large family was also implied in the negative view held of sexual excesses voiced by Plato and the Stoics.

Plato (c.429–347 BC) and Aristotle (c.384–322 BC) went furthest in envisaging the state's policing marriage and eugenically eliminating excess and unfit children. In The Republic Plato spoke of the need to regulate fertility so that offspring would not exceed the means of the community. In *The Laws* he advanced the idea of providing for the stability of the number of plot holders by having one heir per family.[21] Aristotle suggested – as had Plato – that the age of marriage be regulated, and abortion employed to regulate fertility: 'the proper thing to do is to limit the size of each family, and if children are then conceived in excess of the limit so fixed, to have miscarriage induced before sense and life have begun in the embryo.'[22]

Sparta was regarded as remarkable because of its policy of penalizing celibacy and rewarding childbearing. A man was freed of military duties upon the birth of his third son and of taxes with his fourth. But from the fourth century onward concerns were expressed throughout Greece for the need to control population. Phidon of Corinth wanted the numbers of families to remain stable. Philolacus of Thebes had laws passed that, in preventing the parcelling out of land, deterred excessively large families.[23]

It is perhaps not going too far to suggest that the Greeks took it as given that their family system only 'worked' if there were legitimate heirs, but not too many. The simplest way to have achieved this goal would have been to postpone the marriage of women and so limit their potential years of childbearing. But because of the desire to ensure male dominance, women were married off at an early age and could accordingly look forward to a long childbearing career. Moreover, members of the female elite seem to have preferred not to breastfeed and so deprived themselves of the protection against subsequent conceptions offered by extended lactation. They could thus expect their fertile years to be very full, as one pregnancy would be rapidly followed by the next. It followed that the Greeks, deprived of 'natural' defences against conception, had to turn to ideas of artificially controlling procreation.

In order to regulate fertility the Greeks first sought to understand how it functioned. But even when devoting themselves to the discussion of procreation, they revealed themselves as being as preoccupied by the question of who was responsible for new beings as with the question of how they came into existence. The basic question posed was whether men and women played similar roles. Given the patriarchal nature of Greek society it is not surprising that such discussions were coloured by a general assumption of female inferiority. An obvious jealousy of women's procreative power manifested itself in the tales of Zeus giving birth from his head to Athena and from his thigh to Dionysus, and of Aphrodite being born in the foam of the castrated Uranus' sperm. In Aeschylus' *Eumenides* woman was presented as little more than a nest for the growing conceptus: 'She who is called the mother is not her offspring's parent, but nurse to the newly sown embryo. The male – who mounts – begets. The female, a stranger, guards a stranger's child if no god bring it harm.'[24]

Those who denigrated woman's contribution to procreation denied her ability to produce seed. Anaxagoras (c.460 BC), the philosopher friend of Pericles who won fame for having denied the divinity of the heavenly bodies, claimed that males provided the seed and females only the 'ground' in which embryos were reared.[25] Aristotle says of him, 'Anaxagoras and some other philosophers hold that sex is already determined in the sperm. They say that while the father provides the seed, the mother only provides a place for the fetus to develop; that male offspring come from the right testis and female from the left; and that furthermore, male offspring develop in the right side of the womb, females in the left.'[26] Similarly Plato argued that 'the woman in her conception and generation is but the imitation of the earth and not the earth of the woman.'[27] For Diogenes the Cynic (c.400–325 BC) air was the life principle and male semen the 'foam' of the blood; the mother simply reared in the womb the offspring produced by the father.[28]

Aristotle produced the most thorough account of the reasons women could not play an active role in procreation. 'A boy', he asserted, 'actually resembles a woman in physique, and a woman is as it were an infertile male; the female, in fact, is a female on account of an inability of a sort, viz. it lacks the power to concoct semen out of the final state of nourishment (that is either blood, or its counterpart in bloodless animals) because of the coldness of its nature.'[29] Aristotle in short defined woman as a failure. He denied that she produced seed; if she could, he reasoned, she could reproduce by herself. Her menses were, he conceded, analogous to a man's semen, a residue from the blood but less concocted. They provided only the matter or nutritive faculty, whereas the seed provided the perceptive and intellectual faculties for the new being. Aristotle likened the male element operating on inactive female matter to a carpenter working on wood or to rennet changing milk into cheese.[30] If the seed succeeded in impressing form on matter, a male was produced; if it failed, a female resulted.

Aristotle's circular argument was that because women lacked heat they did not produce semen and their failure to produce semen proved they lacked heat.[31] Moreover, since they could not emit semen it followed that, unlike men who had to reach orgasm if conception were to take place, women's pleasure was not required. 'A sign that the female does not emit the kind of seed that the male emits, and that generation is not due to the mixing of both as some hold, is that often the female conceives without experiencing the pleasure that occurs in intercourse.'[32] Indeed Aristotle held that a woman's colder physiology was most influenced by the moon: 'the menstrual discharge in the natural course tends to take place when the moon is waning . . . . that time of the month is cooler and more fluid.'[33] Possibly the fear of female sexual dissatisfaction sent men scuttling in search of arguments that reassuringly explained that a man's failure to arouse his partner was due, not to his incompetence but to her inherently frigid nature.

Aristotle, like his contemporaries, had a limited knowledge of human physiology. He was ignorant of the existence of the ovaries and believed that the male testicles served only as a counterweight to the erect penis. But to believe that his theory was a result of faulty observation would be to misunderstand its purpose.[34] His intent was not to gather evidence but to erect a logical argument that stressed familiar sexual polarities. Aristotle revealed true genius in drawing on a corpus of common anti-female prejudices to produce a comprehensive explanation of generation and development.

The stridency with which male dominance in procreation was trumpeted makes it clear that such claims did not go uncontested. Indeed, the Aristotelian assertion of women's basically passive involvement in procreation was never more than a minority view, running counter as it did to the more commonsense assumption that their contribution was essential. Even the misogynistic Euripides makes Hippolytus complain – in a passage that sounds remarkably like a plea for test-tube babies – of women's crucial role in procreation:

Women! This coin which men find counterfeit!
Why, why, Lord Zeus, did you put them in the world,
in the light of the sun? If you were so determined
to breed the race of man, the source of it
should not have been women. Men might have dedicated
in your own temple images of gold,
silver, or weight of bronze, and thus have bought
the seed of progeny, . . . to each been given
his worth in sons according to the assessment
of his gift's value. So we might have lived
in houses free of the taint of women's presence.[35]

But, argued Parmenides (c.520), both men and women produced semen or seed. Seed from the right testicle in the right side of the uterus produced a boy, both from the left a girl, and the other combinations a boy resembling the mother or a girl resembling the father.[36] Alcmaeon of Croton in the early fifth century BC examined birds' eggs and believed that human offspring likewise developed from female ova.[37] Empedocles (c.450 BC) equated eggs and the seeds of trees. The seeds of men and women came together in the womb; the location in the womb of their mixing determined the sex of the fetus and the heat of the womb parental resemblance.[38] Democritus (c.400 BC), chiefly remembered for the development of atomic theory, likewise asserted that both sexes produced seed; their 'collision' in the womb created life.[39]

In the Hippocratic texts of the late fifth and fourth centuries BC female participation in procreation received its lengthiest treatment.[40] The writer of *On Generation* stated that both partners produced seed (although female seed was thinner than the male's), which explained why children could resemble either parent.

Now that both male and female sperm exist in both partners is an inference which can be drawn from observation. Many women have borne daughters to their husbands and then, going with other men, have produced sons. And the original husbands – those, that is, to whom their wives bore daughters – have as the result of intercourse with other women produced male offspring; whereas the second group of men, who produced male offspring, have yet with again other women produced female offspring. Now this consideration shows that both the man and the woman have male and female sperm.[41]

Seed, according to Hippocratic theory, was drawn from all parts of the body of each parent. The sex of the child and its resemblance to its parents depended on the quality and quantity of seed contributed. But to complicate matters the author of *On Regimen* argued that whether the child was strong or weak (and possibly its sex as well) was also predicated on the environment of the womb, the hot and dry being associated with males and the cold and wet with females. Both works did agree at least on the essential participation of the woman.[42]

Since women, like men, produced seed it followed – according to the Hippocratic theory – that they too would have to experience pleasure to ensure conception. 'Now as regards women in copulation', wrote the author of *On Generation*, 'I assert that when the genitals are rubbed and the womb agitated, there occurs in it a sort of tickling sensation, and the rest of the body derives pleasure and warmth from it. The woman has also a discharge that flows from the body sometimes into the womb so that the womb becomes moist, sometimes outside the womb too when the opening of the womb is wider than it ought to be.'[43] The Hippocratic texts, in assuming that procreation required both the pleasure and the active participation of women, suggested that this was one arena in which women were commonly regarded as being near equals with men.

Although the Greeks differed in their explanation of women's role in procreation, neither the followers of Hippocrates nor those of Aristotle appealed to any notion of supernatural intervention. They preferred to liken the process of childbearing to any number of agricultural and domestic tasks with which they were familiar. Coitus was frequently spoken of as analogous to a sowing of seeds, orgasm to the flare-up produced when wine was poured on a flame, the mixing of semens to a melting together of wax and fat, conception to the curdling of milk, the womb to an oven, the forming of the membrane round the conceptus to a crust hardening on bread or to the scum raised on a boiled liquid, the umbilical cord to a stalk, embryological development to vegetable growth and birth to the falling of ripe fruit.[44] These earthy metaphors were drawn particularly from women's household experiences. Their use implied procreation was marvellous, but not a mystery. They held out the promise that it, like the other challenges posed by nature, could to some extent be understood and controlled.[45]

What were the implications of this procreative ideology? It might be assumed that Aristotle's line of argument, denying women, as it did, any active part in generation, would place the burden of procreative responsibility on the man. Ironically, the followers of Aristotle, like those of Hippocrates, assumed that the onus had to be borne by the woman.

The written evidence suggests that procreative knowledge was first turned to ensuring conceptions. The medical sources contained far more written references to cures for barrenness than to contraceptives.[46] This could be taken as evidence that there was a widespread fear of sterility. The barren wife certainly risked being divorced. But much medical information, supplied as it was by men, also played an oppressive role in forcing women into heterosexual activity.[47] Women were warned, for example, that if they did not marry they would suffer from hysteria. The blood, the Hippocratic physician reported, 'surges up, because of its quantity, to the heart and diaphragm. These parts having become full, the heart becomes torpid; from the torpor numbness results, and from the numbness delirium . . . her visions enjoin her to leap about, to throw herself in wells, or to strangle herself, as if [such things] were good or had any sort of utility.' Coitus was, he concluded matter-of-factly, salubrious in that it kept the womb moist and so eased subsequent menses. 'My advice to young girls . . . is to marry as soon as possible; in effect, if they get pregnant, they will be cured.' 'Among married women', reads the *Diseases of Women*, 'sterile ones are the most susceptible.'[48]

Such was the womb's desire to be filled that it was presented in the texts as 'sucking up' semen. Of course, Plato used not dissimilar anthropomorphic language in describing the penis as 'disobedient and self-willed, like a creature that is deaf to reason, and it attempts to dominate all because of its frenzied lusts'. But the womb could be dangerously obstreperous. In the *Timaeus*, Plato referred to it as an 'animal' whose desire for procreation, if frustrated, resulted in serious complications. Greek physicians noted that in its anger it might 'wander' about the body; a common symptom being breathlessness caused when it pressured the lungs.[49] Luckily the womb had a sense of smell and could be either lured back into place with sweet pessaries or driven down by the patient's inhalation of pungent fumigations.[50]

Once the womb was in place one could proceed with ensuring conception. Greek medical theories stressed the notion that good health and, in turn, successful procreation lay in a balancing of the humours, the hot and the cold, the wet and the dry. Armed with these ideas men and women had recourse to a number of stratagems to guarantee a successful birth. Legumes, cereals and nuts were warming foods and so reputed to promote fecundity. The consumption by the bride of fruits that contained many seeds was also declared to be helpful. Hot ointments and fumigations could be employed to increase the receptivity of the womb. The time of year was also important because, as Aristotle reported, cold weather, cold water and the south wind impeded conception. 'Spring is the best season', stated the Hippocratic texts. 'The man must not be drunk, nor should he drink white wine, but strong unmixed wine, eat very strong food, not take a hot bath, be strong, in good health, abstain from unhealthful foods.'[51]

An interest was taken in predetermining the sex of the offspring. A hot diet produced boys and a cool diet girls. 'Females', declared the author of On Regimen, 'inclining more to water, grow from foods, drinks and pursuits that are cold, moist and gentle. Males, inclining to fire, grow from foods and regimen that are warm and dry. So if a man would beget a girl he must use a regimen inclining to water. If he wants a boy, he must live according to a regimen inclining to fire. And not only the man must do this, but also the woman.'[52] After conception, attempts to determine sex were made based on the belief that males sat on the right side of the womb and females on the left.

It is in this context of the Greeks' belief in the possibility of influencing procreation that their views on fertility control can best be understood. Indeed, most of the references to the placing of curbs on childbearing occur in the very discussions that treat problems of barrenness. Many regarded the issues as two sides of the same coin. But there were obvious differences in emphasis; it was not a straightforward matter of inversion. When the question of barrenness was discussed women were warned of the dangers lack of intercourse posed to their health. But when men chose to limit or avoid fathering children they were reassured that their abstinence was both prudent and healthy. 'Coition', warned

Democritus, 'is a slight attack of apoplexy. For man gushes forth from man and is separated by being torn apart with a kind of blow.'[53] Semen, according to the pessimistic Pythagoreans, was a 'clot of brain containing hot vapor within it' and consequently every sexual pleasure was harmful.[54] Plato, Aristotle and the Hippocratic corpus similarly stressed the need for sexual moderation. Whereas women were depicted in medical writings as requiring intercourse to maintain their well-being, men were presented as the best judges of the propriety of acts that could sap their strength. 'With this restriction on their intercourse', wrote Xenophon of the Spartans, 'the desire of the one for the other must necessarily be increased, and their offspring was bound to be more vigorous than if they were surfeited with one another.'[55]

Those who found abstinence difficult, yet were intent on restricting their fertility, had to turn to other means. Coitus interruptus was and is among the simplest forms of contraception, but there are remarkably few references to its employment in ancient Greece. Possibly Plato was referring to it when he spoke of 'sowing seed on stoney ground where it cannot grow fruit', and it might have been what Herodotus (c.484–420 BC) meant when he reported that Peisistratus, the tyrant of Athens, 'as he had already sons who were young men . . . therefore not desiring that children should be born to him from his newly-married wife, he had commerce with her not in the accustomed manner.'[56] The most famous references to withdrawal occurred in poetry. Archilochus of Paros, a seventh-century BC mercenary and poet, seemed to suggest coitus interruptus when describing the seduction of the younger sister of his fiancée:

> So much I said, but then I took the girl into the flowers in
> bloom and laid her down, protecting
>   her with my soft cloak, her neck held in my arms. Though
> out of fear like a fawn she hindered, I encouraged
>   her and her breasts with my hands gently grasped. She,
> then and there, herself showed young flesh – the onset
>   of her prime – and, all her lovely body fondling, I also let
> go with my force, just touching, though her tawny
>   down.[57]

If coitus interruptus was in the ancient world, as it was to be in nineteenth-century Europe, the main form of contraception, it is possible that references to it are scarce simply because there was no need or occasion to describe or report its employment. It may be that coitus interruptus – because it required a sacrifice of pleasure that few men were prepared to make – was not widely employed. The extraordinary value given male semen in the Aristotelian texts certainly provided a rationale for men's hostility to employing such methods. Even in modern times some cultures avoid the use of coitus interruptus and the same might have been true in the ancient world. But it is hard to believe, given the learned Greeks' sophisticated understanding of the process of procreation, that they were ignorant of the method's effectiveness. References are certainly made in the medical texts to specific types of body movements during and immediately after coitus which could inhibit or favour fertilization. In *On Generation* a suggestive passage reads: 'When a woman has intercourse, if she is not going to conceive, then it is her practice to expel the sperm from both partners whenever she wishes to do so. If however she is going to conceive, the sperm is not expelled, but remains in the womb.'[58]

Non-vaginal penetration would, of course, not be procreative. The Greek enthusiasm for homosexuality might well have popularized anal intercourse in heterosexual relationships. K.J. Dover has noted that when heterosexual scenes were depicted in Greek art they often suggested sodomy. He further speculates that the *hetairai* or courtesans employed anal intercourse as a birth-control method.[59] Himes notes as well that neither the Quran nor the Talmud forbad anal intercourse with one's wife.[60]

If withdrawal is classed as a 'male' form of contraception, the employment of occlusive pessaries, plugs and potions can be viewed as 'female' forms. Here the sources are more abundant and they make it clear that limitation of births was primarily a woman's business.[61] Even so we probably will never have a full account. The texts written by men necessarily provide only a hazy picture of women's actions and motives. Since breastfeeding inhibits ovulation, the most 'natural' way in which women could have protected themselves from a subsequent pregnancy would have been by extending their nursing of a first child. It appears, however, that upper-class Greek women sent their children to wet nurses, which meant that they had to seek other forms of protection.[62]

A number of herbal potions were believed by the Greeks to have a contraceptive effect. In this context it is noteworthy that the

Greeks had a word for the contraceptive – *atokion* – whereas in Latin there existed only a vague term – *venenum* – which meant 'poison'.[63] Even so it was not always clear whether the purpose of a brew was to prevent conception or terminate it. The *De materia medica* of Dioscorides (AD 40–80), in adding to the earlier herbal information of Theophrastus (*c.*300 BC) listed many recipes for drinks containing purportedly sterilizing elements such as the leaves or bark of hawthorn, ivy, willow and poplar. Boy-cabbage if drunk in goat's milk was reputed to excite the sexual impulse, but diminished it if eaten dry. Juniper berries placed on the penis or in the vulva was claimed to produce temporary sterility.[64] 'Misy', which appears to refer to copper sulphate, was recommended in the Hippocratic works where one disciple wrote, 'If a woman does not wish to become pregnant, dissolve in water misy as large as a bean and give it to her to drink, and for a year she will not become pregnant.'[65]

Potions were supplemented by recourse to various barrier methods of contraception. Dioscorides suggested anointing the genitals with cedar gum and applying alum to the uterus. Such substances would be regarded today as effective, inasmuch as they could not immobilize sperm. But as Aristotle explained it in *Historia Animalium*, 'by anointing that part of the womb on which the seed falls with oil of cedar, or with ointment of lead or with frankincense, commingled with olive oil', prevention was attained in making the womb a 'smooth' and thus an inhospitable environment to seed.[66]

Dioscorides referred to a peppermint and honey suppository employed prior to coitus and a peppery pessary to be used after coitus. According to Hippocratic theory such suppositories were effective not because they provided a barrier but inasmuch as they dried out the uterus.[67] Several Egyptian papyri contained references to plugs of honey, gum, acacia and crocodile dung. These recipes were employed by the Arabs and later reported in the west by Constantine the African.[68]

Attempts might have been made by Greek women to employ the rhythm method, though presumably with poor results; it was believed that conception was likely to occur either immediately before or after menstruation. The Hippocratic writer of *On Fleshes* noted that the *hetairai* or courtesans knew when they had conceived; the same was said in *On Generation* of 'experienced women'.[69] If all else failed recourse could be made to magic in the form of protective amulets and talismans. Dioscorides credited the asparagus root amulet with ensuring barrenness. Concoctions made up of a mule's kidney and the urine of a eunuch were declared by believers in sympathetic magic also to inhibit potency.[70]

Most of these contraceptive practices referred to stratagems employed by women; this was clearly 'female knowledge' of which male writers were often simply the chroniclers. Obviously many of the methods could not 'work' in the sense of having the desired physiological effect, but they did play a positive psychological role. Women saw themselves as not passive but having some control over their fates. Whatever the effectiveness of these contraceptives, their use demonstrates the serious intent with which women's control of procreation was pondered and pursued.

Women naturally preferred to control their fertility by some form of contraception because recourse to abortion put them at risk. But references to abortion are far more common in the ancient world than references to contraception.[71] There were good reasons why this would be the case. Contraception (in particular coitus interruptus, reliance on some sort of rhythm method or non-vaginal intercourse) was an intimate act that in most cases was neither reported nor taught. Abortion, on the other hand, often required some assistance or instruction. Self-induced miscarriages that went wrong were, the Hippocratic texts noted, necessarily brought to public attention. 'When the woman is afflicted with a large wound as a consequence of an abortion, or the womb is damaged by strong suppositories, as many women are always doing, doctoring themselves, or when the fetus is aborted and the woman is not purged of the afterbirth, but the womb inflames, closes, and is not purged, if she is treated promptly she will be cured, but will remain sterile.'[72]

The Greek medical texts discussed numerous abortion techniques including the use of perforations, pessaries, oral potions, suppositories, fumigations and poultices. In addition jumping, excessive coition, fevers, vomiting and bleedings were reported as playing a role in bringing on miscarriages.[73] Physicians knew miscarriages could be induced, but were cautious in making such attempts. 'Abortions are more dangerous than normal births', warned the author of *Illnesses of Women*, 'for they are more difficult. One cannot bring on an abortion without violence, drugs, potions, foods, suppositories, or something else. But violence is dangerous, for the uterus may ulcerate or inflame.'[74]

The greatest dangers were posed by the mechanical methods that entailed perforation of the sac in order to precipitate expulsion. Fumigations were first employed to soften the cervix and then dilators of wood, tin or lead inserted.[75] Wool and cotton tampons and suppositories were directed at dilating the cervix. Pessaries, consisting of a mixture of irritating drugs in an oil or grease base, were turned to the same purposes. Cataplasms or poultices – such as resin placed on the lower belly – were thought to work by raising the temperature of the womb.

The Ebers Papyrus of ancient Egypt contained recipes for douches to regulate the menses and to hurry labour. For abortion a recommendation was made for the employment of a pessary of dates, onions and the fruit of the acanthus crushed in honey, sprinkled on a cloth and applied to the vulva.[76] The fullest account in the ancient world of menses-inducing drugs was contained in Dioscorides' herbal. The list included bryonia used as a tampon, anagyris potions, fumigations of balsam and cardamom, tampons of the root of gentiana and the leaves of heliotrope, macerated madder, vaginal infusions of lupins, white and black hellebore in potions and pessaries, sticks or pencils of saltpetre, decoctions of Cretan thyme, and various mixtures of peony, rue, soapwort, shepherd's purse, absinthe, edderwort and Greek cyclamen. Wild rue was reputed by many both to congeal sperm and to precipitate miscarriages. The Hippocratic corpus contains several references to the abortive powers of Cretan poplar, batrachion, wild cucumber and chalbane.[77]

Medical writers described abortion as a practice to which women sometimes secretly had recourse, but there is no evidence in the texts of the early lawgivers, such as Lycurgus, mythical founder of Sparta, and Solon of Athens, of any laws against abortion *per se*. Plato actually called for all conceptions in women over the age of forty to be aborted as part of state policy. Lycurgus was reported as having dissuaded his wife from aborting her first husband's child, but as Plutarch tells the story he was motivated by a concern for the safety of the woman, not the fetus.[78]

Abortion was considered by many of the cults to be a cause of impurity, but so too was childbirth. Women who had experienced either were forbidden entry into religious sanctuaries until a specified period of time had lapsed. An inscription of c.100 BC, at a temple in Philadelphia in Lydia dedicated to Dionysus forbade the entry of those who employed aphrodisiacs, abortifacients and anticonceptual magic. In Hellenistic Egypt birth, abortion and exposure were all listed in an inscription of the Ptolemies as causes of impurity.[79]

If the inducement of miscarriage were tolerated, one might ask why the Hippocratic Oath contained its famous injunction that doctors foreswear abortion. 'Neither will I administer a poison to anybody when asked to do so, nor will I suggest such a course. Similarly I will not give to a woman a pessary to cause abortion. But I will keep pure and holy both my life and my art.'[80] It is not clear what this represented. Edelstein argued that in fact this was a later Pythagorean addition to the corpus that reflected, not medical, but philosophical concerns. The teachings of the ascetic Pythagorean cult, which included a hostility to surgery, ran counter to much Greek medical theory and practice. Indeed, the cult's belief in life starting at the moment of conception seemed more reflective of the mystery religions. Others have suggested that the injunction against abortion, whatever its source, might only signify that doctors were normally to leave both births and abortions to the jurisdiction of midwives. The Hippocratic corpus does contain, however, a remarkably detailed description of an abortive technique recommended by a physician:

> It was in the following way that I came to see a six day old embryo. A kinswoman of mine owned a very valuable singer, who used to go with men. It was important that this girl should not become pregnant and thereby lose her value. Now this girl had heard the sort of thing women say to each other – that when a woman is going to conceive, the seed remains inside her and does not fall out. She digested this information, and kept a watch. One day she noticed that the seed had not come out again. She told her mistress, and the story came to me. When I heard it, I told her to jump up and down, touching her buttocks with her heels at each leap. After she had done this no more than seven times, there was a noise, the seed fell out on the ground, and the girl looked at it in great surprise.[81]

The author went on to describe in detail the membrane and blood clots of what sounds like a seven to ten week old conceptus, but which he called a 'six day old embryo'. Since human life was not believed to be present until well along in the gestation period, the manoeuvres so calmly chronicled in this account might have been judged as more contraceptive than abortive in nature.

It was common knowledge that midwives provided abortions. In *Theaetetus*, Plato presented Socrates (whose mother Phaenarete was purportedly a midwife) describing their skills:

SOCRATES: And it is more than likely, is it not, that no one can tell as well as a midwife whether women are pregnant or not?

THEAETETUS: Assuredly.

SOCRATES: Moreover with the drugs and incantations they administer, midwifes can either bring on the pains of travail or end them at their will, make a difficult labor easy, and at an early stage cause a miscarriage if they so decide?

THEAETETUS: True.[82]

For the Greeks nascent life had only limited rights. Philosophers taught that a male conceptus was not a rational or ensouled being until thirty days (Hippocrates) or forty days (Aristotle) after conception; a female not until after eighty or ninety days. Female seed, being thinner than the male, took longer to coagulate; the male fetus began to move at three months, the female at four months. The Greeks envisaged the existence of a variety of souls, nutritive for plants, sensitive for animals, rational for humans. The fetus, in moving through these various levels, could thus be viewed as alive from an early stage, but only in the same way a vegetable was. Indeed, Aristotle held that even before conception semen and menstrual fluid had souls. The Jews expressed a similar concern for the stages of embryological development, Exodus 21:22–3 calling for fines for damage to the fetus, but only after it was determined to be 'alive'.

The general view of the ancient world was that a fetus was never more than potentially human. Stoics reflected this common sentiment in regarding it as a part of the mother until its birth. Abortion therefore presented an easier moral problem for the ancients than today inasmuch as they simply assumed that life was not present until parturition.[83] Indeed, unmarried daughters were expected to seek abortion in order to save themselves and their fathers from dishonour; the law of Solon, according to Plutarch, allowed the father to sell his dishonoured daughter into slavery. Married women were supposed to obtain the permission of their husbands before aborting, it only being considered 'wrong' if carried out counter to his wishes.

The point was not to outlaw abortion, but rather to assert that the husband was the only authority recognized as competent to judge the issue of whether or not an abortion was warranted. Such sentiments were reflected in Antigene's wife being accused of aborting to deprive her husband of heirs. Similarly Cicero recalled, 'I remember a case which occurred when I was in Asia: how a certain woman of Miletus, who had accepted a bribe from the alternative heirs and procured an abortion by drugs, was condemned to death: and rightly, for she had cheated the father of his hopes, his name of continuity, his family of its support, his house of an heir and the Republic of a citizen-to-be.'[84] Men's suspicion of women's abortions also implied a fear that recourse to such operations might hide the result of adulterous affairs. But the very fact that sanctions were threatened against women having abortions without their husbands' permission presupposes that women were in fact acting on their own. As Plutarch's account of Lycurgus implies, it was difficult to police such activities, and men might well find themselves reduced to the position of having to cajole wives into completing a pregnancy.

The public tolerance of abortion – which might seem surprising – is made more understandable when placed in the context of the exposing of children. Indeed, Aristotle argued that abortion would be necessary if the abandonment of children were not permitted:

> As to exposing or rearing the children born, let there be a law that no deformed child shall be reared; but on the ground of number of children, if the regular custom hinder any of those born being exposed, there must be a limit fixed to the procreation of offspring, and if any people have a child as a result of intercourse in contravention to these regulations, abortion must be practised on it before it has developed sensation and life.[85]

The extent to which exposure was carried out is difficult to determine. Certainly the theme of the abandoned and rescued child was popular; it is basic to the story of Oedipus, for example. It says something of the 'naturalness' with which the practice was viewed by the Greeks that Plato presented Socrates playfully using the image of exposure when examining a fresh idea produced by his disciple Theaetetus:

SOCRATES: Shall we say that's your new-born child, so to speak, and the product of my midwifery? What do you say?

THEAETETUS: I'm obliged to agree, Socrates.

SOCRATES: So this is what we've produced at long last, whatever exactly it turns out to be. And now that the birth is over, we must hold its inspection ceremony, literally circling all round it in our argument, and looking to see that if what we've produced isn't worth bringing up, but a falsehood, the result of a false pregnancy, the fact doesn't escape us. Or do you think you ought, whatever happens, to bring up your offspring and not do away with it?[86]

As Socrates implied, the Greek father had no duty to accept his child; rather he decided its fate on the fifth, seventh or tenth day.[87] A divorced woman had the option of exposing a child if the father did not recognize it. The naming ceremony signified public acceptance of the newborn. Given the high death rate of infants, taking such a wait-and-see attitude before embracing a new family member might well have made psychological sense. Given the fact that most accounts of exposure are drawn from literary works, it is difficult to say much about the actual extent of the practice. It is unlikely that it was practised by the elite. Probably most of the children exposed were born to the impoverished or out of wedlock and their abandonment was an act of desperation. In the comedies and tragedies the exposed child was usually the result of a rape.

The evidence also suggests exposure (for which the Greeks used the euphemism 'apothesis' or disposal) was employed as a eugenic practice. 'There certainly should be a law', asserted Aristotle, 'to prevent the rearing of deformed children.'[88] The malformed of

Sparta were exposed, wrote Plutarch, 'in the conviction that the life of that which nature had not well equipped at the very beginning through health and strength was of no advantage either to itself or to the state'.[89] But how common such actions were is difficult to determine. Those scholars who have questioned the extent of exposure in the Graeco-Roman world note that Christian opponents of paganism played a key role in popularizing the idea that such barbarous acts were customary. But pagans also opposed exposure as cruel and unnatural.[90]

The newborns who were abandoned were customarily left with a trinket or toy in a specific place – such as near a temple or crossroads – where those seeking offspring could easily find them. If the child survived and was rescued it could be raised as either freeborn or slave; since the rights of the biological parents were never lost it could not be adopted. In the Greek comedies it was suggested that barren, wealthy wives passed off such foundlings as their own. The likelihood is that most of the rescued met less fortunate fates as beggars, slaves or prostitutes.

Exposure, unlike abortion, obviously did not threaten women's health; for psychological and moral reasons, however, it was likely to be contemplated only with dismay. It was, of course, the Greek father – not the mother – who had the right of exposing the newborn child.[91] It was assumed that both exposure and infanticide were used particularly to dispose of female children. 'Even a poor man will bring up a son', noted Posidippus (c.300 BC), 'but even a rich man will expose a daughter.'[92] It certainly was the case that when children were listed by a father the girls were often 'forgotten'. It was once argued that the reason prostitutes were needed in such numbers was that the exposure and infanticide of girl babies created a serious sex ratio imbalance.[93] More recently it has been pointed out that there is little hard data to back up such claims.[94] Archeological and tomb evidence that suggested an unbalanced sex ratio that could only have resulted by a disposal of females has been discounted.[95] Moreover, the tirades of women against males that appear in literary productions such as *Medea* and *Lysistrata* make no mention of exposure.[96] If it had been employed disproportionately against females one would expect it to have been cited. The argument has also been made that boys who could make a claim on the equal division of the estate were more likely than girls to be abandoned.[97] This makes sense if one assumes that sexual prejudice would not over-ride economic calculation. But whatever the reality of the situation, the public acceptance of the father's theoretical power to expose his children starkly demonstrates how far the Greeks were prepared to go in pruning the family of superfluous members.

The discussion of exposure provides the most dramatic evidence of the notion, broached in the first pages of this chapter, that the Greeks could not disentangle the issue of fertility control from concerns pertaining to the roles men and women played within the family. Women and men no doubt shared the view that on occasion attempts might have to be made to limit conceptions, but they necessarily differed on the 'how' and the 'why'. Males were preoccupied with protecting their patrimony; it was difficult for them to appreciate female concerns – with high infant mortality, still births, poor maternal health, unhealthy children – which were more medical than economic in nature. Physicians showed little interest in fertility-control methods like coitus interruptus which demanded that the male exert some self-control; far more attention was paid to the father's right to expose his child. Contrariwise, women experimented with contraceptives and one gains, even through the medium of male texts, the impression that women felt that abortion, for all the risks that it posed, offered some margin of independence. In examining the different types of family planning techniques the natural tendency is to move from those we think least effective – the various contraceptive potions – to the most effective – abortion and exposure. It is quite wrong, however, to assume that the former were therefore less important than the latter. To do so is to turn our attention from private to public events, from the least to the most likely actions to be verified by men, and from the female to the male sphere.

In the Greek popular cultural context, women clearly were expected to assume responsibility for births, but this warred against the notion that all major decisions had to be made by men. Within the Aristotelian theory of generation the argument was made that women played in procreation – as in politics – an inherently passive role. It followed that women's attempts to exert some control over their bodies would be viewed as potentially threatening. Prostitutes were thought to be particularly know-ledgeable in such questions. Apollodorus, in his speech condemning the courtesan Neaera, warned that if she were acquitted other poor women would be attracted to prostitution and enjoy 'the impunity to breed children as they please'.[98] The Hippocratic works, unlike Aristotle's, presented women playing an active role in conception, but they too contained complaints that ordinary women would not 'obey' their doctors and that they lied about their abortions and miscarriages.[99] 'For they say what they know', complained one male physician, 'and they will always continue to do so. For they could not be persuaded either by fact or by argument that they know anything better than what goes on in their own bodies. Anyone who wishes to assert otherwise is at liberty to do so, but the women . . . decide the contest and give the prizes.'[100]

Notes

1 Polybius, *The Histories*, tr. W. R. Paton (Harvard University Press, Cambridge, Mass., 1927), 36.17.5–7.
2 J. Lawrence Angel, 'The Basis of Paleodemography', *American Journal of Physical Anthropology*, 30 (1969), pp. 427–38; Sarah B. Pomeroy, *Goddesses, Whores, Wives, and Slaves in Classical Antiquity* (Schocken, New York, 1975), p. 68; Peter Garnsey, *Famine and Food Supply in the Graeco-Roman World: Responses to Risk and Crisis* (Cambridge University Press, Cambridge, 1988), pp. 64–8.
3 Aristotle, *Politics*, tr. John Warrington (Dent, London, 1959), 2.1272a; K. J. Dover, *Greek Homosexuality* (Duckworth, London, 1971).
4 See Emiel Eyben, 'Family Planning in Graeco-Roman Antiquity', *Ancient Society*, 11–12 (1980–1), pp. 5–81.
5 Plato, *The Laws*, tr. R.G. Bury (Harvard University Press, Cambridge, Mass., 1942), 5.740.
6 Eva C. Keuls, *The Reign of the Phallus: Sexual Politics in Ancient Athens* (Harper and Row, New York, 1985).
7 Hesiod, *Theogony; and Works and Days*, tr. M. L. West (Oxford University Press, Oxford, 1988), 580–612; Hugh Lloyd-Jones, *Females of the Species: Semonides on Women* (Duckworth, London, 1975).
8 Demosthenes, 'Against Neaera', *Private Orations*, tr. A. T. Murray (Harvard University, Cambridge, Mass., 1939), 122.
9 Marilyn B. Arthur, 'Origins of Western Attitudes Towards Women', *Arethusa*, 6 (1973), p. 17.
10 S. C. Humphrey, *The Family, Women and Death: Comparative Studies* (Routledge, London, 1983).

11 On Sparta see Cicero, *Tusculan Disputations*, tr. J. E. King (Harvard University Press, Cambridge, Mass., 1943), 2.15–36.
12 Aristotle, *Politics*, 7.1335b; S. G. Cole, 'The Social Function of Rituals of Maturation: The Koureion and Arkteia', *Zeitschrift für Papyrologie und Epigraphik*, 55 (1984), pp. 233–44.
13 Plutarch, 'Solon', in *Plutarch's Lives*, tr. Bernadette Perrin (Harvard University Press, Cambridge, Mass., 1919), 20.2–4.
14 Herodotus, *The History of Herodotus*, tr. G. C. Macaulay (Macmillan, London, 1914), 5.39.
15 W.K. Lacey, *The Family in Classical Greece* (Thames and Hudson, London, 1968), p. 107.
16 David M. Schaps, *Economic Rights of Women in Ancient Greece* (Edinburgh University Press, Edinburgh, 1979), pp. 31–41.
17 Kathleen Freeman, *Ancilla to the Pre-Socratic Philosophers* (Harvard University Press, Cambridge, Mass., 1984), fragment 276–7, p. 116.
18 Philip Slater, *The Glory of Hera: Greek Mythology and the Greek Family* (Beacon, Boston, Mass., 1968).
19 Hesiod, *Works and Days*, 376–7.
20 Freeman, *Ancilla*, fragment 49, pp. 149–50.
21 Plato, *Republic*, tr. A. D. Lindsay (Dutton, New York, 1957), 5.459d–461c; Plato, *Laws*, 5.740.
22 Aristotle, *Politics*, 5.1335b.
23 L. P. Wilkinson, *Classical Attitudes to Modern Issues* (Kimber, London, 1979), pp. 18–20.
24 *Eumenides*, 658–62, cited in Pomeroy, *Goddesses*, p. 65. See also Euripides, *Orestes*, 550–8; Plato, *Timaeus*, 91. In practice the laws of incest held that marriages between a mother's children were forbidden while those between a father's were allowed.
25 Kathleen Freeman, *The Pre-Socratic Philosophers* (Blackwell, Oxford, 1949) p. 272.
26 Aristotle, *Generation of Animals*, tr. A. L. Peck (Harvard University Press, Cambridge, Mass., 1943), 763b.
27 Plato, *Menexenus*, in *The Dialogues of Plato*, tr. B. Jowett (Clarendon, Oxford, 1953), 1.238.
28 Freeman, *Pre-Socratic Philosophers*, p. 283.
29 Aristotle, *Generation of Animals*, 728a; Mary Anne Cline Horowitz, 'Aristotle and Women', *Journal of the History of Biology*, 9 (1976), pp. 183–214.
30 In Job, X:10 the same metaphor was employed: 'Hast thou not poured me out as milk, and curdled me like cheese?'
31 Anthony Preus, 'Science and Philosophy in Aristotle's *Generation of Animals*', *Journal of the History of Biology*, 3 (1970), pp. 1–52; Prudence Allen, *The Concept of Woman: The Aristotelian Revolution, 750 BC–AD 1250* (Eden Press, Montreal, 1985).
32 Aristotle, *Generation of Animals*, 728a–b.
33 Aristotle, *Generation of Animals*, 738a.
34 The Hippocratic treatises held that the seed came from all parts of

the body and only passed through the testicles. Castration was believed to cause sterility inasmuch as it closed the seminal passages; an incision made by the ear was thought similarly to interrupt the seed sent from the brain. See *On Generation*, 2.1, in Iain M. Lonie, *The Hippocratic Treatises 'On Generation', 'On the Nature of the Child', 'Diseases IV'* (Walter de Gruyter, London, 1981).

35 Euripides, *Hippolytus*, tr. David Grene, in *Euripides 1*, eds David Grene and Richmond Lattimore (University of Chicago Press, Chicago and London, 1955), 616–24.

36 Leonardo Taran, *Parmenides* (Princeton University Press, Princeton, NJ, 1965), pp. 171–2; see also pp. 263–5.

37 Freeman, *Pre-Socratic Philosophers*, p. 138.

38 Freeman, *Pre-Socratic Philosophers*, pp. 193–5.

39 Freeman, *Pre-Socratic Philosophers*, pp. 306–7.

40 It is unlikely that any of the extant writings of the Hippocratic school were actually written by Hippocrates of Cos (*c*.469–399 BC), the 'father of Greek medicine'.

41 *On Generation*, 7.1, pp. 3–4; and see also *On Regimen*, tr. W. H. S. Jones (Heinemann, London, 1931), 1, 28–9.

42 *On Regimen*, 1, 27.

43 *On Generation*, 4.1. Comedies such as Aristophanes' *Lysistrata* also assumed that women liked sex at least as much as men.

44 *On the Nature of the Child*, 12.6, 17.1, 22.1, and see also G.E.R. Lloyd, *Polarity and Analogies* (Cambridge University Press, Cambridge, 1966), pp. 345, 347, 367, 369.

45 The most famous example was the author of *On the Nature of the Child*, 29.2, asserting that if each day for twenty days a fertilized egg was opened the wonders of embryological development would be revealed, 'making allowance of course for the degree to which one can compare the growth of a chicken with that of a human being'.

46 Some sterility may have been caused by lesions and poisonings resulting from the consumption of powerful contraceptive and abortifacient potions and pessaries, which will be discussed below. See Marie-Thérèse Fontanille, *Avortement et contraception dans la médecine Gréco-Romaine* (Laboratoires Searle, Paris, 1977), pp. 146–8.

47 See Aline Rousselle, 'Observation féminine et idéologie masculine: le corps de la femme d'après les médecins grecs', *Annales* 35 (1980), pp. 1089–115.

48 *Diseases of Young Girls*, cited in Monica Helen Green, 'The Transmission of Ancient Theories of Female Physiology and Disease Through the Early Middle Ages', unpublished Princeton University PhD, 1985, pp. 17–18; Hippocrates, *Diseases of Women I*, tr. A. Hanson, *Signs*, 1 (1975), pp. 567–84.

49 Plato, *Timaeus*, tr. R.G. Bury (Harvard University Press, Cambridge, Mass., 1961), 91c. See also Mary R. Lefkowitz, *Heroines and Hysterics* (Duckworth, London, 1981), pp. 12–18; Helen King,

'Bound to Bleed: Artemis and Greek Women', in *Images of Women in Antiquity*, eds Averil Cameron and Amelie Kuhrt (Croom Helm, London, 1983), pp. 109–27.

50 Not until Herophilus (fl.300 BC) would there be any understanding of the function of the ovaries; see Paul Potter, 'Herophilus of Chalcedon: An Assessment of his Place in the History of Anatomy', *Bulletin of the History of Medicine*, 50 (1976), pp. 45–60.

51 Aristotle, *Generation of Animals*, 4.2.766b–c, 767 a 35, and *Politics*, 7.1335b; Anthony Preus, 'Biomedical Techniques for Influencing Human Reproduction in the Fourth Century BC', *Arethusa*, 8 (1975), p. 243.

52 *On Regimen*, 1.27; Hans Licht, *Sexual Life in Ancient Greece* (Routledge, London, 1932), pp. 364–71.

53 Freeman, *Ancilla*, fragment 32, p. 99.

54 Michel Foucault, *The Use of Pleasure*, tr. Robert Hurley (Pantheon, New York, 1985), p. 130.

55 Xenophon, 'Constitution of the Lacedaemonians', in *Scripta Minora*, tr. E. C. Marchant (Harvard University Press, Cambridge, Mass., 1962), 1.5–6.

56 Plato, *Laws*, 5.740; Herodotus, *History*, 1.61.

57 Mary Lefkowitz and Maureen B. Fant eds, *Women in Greece and Rome* (Samual Stevens, Toronto, 1977), p. 74.

58 *On Generation*, 5.1.

59 Dover, *Greek Homosexuality*, pp. 100–1.

60 Norman E. Himes, *A Medical History of Contraception* (Williams and Wilkins, Baltimore, 1936), p. 17.

61 Only ten of a catalogue of 413 fertility-regulating recipes drawn from Greek and Roman sources were meant to be employed by men; all were forms of genital ointment; see Fontanille, *Avortement et contraception*, pp. 78–119.

62 Some elite Greek women did nurse; see Mark Golden, 'The Effects of Slavery on Citizen Households and Children', *Historical Reflections/ Réflexions historiques*, 15 (1988), p. 456.

63 Wilkinson, *Classical Attitudes*, p. 41.

64 John M. Riddle, *Dioscorides on Pharmacy and Medicine* (University of Texas Press, Austin, 1985), pp. 59–63.

65 'De la nature de la femme', in *Oeuvres complètes d'Hippocrate*, ed. E. Littré (Baillière, Paris, 1853), vol. VII, p. 98, and see also 'Des maladies des femmes', vol. VIII, p. 141.

66 Robert T. Gunther, *The Greek Herbal of Dioscorides* (Oxford University Press, Oxford, 1934); Aristotle, *Historia Animalium*, tr. A.L. Pleck (Harvard University Press, Cambridge, Mass., 1965), 7.3.583a.15–27.

67 Hippocrates, 'De la nature de la femme', Littré, vol. VII, p. 415.

68 Himes, *Contraception*, pp. 59–68. The goat's bladder employed by Prokris to protect her from the serpents and scorpions in the semen of Minos, king of Crete, sounds very much like a contraceptive

sheath. See John Scarborough, *Roman Medicine* (Cornell University Press, Ithaca, NY, 1969), p. 209; B. E. Finch and H. Green, *Contraception Through the Ages* (Thomas, Springfield, Mass., 1963), p. 47.

69 G. E. R. Lloyd, *Science, Folklore and Ideology: Studies in the Life Sciences in Ancient Greece* (Cambridge University Press, Cambridge, 1983), p. 78.

70 Dioscorides, *De materia medica*, 1.104.

71 Enzo Nardi, *Procurato aborto nel mundo Greco Romano* (Giuffre, Milan, 1971), pp. 136–7.

72 Hippocrates, 'Des maladies des femmes', Littré, vol. VIII, p. 141.

73 *On Generation*, 10.1.

74 *On the Illnesses of Women*, cited in Preus, 'Biomedical Techniques', p. 253

75 John Stewart Milne, *Surgical Instruments in Greek and Roman Times*, (Clarendon, Oxford, 1907), pp. 81–2.

76 Cyril P. Bryan, *The Ebers Papyrus* (Bles, London, 1930), pp. 82–3.

77 M. Moissides, 'Contribution à l'étude de l'avortement dans l'antiquité Grecque', *Janus*, 26 (1922), pp. 59–85, 129–34; Wolfgang Jochle, 'Menses-Inducing Drugs: Their Role in Antique, Medieval and Renaissance Gynecology and Birth Control', *Contraception*, 10 (1974), pp. 425–39.

78 Plutarch, 'Lycurgus', in *Plutarch's Lives*, 3.

79 R. Crahay, 'Les moralistes anciens et l'avortement', *L'Antiquité classique*, 10 (1941), p. 17.

80 Ludwig Edelstein, 'The Hippocratic Oath', *Supplement to the Bulletin of the History of Medicine*, 1 (1943), pp. 1–64; Paul Carrick, *Medical Ethics in Antiquity: Perspectives on Abortion and Euthanasia* (D. Reidel, Dordrecht, 1985).

81 *On the Nature of the Child*, 13.1–2.

82 Plato, *Theaetetus*, tr. John McDowell (Clarendon, Oxford, 1973), 149c–d; Julius Tomen, 'Socratic Midwifery', *Classical Quarterly*, 37 (1987), pp. 97–102.

83 Sheila K. Dickinson, 'Abortion in Antiquity', *Arethusa*, 6 (1973), pp. 159–60.

84 Richard Harrow Feen, 'Abortion and Exposure in Ancient Greece: Addressing the Status of the Fetus and "Newborn" from Classical Sources', in *Abortion and the Status of the Fetus*, eds William B. Bondeson and H. Tristram Engelhardt (D. Reidel, Dordrecht, 1983), p. 290; A. R. W. Harrison, *The Law of Athens* (Clarendon, Oxford, 1968), pp. 72–3; Cicero, 'In Defence of Cluentius', *The Speeches*, tr. H.G. Hodge (Harvard University Press, Cambridge, Mass., 1927), 11.32.

85 Aristotle, *Politics*, 7.1335b.

86 Plato, *Theaetetus*, 161a.

87 Harrison, *The Law of Athens*, pp. 70–1.

88 Aristotle, *Politics*, 7.1335b.

89 Feen, 'Abortion and Exposure', p. 286.
90 H. Bolkestein, 'The Exposure of Children at Athens', *Classical Philology*, 17 (1922), pp. 222–39; A. Cameron, 'The Exposure of Children and Greek Ethics', *Classical Review*, 46 (1932), pp. 104–14.
91 In Sparta it was the state rather than the individual father that decided on the exposure of the malformed. See Eyben, 'Family Planning', p. 23.
92 Eyben, 'Family Planning', p. 16; Pomeroy, *Goddesses*, p. 46; Sarah B. Pomeroy, *Women in Hellenistic Egypt* (Schocken, New York, 1984), p. 111.
93 Claude Vatin, *Recherches sur le mariage et la condition de la femme mariée à l'époque hellénistique* (Boccard, Paris, 1970), p. 239; and see also Sarah Pomeroy, 'Infanticide in Hellenistic Greece', in Cameron and Kuhrt, *Images of Women in Antiquity*, pp. 207–22.
94 Louis R. F. Germain, 'Exposition des enfants nouveau-nés dans la Grèce ancienne: aspects sociologiques', *Recueils Jean Bodin*, 35 (1975), pp. 211–46.
95 Donald Engels, 'The Problem of Female Infanticide in the Graeco-Roman World', *Classical Philology*, 75 (1980), pp. 112–20.
96 Feen, 'Abortion and Exposure', p. 287.
97 A.W. Gomme, *The Population of Athens in the Fifth and Fourth Centuries BC* (Oxford University Press, Oxford, 1933), pp. 79–80.
98 Demosthenes, 'Against Neaera', 113.
99 Hippocrates, 'Épidémies I', Littré, vol. II, p. 649; see also Paul Diepgen, *Die Frauenheilkunde der Alten Welt* (Bergmann, Munich, 1937).
100 Hippocrates, 'Du foetus de sept mois', Littré, vol. VII, p. 141, cited in Lloyd, *Science, Folklore and Ideology*, p. 77.

2

Fertility Control in Rome

'For a woman forbids herself to conceive and fights against it'
Lucretius (*c.* 50 BC), *De rerum natura*

Rome differed from the Greek city states in at times actively seeking to encourage population growth. The ideas in Metellus Macedonicus' famous speech of 131 BC that suggested making marriage compulsory were repeated in Cicero's oration, 'Pro Marcello', of 46 BC, and later still by the emperor Augustus. Some concrete demonstrations of concern for fertility were expressed in legislation. In 59 BC Julius Caesar had land allotted to fathers of three or more children. Augustus sought by legislation in 18 BC and AD 9 to reform the morality of the wealthy and ambitious elite; his laws on the one hand pressured widows to remarry and on the other punished celibacy and childlessness. Fathers were given political privileges and mothers of three or more children escaped tutelage. But only the propertied were hit by the statutes that restricted the rights of the unmarried and childless to make wills or leave legacies, and they soon found loopholes in the law.[1] Trajan's alimentary system (AD 98–117) was more innovative in that it offered aid to the prolific lower orders, but it was limited in effect.[2] Roman law provided only meagre rewards for large families; the employment of fertility-control measures was never seriously curbed. When all was said and done the Romans' adherence to the concept of a father's unlimited powers over his family – *patria potestas* – effectively limited the state's ability to interfere in questions pertaining to marriage, exposure, contraception and abortion.

What made the Roman family unique was the apparent tyranny exercised by the father. Roman fathers were, to the amazement of the Greeks, declared to have complete power until death over both their married and unmarried children. Fathers were believed even to have the right to put their offspring to death. Such severity was viewed with distaste from the time of Livy (59 BC–AD 17) and not employed in the empire.[3] But in theory children could still be treated like slaves; the birth of new heirs from second marriages always posed the threat of disinheritance.

The Romans were positively fixated by an ideal of the self-controlled, aggressive, virile male. To achieve this status boys were subjected to a cruel and demanding education.[4] In practice most families no doubt had to face no more than the usual generational frictions. But the existence of tension-ridden households in which the children's independence was only fully assured by the death of the patriarch made the Roman preoccupation with patricide understandable.

In theory the father was all-powerful; in fact in poorer households he was not. Among the plebs there existed a matrifocal world in which children took the mother's name; and they only recognized the father if he was a member of the household. And elite children once out of the paternal home were fairly free of such tyranny. Moreover, the father's awesome power was soon cut short by his limited average life expectancy. It has been suggested that only about half the daughters who married in their teens still had a living father.[5]

Roman males' sexual concerns were primarily proprietary. They did not think of the family as a 'natural' construct. The maintenance of family prestige and wealth required, they assumed, the adoption of marriage tactics in which, ideally, women and children were employed as pawns by dispassionate males. Accordingly the Roman family, though basically conjugal and nuclear, was, like its Greek counterpart, a flexible unit that could be expanded or contracted. The *familia* might include slaves, wet nurses, tutors and foster children in addition to its 'natural' members – the wife and children – who were all subject to the dictates of the *pater familias*.[6] Family members were tied to kin primarily by material interests; to prevent property being lost to outsiders it was permissible to resort to an endogamous marriage.[7] Rome was not like Egypt where sibling unions were common, but a Roman could – like a Greek – marry his niece.[8]

The Roman marriage was a completely private arrangement. For the propertied its most important aspect was the dowry contract;

they believed there was no reason why marriages could not be both arranged and happy. Such parental involvement was necessary because the Romans further assumed, as did the Greeks, that family order was best assured if an age gap of about ten years separated the bride and groom. Evidence drawn from epitaphs has been employed to suggest that, although Roman girls did not reach sexual maturity until at least fourteen, many were married off as early as twelve, and half were wives by the age of fifteen. Their husbands, on the other hand, wed in their twenties. Such disparities in age and experience could result in terrified young brides being in effect raped on their wedding night.[9] Recent reinterpretations of the evidence suggests that such early marriages were not common. Elite young daughters were for dynastic reasons married off at an early age; women lower down the social hierarchy – who were expected to be workmates as well as wives – were more likely to marry from fifteen on.[10] In Roman Egypt females married at fifteen to sixteen and males from eighteen.

Marital affection was applauded, but not thought to be absolutely necessary for a successful union. Should a marriage fail, divorce was easy. The dowry was returned with the woman, but the Greek tradition of the father taking his daughter away from the husband was not followed. Frequent divorce was not necessarily a sign that the Romans were preoccupied by the pursuit of love and affection. Divorces were sometimes sought simply to allow new marriage alliances to be forged. But such divorces, if they violated an otherwise stable union and were pursued solely for material gain, were considered morally reprehensible.[11]

Paul Veyne has argued that a slow shift occurred in the first century AD, from the idea of marrying simply to breed, to that of marrying for conjugal affection. Seneca (4 BC–AD 65), the Stoic philosopher, and Pliny the Younger (AD 61–112), the celebrated letter writer, certainly struck a sentimental tone in discussing marriage. The wife – once classed with the domestics – was increasingly described as a friend. But one would be mistaken in assuming that some new age of romance had dawned. The distinction between romantic and companionate love continued to be made. Concord rather than passion was the goal. Love tended to be associated with the irrational lusts of extramarital affairs.[12] Plutarch (AD 46–119), for example, hailed marriage as a brake on the sexual passions and a school for order and domestication. Of course, such idealistic speculations were a luxury limited to the citizen elite. Since slaves had traditionally not been allowed to marry, the legally 'married' made up only a small proportion of the population. For the masses living in free unions it is doubtful if any transition in attitudes towards conjugal unions ever took place. But a dramatic change did occur in practice; from the second century onward the right of legal marriage was extended even to slaves.[13]

No direct written testimony was left by Roman women, but we do know more about them than was once thought possible.[14] The evidence indicates that they were freer than their secluded Greek sisters. By the mid-fifth century BC they could, if formally represented by a male, inherit, own and bequeath property. Although it is important not to exaggerate the 'freedom' enjoyed by Roman women, it appears that, whereas they had once married under the system of *cum manu* which gave control of their dowry to their husbands, from the second century BC they increasingly retained such control by marrying *sine manu*.[15] Elite Roman daughters, according to Hallett, also enjoyed higher esteem than their Greek counterparts, retaining ties with their father, whose name they bore.[16] Even after marriage they remained members of their family of origin.

Wives of elite families were not thought to be unusual if they had limited contact with their husbands. Cool conjugal relations did not have to be a source of anxiety.[17] The woman looked to her children – particularly her dutiful sons – for emotional support. The eldest might indeed be closer to her in age than her husband was. Even so, Roman culture glorified the ideal mother as forceful and rational; not as particularly more tender toward her children than the father. If her marriage failed, a Roman woman could – with the assistance of her father – obtain a divorce. On separation she had her dowry returned. After her father's death she could marry as she pleased. Rich widows were free to remarry, but some opted to take lovers. In law women's subservience and deference to males was asserted, but in practice – as the careers of Fulvia, Messalina and Agrippina attested – some Roman women enjoyed a good deal of independence. Folk beliefs even credited women with semi-magical powers. Their milk, asserted Pliny the Elder (AD 23–79), credulous collector of arcane information, could cure fevers and gout, their hair if burnt soothed warts and sores, and their menstrual fluid – most potent of all – could kill vermin, worms and beetles, destroy crops, blight bee hives, rust brass, tarnish mirrors, blunt razors and cause mares to miscarry.[18]

Despite such purported powers, Roman women, like their male counterparts, could anticipate a short life span. About half the population reached age twenty, a third forty, a sixth sixty. High mortality rates meant many were widowed and remarried.[19] Few children had living grandparents. Ensuring a continuation of the family line by seeing at least one heir survive adolescence could only be an ambition, never a certainty.

The Romans married in order to have a family, or as the physician Soranus put it unromantically, 'women usually are married for the sake of children, and not for mere enjoyment.'[20] Aulus Gellius (c.130–c.180) stated that couples took an oath that they married for the purpose of having offspring and recalled that a husband accordingly had divorced a loved wife who proved to be barren.[21] But there were far more practical reasons why the Roman couple's first concern was to have children and to ensure their survival. On them depended the conservation of the household, the maintenance of the estate, the carrying on of the family name, the forging of family alliances, the provision for the elderly in old age and the performing of funeral rites after their passing.[22] The son carried the hopes and plans of the family. The girl's marriage settlement was said to be a burden, but the provision of such dowries and the alliances they cemented provided a family with social éclat. Fertility was praised and rewarded. Motherhood enhanced a woman's status; indeed, under Augustus a woman who had borne three children was given special rights.

Heirs were so important that the Romans tolerated a variety of curious marriage arrangements in order to obtain them. There were exceptional cases of fertile wives being 'shared'. Plutarch left an account of Cato divorcing his wife Marcia so she could marry and bear an heir for a friend and later remarry Cato.[23] There were also a number of famous examples of men forging alliances by marrying off their already pregnant wives to friends; for example, Livia had already been made pregnant by Claudius Nero before her marriage to Augustus.[24] Augustine (AD 354–430) similarly reported cases of 'surrogate motherhood' in the empire when an infertile wife gave permission for her husband to have by another woman a child which the wife raised as her own.[25] Men's fear of not passing on their property to rightful heirs led to equally innovative practices. Husbands were made anxious by stories of adulteries which resulted in illegitimate claimants and abortions that extinguished legitimate inheritors. On occasion pregnancies were actually policed. Widows suspected or claiming to be pregnant were shut up until the birth by relatives to prevent the substitution of foundlings.[26]

If one did not have natural children one could always resort to adoption. Indeed, the Augustan legislation that required one to be a 'father' to fill certain posts sometimes necessitated such a strategy. In the main adoption was employed by the Romans, as by the Greeks, to control inheritances. Sons-in-law were adopted. Augustus, grand-nephew of Caesar, was for political purposes declared in the will of the latter to be his son. Adoption was yet another sign of a father's power inasmuch as it could be employed to usurp a rightful heir; Cicero (106–43 BC) and Ulpian (fl. AD 200) accordingly attacked the cruelty of men who adopted in order to disinherit their natural children.[27] But in the normal course of events a Roman married 'in order to have sons', as the formula went, and had no thoughts of either adoption or surrogacy. If it seemed necessary to either curb or increase fertility a couple would presumably first seek the aid of magic or medicine.

The Romans relied heavily on Greek medicine for their understanding of reproduction – indeed, the leading physicians of the empire were Greek – but the Romans tended to take a more pessimistic view of health. The Hippocratic texts assumed that the body was basically healthy and did not stress the need for moderation. But physicians practising in Rome like Galen tended to present the body as continually deteriorating, and simply equated health with the absence of disease. Their clients were clearly preoccupied with corporal fragility and exhibited an intense interest in diet and regimen.[28] It is in this context that the Roman discussion of procreation has to be located.

Soranus of Ephesus, a Greek physician who practised in the time of Trajan (AD 98–117) and Hadrian (AD 117–38), was Rome's greatest writer on gynaecology. He employed the knowledge of the Alexandrian anatomists to discount the idea of the wandering womb and rejected Hippocratic ideas concerning the humours and sexual polarities. He denied that women possessed seed, while at the same time he argued against Aristotle's view that males and females were radically different. Countering the Hippocratic writers who stressed the idea that female health depended on regular menstruation, Soranus went so far as to assert that it was basically harmful. He pointed out that female singers, athletes and many robust women both young and old did not menstruate. Soranus likewise played down the Hippocratic stress on women's need for intercourse. Virginity was healthy, he argued, and coition exhausting. 'Both menstruation and pregnancy are useful for the propagation of men', he wrote, 'but certainly not healthful for the childbearer.'[29] Pregnancy was accompanied by inconveniences and cravings, and led to premature senility. The woman made old before her time by repeated birthings he likened to an exhausted field. Soranus recognized that the social pressures to marry and bear children were overwhelming; his advice was that the good wife and mother be wise enough to conserve her health by insisting upon periodic abstinence.[30]

Galen of Pergamum (AD 129–99), an attendant of the emperor Marcus Aurelius and the most influential of the ancient anatomists, advanced a slightly different interpretation of intercourse. He provided essentially a synthesis of Aristotelian and Hippocratic theories concerning conception, accepting the importance of the humours and the two-seed theory of procreation.[31] Although he, like Aristotle, assumed the woman lacked heat and confused menstrual fluid with a woman's 'seed', he did recognize the importance of the ovaries.[32] He denied the womb's ability to 'wander', while retaining the idea that it was the seat of most of women's diseases.[33] He argued, in opposition to Soranus, that if either the seed or the menses were not expelled they could become harmfully noxious. The retention of semen was, he asserted, a 'burden' to women and could result in hysteria. Sexual intercourse was therefore necessary for health.[34] 'It is evident', he concluded, 'that a chaste person does not indulge in sexual intercourse for pleasure, but with the intention to relieve this urge, as if this were not associated with pleasure.'[35]

The medical literature suggested that the Romans, far from being unthinking hedonists, viewed sexuality with some anxiety. Whether one followed Soranus or Galen one came away with the conviction that procreation was a problematical undertaking. But at the same time such writings carried the assurance that doctors could offer advice to those seeking to ensure a conception, advice that complemented or competed with folk wisdom.

Some took great pains to ensure the wife's fertility.[36] Soranus assumed that even before marriage, midwives would be sent by the groom's family to examine the uterus and physiognomy of the future wife. Soranus had nothing to say against such customs, but he did attack as useless the practice of seeking to test the woman's fecundity with fumigations and suppositories. Once the couple was married and bedded the question arose as to which positions were most advantageous. Soranus declared (as had the philosopher Lucretius) that the married should mate like animals, *a tergo*, if they wished to ensure a conception. The contrary view was advanced by Artemidorus (106–48 BC) in *The Interpretation of Dreams*, where he catalogued a number of positions, but concluded that 'men invented all the other positions as a result of wantonness, licentiousness, and intoxication, and that only the face-to-face position was taught them by nature.'[37]

What time was most propitious? Paul of Aegina followed Galen in declaring that coition was 'the best possible remedy for melancholy' inasmuch as it relieved plethora, promoted growth, restored the appetite and freed the mind. But to bear its demands – particularly for those of a dry and cool disposition – warming foods such as molluscs, pot herbs, rocket, turnip, pulse, peas and beans were required. After eating and before sleep, he claimed, was the most opportune occasion for intercourse: 'This too is the fittest time for procreation on many accounts, and because that the woman falling asleep is the more likely to retain the semen.'[38] A warm bath or rubdown which relaxed the woman's body was, according to Soranus, also helpful.

Roman doctors tended to follow Hippocrates in believing that both men and women produced seed. The Latin sexual vocabulary contained many agricultural analogies referring to a man's 'ploughing' and the woman's 'grinding mill or mill stones'.[39] Both sexes were portrayed as playing active roles. Oribasius and Galen claimed that women knew when they conceived. Pliny the Elder and Lucretius noted that some barrenness was due to incompatibility.[40] Like Soranus and Galen they believed that the woman's pleasure was required for procreation to take place. According to Soranus the uterus dilated 'as in the desire of intercourse for the reception of seed.'[41] The vital function of the clitoris was well understood.

In case of impotence doctors recommended the consumption of narcissus root, chick peas, pine nuts, seed of nettle or anise, and drinks of pepper, rocket and saffron. Pliny the Elder reported the popular beliefs that satyrion, crocodile feet, myrrh, rocket, pepper, mare's sweat and dried horse testicles all acted as aphrodisiacs, that mistletoe helped women conceive, and that drinks based on the sap of fleawort and the thistle assured the birth of boys.[42]

Childbearing was so important that some, convinced that their barrenness was caused by their enemies' recourse to black magic, sought to protect themselves with talismans and pendants. The poet Ovid (43 BC–AD 17) spoke of charms – by knottings, poisoned drinks and incantations – used to cause impotence.[43] In response, urine could be used medicinally, suggested Pliny the Elder; especially 'that of eunuchs to counteract the sorcery that prevents fertility'.[44] But Plutarch warned women against using love potions and magic on their spouses.[45]

In labour, sympathetic magic might also be called upon. Sitting by a pregnant woman with legs crossed or fingers interlaced was thought to impede delivery. 'It is said', reported Pliny the Elder, in his catalogue of popular beliefs, 'that difficult labor ends in delivery at once, if over the house where there is a lying-in woman there be thrown a stone or missile that has killed with one stroke each three living creatures – a human being, a boar, and a bear.'[46] Sowbread root worn as an amulet was also thought to speed expulsion.[47]

If the Roman couple's first concern was to have children, their second was not to have too many. Though children were commonly expected to follow marriage, the Roman elite did not relish the prospect of their urbanized, civilized style of life being jeopardized by a hoard of infants. The custom that required the equal division of the estate among one's children was the main reason usually advanced to explain why Roman families were so small. Even the intermittent attempts of the state to encourage population growth proved futile. The repeal of such sanctions, which would have forced the poet Sextus Propertius (c.50–16 BC) to give up his mistress, led him to exult,

> The law's repealed at last, that threatening law
> that might have riven heart from loving heart,
> though Jove himself could not divide true lovers . . .
> I shall beget no sons to swell Rome's glory;
> not of my sons shall historians tell . . .

Let me be your one joy; you at my side,
I have no need of sons to feed my pride.[48]

But most who questioned the wisdom of excessive childbearing
were motivated, not by romance, but by the hard-headed
realization that too many children posed a threat to the household.
Pliny the Younger noted that he lived in 'an age when even one
child is thought a burden'.[49] Seneca called them a civic charge.[50]
Childless widows and widowers whose age guaranteed that their
estate would not have to be shared with offspring were, according
to the satirists, the favourite targets of legacy hunters. 'No one
brings up children', claimed Petronius (d. AD 65/6), 'because
anyone who has heirs of his own stock is never invited to dinner or
the theatre.'[51] Even the purported advantages of children were
questioned. 'The most fatuous thing in the world', Seneca sourly
concluded, 'is to marry and have children in order to perpetuate
one's name, or to have support in old age, or to secure that you
have an heir.'[52]

Although the limited evidence makes it impossible to advance
precise figures, it is probable that Roman elite couples enjoyed on
average at least fifteen years of married life, but rarely had more
than two or three children. Indeed, almost all the emperors between
14 and 200 AD had to adopt heirs. Most funeral inscriptions noted
only one or two children per family. To have three or more was
considered exceptional.[53] The remarkable infertility of the Roman
elite has been attributed to everything from racial degeneration to
lead poisoning; lack of evidence has led to the discounting of such
interpretations.[54] But it is equally difficult to determine precisely
the effects of conscious efforts to control fertility; what is clear is
that such attempts were made. Because of high infant mortality rates
the Romans could not, of course, concentrate their childbearing into
a few short years with the confidence that one or two heirs would
survive.[55] More flexible responses depending on circumstances had
to be made, the assumption being that intervention anywhere
along the continuum that ran from conception to birth was
legitimate. Most often means were probably taken to space
pregnancies or end them when they proved inconvenient or
dangerous. For the Romans it was not just a question of whether or
not to conceive but whether to impede or encourage conception,
gestation, abortion and infant survival.

'Fertility control', claims Brent D. Shaw, 'for most families limited itself to the practical solutions of killing, sale or exposure of excess surviving children.'[56] Exposure was the most dramatic way of disposing of unwanted infants. The practice is glimpsed through a romantic haze in Longus' account of Daphnis raised by a she-goat and Chloe left with nymphs.[57] The historian Tacitus (AD 55–120) was more forthcoming when he paused in his description of the 'preposterous and mean' customs of the Jews to admit that they did possess one praiseworthy custom: 'they take thought to increase their numbers; for they regard it as a crime to kill any late born child.'[58] The Egyptians were also opposed to the exposure of unwanted neonates, which they regarded as a Greek custom. Rescued foundlings in Roman Egypt were, in remembrance of their place of retrieval, often given the name Kopreus, meaning 'off the dunghill.[59]

By 'late born' Tacitus meant a child who unexpectedly came on the scene after the father had made up his will. A Roman father would not kill such a child, but was within his rights if he abandoned it. The ritual was for a Roman citizen to 'take' a child by picking it up from the floor where the midwife placed it immediately after birth. The family interests, as interpreted by the *pater familias*, dictated whether or not the baby was accepted. Widowed and unmarried women of the elite enjoyed the same power.

Soranus was contemptuous of the Germans and Scythians who only raised newborns that survived the test of an icy bath, but he assumed that abnormal babies would be dispatched by the midwife or abandoned for eugenic reasons.[60] 'Monstrous offspring we suppress', Seneca calmly agreed, 'and we drown infants that are weakly or abnormal.'[61] But Seneca demonstrated the ambivalence of the Romans, in also asking:

> Would any man judge his children so unfairly as to care more for a healthy son than for one who was sickly, or for a tall child of unusual stature more than for one who was short or of middling height? . . . Parents lean with more affection towards those of their offspring for whom they feel pity. Virtue, too, does not necessarily love more deeply those of her works which she beholds in trouble and under heavy burdens, but, like good parents, she gives them more of her fostering care.[62]

Seneca was talking about a child, not a newborn, but the concern he expresses implies that abandonment would not be turned to without serious reason.

'The poor do not bring up children', declared Plutarch, but there is little evidence that exposure was resorted to by any except the desperate.[63] Nor should it be assumed that since some children were abandoned the remainder were not cherished. 'Others expose them in some desert place', asserted Philo (30 BC–AD 40), the philosopher of Hellenistic Judaism, 'hoping or so they assert, that the infants may be rescued but in reality leaving them to suffer the most terrible fate.'[64] But even the impoverished obviously nourished the faint hope that an abandoned child would be found and adopted. That foundlings did survive was implied by the existence of legal statutes dealing with their rights and obligations.[65]

It appears that more girls than boys were exposed. In an otherwise unremarkable letter written in Egypt under Roman rule Hilarion instructed his wife Alis, 'If, as may well happen, you give birth to a child, if it is a boy let it live, if it is a girl, expose it.'[66] A husband in Ovid's *Metamorphoses* similarly told his spouse, 'If by chance your child should prove to be a girl – I hate to say it, and may I be pardoned for the impiety – let her be put to death.'[67] Some have gone so far as to suggest that perhaps 10 to 20 per cent of female infants were exposed, but there is little supportive evidence of any resulting imbalance in the sex ratio.[68] Whatever the numbers involved, the public acceptance of the principle of exposure was a clear demonstration of the power of the Roman father. The exposure of female babies was one link in the chain of the sexual exploitation of women that led on to slavery and prostitution.

By the late republic, concerns for population growth led to the apparent invention of the 'law of Romulus' to oppose the exposure of sons and first daughters.[69] By the time of the Severi (AD 193–211), abandonments were being described as murder though still not officially condemned. In AD 318, Constantine declared that a father's murder of his children was a crime; no clear stance was taken on infanticide. At the end of the fourth century, Valentinian, Valens and Gratian criminalized child murder, and fathers who abandoned their children now lost their rights to them. But even the Christian emperors remained ambivalent as regards exposure;

in AD 529 Justinian only went as far as outlawing the enslavement of foundlings.[70]

Exposure was, for the self-centred father, the simplest form of fertility control. He could sire as many children as desired and then abandon the excess. Roman women presumably stoically shared the belief that, to protect the well-being of the household, circumstances might require newborns to be exposed.[71] But it obviously would have been more in the women's interests if they employed contraceptives to avoid pregnancies or abortifacients to terminate them rather than risk the physiological dangers of carrying a pregnancy to term and the psychological stress of abandoning an infant.

Upper-class women had good reasons to be particularly interested in contraception. They tended to marry earlier than plebians and therefore had a potentially longer childbearing career. The impression is given that they were also less likely to breastfeed and so deprived of the natural protection associated with extended lactation. And finally, they could entertain the serious expectation that by restricting their fertility they could provide a more secure inheritance for their already existing children. Indeed, their attempts to limit family size suggest not so much an antipathy for the young as a concern for their well-being. In short, they had the most to gain from controlling fertility; the most to lose if they did not.

This does not mean, of course, that poor women might not also have had good reasons for seeking to avoid unwanted pregnancies. Dio Chrysostom, after noting that some freeborn women in order to cloak their infertility took in abandoned children, stated:

> but in the case of slave women, on the other hand, some destroy the child before birth and others afterwards, if they can do so without being caught, and yet sometimes even with the connivance of their husbands, that they may not be involved in trouble by being compelled to raise children in addition to their enduring slavery.[72]

Unfortunately, sources that depict the childbearing experiences of the lower orders are exceedingly rare.

The man was primarily interested in the number of children among whom his estate would be divided; the woman was as concerned with when children were born as with how many she had. Her health depended on it. Such anxieties were reflected in the call made by Soranus and Oribasius for the spacing of births, or at the very least for the postponement of the marriage of young girls.[73]

The simplest way to postpone or space births was by abstaining from sexual relations. Some husbands were ascetic. Plutarch praised the practice of abstinence with one's wife as a training for doing without other women.[74] Diet was employed by the more cautious to damp down desire. A dry diet, a hard bed and sombre stories were recommended by Soranus. Paulus Aegineta reported that cooling vegetables like rue, lettuce and linseed blunted venereal appetites, a plate of lead tied to the loins prevented arousing dreams, and dustings of rue or chaste tree sprinkled on the bed ensured continence.[75]

Males seemed to have been more interested in the benefits abstinence offered their health than in the protection against pregnancies it promised their spouses. Epicurus said all coitus was bad. Rufus of Ephesus (fl.AD 100) came close to agreeing and pointed out that the accompanying loss of heat suffered by men – but not women – resulted in indigestion, memory loss, spitting of blood and fading of sight and hearing.[76] Soranus agreed that excessive coition was dangerous. Caelius Aurelianus, who translated and abridged Soranus, claimed that venery contributed to pleurisy, apoplexy, madness, paralysis, nephritis and haemorrhaging. He went on to assert, in attacking Asclepiades' argument that coitus could cure epilepsy, that coition was itself 'minor epilepsy'.

> For it causes a motion of the parts like that in epilepsy; various parts are subjected to spasms, and at the same time there occur panting, sweating, rolling of the eyes and flushing of the face. And the completion of coitus brings with it a feeling of malaise along with pallor, weakness, or dejection.

Coition, he concluded, exacerbated mania, 'for it not only deprives the body of strength but also agitates the soul'.[77] Celsus (fl.AD 20) took a more moderate line in arguing that although intercourse was tiring it only had to be avoided during the day, in summer and before either work or meals. 'Concubitis indeed is neither to be desired overmuch, nor overmuch to be feared; seldom used it braces the body, used frequently it relaxes.'[78]

Aline Rousselle argues that this fear of sexual excesses was important in that it resulted in a decline in rates of intercourse. 'This is doubtless one of the factors', she writes, 'on the male side, responsible for the fall in the number of births among the upper classes of the Roman empire.'[79] It is difficult to imagine, however, how one could either prove or disprove such a theory.

Abstinence might have been employed only as long as a wife nursed to ensure that a conception did not dry up her milk supply. Doctors recommended that children in elite families be breastfed up to three years.[80] Sexual continence was advised since coition was known to 'spoil' the milk. If such advice was followed it would clearly have provided a spacing of births, but women members of the elite chose not to nurse. In contrast to them, Tacitus held up for praise German mothers. They, he asserted, raised households of children 'filling out amid nakedness and squalor into that girth of limb and frame which is to our people a marvel. Its own mother suckles each at her breast; they are not passed on to nursemaids and wet-nurses.'[81] Pliny the Younger and Seneca, who were themselves childless, suggested that women frivolously resorted to birth control simply out of pure selfishness.[82] The evidence suggests it would be closer to the mark to say that women turned from natural to artificial methods of protection.[83]

Should a wife decide to nurse or for some other reason wish to abstain from intercourse her husband might seek gratification elsewhere. Indeed, Plutarch suggested that if a man was dissolute with other women he was in fact showing respect for his wife.[84] Reports of married women's hysteria were possibly due to their husbands' commonly preferring the company of others.[85] A man could, of course, have recourse to prostitutes or slaves. Slaves had no right to refuse; there was no concept of slave rape. They could always be coerced, as Petronius, Martial and Horace noted, into providing sexual services. Children had by slaves were not recognized. Though some were freed and others raised in the family like pets, they placed no real burden on the family economy. Slavery necessarily affected private life in instilling in many men a crass, exploitative approach to sexuality. Indeed, one explanation for the idealistic view taken of male homosexual love was that it had to be won; sex with inferiors such as women and slaves could be perceived as inevitably corrupted by coercion.[86]

It is possible that married men were instructed by prostitutes on contraceptive practices. A rare reference to coitus interruptus is found in the poet Lucretius' (c.95–55 BC) statement that prostitutes 'indulged in such motions, for their own purposes, that they might not often be quickened and lie pregnant'.[87] Wet nurses, who depended on not getting pregnant in order to continue their livelihood, might also have employed coitus interruptus. Roman wet-nursing contracts customarily required the woman to avoid getting pregnant for between six months and three years. 'So long as she is duly paid she shall take proper care', read one such document, 'both of herself and of the child, not injuring her milk nor sleeping with a man nor becoming pregnant.'[88] Jewish rabbis similarly recommended the policy of 'threshing inside and winnowing outside' while a woman was breastfeeding.[89] Perhaps the ubiquity of coitus interruptus accounts for its being so infrequently noted. It is striking, however, that the few references made in Roman times to withdrawal – which is usually assumed to be a male form of contraception – referred to women's being the active party. It seems safest to conclude that men left the problem of avoiding pregnancy largely to them.[90]

It was certainly the case that Roman writers attributed their society's low fertility to women's pursuit of their own interests. Seneca protested that women were becoming as bad as men in their pursuit of pleasure. Though destined by nature to be passive partners they were proving to be competitive even in love.[91] The satirist Juvenal (AD 67–127) complained that women readily turned to drugs both to prevent conceptions and to end them.[92] But, as one historian has noted, to rely on such literary evidence can result in limiting one's knowledge to that of the 'night-club society' of the ancient world.[93] A more serious appraisal of women's options was presented in the contemporary medical literature.

Soranus' first suggestion for those seeking to avoid conception was to beware 'having sexual intercourse at those periods which we said were suitable for conception'. By this he meant that the woman should employ a rhythm method and avoid sex during the days immediately following menstruation.[94] Caelius Aurelianus, Mustio (sixth century) and Oribasius concurred; Galen stated that some women knew when they had conceived.[95]

Particular movements and positions were also thought to impede conception. 'For a woman forbids herself to conceive and fights against it', declared Lucretius, 'if she aids the man's actions by the movement of her hips, and by the flexible writhing of her breast; for she turns the share clean away from the furrow and makes the seed fail of its place.'[96] It was this variant of coitus interruptus that was recommended by Soranus:

> And during the sexual act, at the critical moment of coitus when the man is about to discharge the seed, the woman must hold her breath and draw herself away a little, so that the seed may not be hurled too deep into the cavity of the uterus. And getting up immediately and squatting down she should induce sneezing and carefully wipe the vagina all around; she might even drink something cold.[97]

This belief in the efficacy of sneezing continues to be reported in the twentieth century.

Soranus' reference to a cold drink may link with the fact that the Romans, like the Greeks, had recourse to herbal contraceptive teas. Pliny the Elder noted that Homer called the willow 'fruit losing' because it lost it seeds quickly; for that reason, continued Pliny, 'it is well known that willow seed taken as a drug produces barrenness in a woman.'[98] Bryony mixed with ox urine caused impotence.[99] Soranus described the use of wine, rue, wallflower seed, myrtle, myrrh and white pepper.[100] Dioscorides (fl.AD 50) listed nine plants endowed with contraceptive properties.[101]

Roman women also employed a variety of barrier methods of birth control. Pliny the Elder in discussing the cedar stated, 'Gossip records a miracle: that to rub it all over the male part before coition prevents conception.' Presumably he was referring to cedar gum, as had Dioscorides.[102] The Christian apologist Tertullian (AD 155–220) spoke of the Roman use of pessaries. Tampons and plugs were also employed. Dioscorides provided recipes for pessaries and sticky mixtures of peppermint, cedar gum, alum, and axe-weed in honey.[103] Oribasius and Aetius of Amida prescribed basically the same recipes.[104] Such plugs usually consisted of wool soaked in a viscous substance such as honey, olive oil, white lead or alum. Soranus provided the fullest account of the use of such substances:

> It also aids in preventing conception to smear the orifice of the uterus all over before with old olive oil or honey or cedar

resin or juice of the balsam tree, alone or together with white lead; or with a moist cerate containing myrtle oil and white lead; or before the act with moist alum, or with galbanum together with wine; or to put a lock of fine wool into the orifice of the uterus; or before sexual relations to use vaginal suppositories which have the power to contract and to condense. For such of these things as are styptic, clogging and cooling cause the orifice of the uterus to shut before the time of coitus and do not let the seed pass into its fundus.[105]

Today's doctors would agree that such substances that either immobilized or blocked the entry of sperm clearly could be effective. But Soranus, like his Greek forebears, believed that these substances' humoral ability to cool and so shut the uterus – and not simply the physical impediment they provided – was the basis of their contraceptive powers. Indeed, he suggested that some of the suppositories be removed just before intercourse.

The Romans appear to have employed douches. Soranus mentioned a mixture of alum and wine. The poet Martial referred to the use of sea water as a spermicide.[106] Ovid suggested that cold water was as important to women as coitus interruptus was to men.[107] Caelius Aurelianus recommended a mixture of brine and vinegar.[108] Remarkably similar vinegar or lemon-juice solutions were still being approved of by birth-control advocates in the early twentieth century. If the Romans used them only after coition they would have a limited effect; if employed both before and after they would have been successful.

Soranus scoffed at the use of prophylactic amulets and talismans, but the Romans employed both magic and medicine in order to control procreation. Aetius described the effectiveness of wearing a weasel liver.[109] A spider's egg containing two worms, if attached to the body with deer skin before sunrise, would, reported Pliny the Elder, prevent conception for a year. Pliny, though personally opposed to contraception, offered such information with the admission that some women obviously needed protection from an excessive fecundity.[110]

Most Roman women presumably shared Soranus' view that 'it is much more advantageous not to conceive than to destroy the embryo'.[111] But they might, if contraception failed, attempt to procure an abortion. They had no legally codified 'right' to do so,

but operated in an informal space where their prerogative to take
defensive action was conceded by the community. Their recourse
to such practices, demonstrating as it did an ability to control their
own bodies, was viewed by some men with distrust. Such was the
concern that a man not be deprived of 'his' child that in the second
century Rutilius Severus obtained an order to have his divorced
wife's womb guarded.[112] Ovid claimed that Roman matrons once
successfully carried out a 'birth strike' to force the return of a lost
privilege:

> Afterward the honor was taken from them, and every matron
> vowed not to propagate the line of her ungrateful spouse by
> giving birth to offspring; and lest she should bear children,
> she rashly by a secret thrust discharged the growing burden
> from her womb. They say the Senate reprimanded the wives
> for their daring cruelty but restored the right of which they
> had been mulcted.[113]

Ammianus Marcellinus, the fourth-century historian, retold the
story of the empress Eusebia, wife of Constantius, administering
abortifacients to prevent her rival Helen from producing an heir.[114]
Most moralists credited women with more mundane motives.
Seneca praised his mother for not frivolously resorting, like so
many of her peers, to abortion:

> You have never blushed for the number of your children, as if
> it taunted you with your years, never have you, in the manner
> of other women whose only recommendation lies in their
> beauty, tried to conceal their pregnancy as if an unseemly
> burden, nor have you ever crushed the hope of children that
> were being nurtured in your body.[115]

Plutarch condemned 'licentious women who employ drugs and
instruments to procure abortion for the sake of conceiving
again'.[116] Pliny the Elder moralized, 'In the human race the males
have devised every out-of-the-way form of sexual indulgence,
crimes against nature, but the females have invented abortion.
How much more guilty are we in this department than the wild
animals.'[117] Ovid provided perhaps the most famous depictions of
abortion in poems thirteen and fourteen of his *Amores*. The male
narrator ostensibly protested that abortion, motivated by female

egoism and self-centredness, threatened society with depopulation, but made it clear that his real concern was for his own happiness which had been jeopardized by his mistress's daring.[118] The Romans rarely referred to a woman being coerced by her spouse into having an abortion.[119] This, of course, did not pose a problem inasmuch as a woman was obliged to obey her husband; a woman aborting for her own purposes raised the spectre of insubordination.

If men opposed abortion it was because they thought that it threatened their interests, not that it violated fetal life. The Romans shared the Greek view that the fetus had no independent existence until birth. For example, the neo-Platonist philosopher Porphyry (AD 232–305) argued in *Pros Gauron* that the embryo was little more than a vegetable.[120] Stoics like Seneca viewed the inducement of miscarriages as a female foible comparable to the wearing of make-up. Accordingly, abortion and contraception were not as distinctly separated in the Roman mind as they would be in later societies. Soranus was clearly preaching to the unconverted when he felt it necessary to stress that 'A contraceptive differs from an abortive, for the first does not let the conception take place, while the latter destroys what has been conceived. Let us, therefore, call the one "abortive" (*phthorion*) and the other "contraceptive" (*atokion*). And an "expulsive" (*ekbolion*) some people say is synonymous with an abortive.'[121] Such fine distinctions were seldom made.

A variety of herbal means were believed, in Soranus' words, 'not only to prevent conception, but also to destroy any already existing'.[122] Pliny the Elder noted that the ground-pine was called 'abiga' because it caused abortion; so did potions of hemionion and bracken.[123] The herbalist Dioscorides described over twenty-five plants that had abortifacient properties. Paulus Aegineta provided recipes for ten brews.[124]

Roman doctors discussed the same methods as those referred to in the Hippocratic corpus – violent exercises, bleedings, pessaries and injections.[125] Aretaeus (fl. AD 200) mentioned in passing 'the application of a pessary to induce abortion'.[126] Soranus described the use of vaginal suppositories, bleedings, hot baths, injections of warm oil and rue, and poultices of linseed, fenugreek, mallow and wormwood, but warned of the dangers of surgical intervention. He also indicated that women doctored themselves when he cautioned against the use of 'squirting cucumber, black hellebore, pellitory, panax balm, drugs which women have often used also for abortion'.[127]

From Soranus' and Galen's writings it was made clear that even when a doctor was in attendance the physical examination of a woman would be carried out by a midwife. For assistance in aborting, wealthy women could turn to midwives – *obstetrices* – and women doctors – *medicae*.[128] Juvenal claimed that poor women could go to quacks, but chose not to:

> Yet these the pangs of childbirth undergo
> And all the yearnings of a mother know.
> These, urged by want, assume the nurse's care,
> And learn to breed the children whom they bear.
> The rich shun toil and danger; for, though sped,
> The wealthy dame is seldom brought to bed:
> Such the dire power of drugs, and such the skill
> They boast to cause miscarriages at will.[129]

There were doctors who provided abortions, but Soranus noted that some would not countenance the practice and others such as himself would only provoke a miscarriage if the mother's life was in danger. Galen did discuss abortifacients, but was equally circumspect.[130]

Neither contraception nor abortion *per se* was treated as illegal. It was true that abortion as a cause rather than as an end was criminalized at the end of the second century. 'The divine Severus and Caracalla decreed that a woman who procured an abortion should be sent into exile for a fixed term by the official for it would seem unworthy that she should have deprived her husband without incurring a penalty.'[131] Brunt suggests that abortion against a husband's wishes was a matrimonial offence punishable by a forfeiture of one-eighth of the dowry after divorce.[132] But as the statute made clear, the practice was only considered a crime if it was carried out counter to a husband's wishes. He, not the fetus, was the wounded party. Thus Nero found it possible to justify a divorce suit by charging his wife Octavia with having aborted. Similarly, abortifacients were outlawed under Caracalla not because they threatened the embryo but because they were – like love potions and aphrodisiacs – believed to endanger the woman who employed them.[133]

The evidence suggests that fertility control was openly employed as long as women enjoyed a margin of freedom in the wealthy and urbanized empire. In a society that prided itself on its rationalism and individualism such methods obviously had a place. But it was not an age, as the popular historians would have it, of pagan sensuality and unbridled lust. The men and women of the time suffered, as we have seen, from the anxieties and constraints peculiar to their epoch. And an obvious waning in the discussion of contraception and abortion, and possibly in their use as well, occurred from the fourth century onward as religion and irrationalism spread and the status of women declined.

But even earlier, in the second century, a shift in the tenor of the times was marked by a philosophical turning inward. The Stoic Musonius Rufus (AD 30–100) led the way in rejecting the selfishness that had previously marked marriage strategies. He presented a new, monogamous, dehedonized, procreative form of marriage.[134] Sexual intercourse in such a union would only be lawful when undertaken for the purpose of procreation. The emperors, he argued, had already attempted to bring about such a state of affairs:

> For this reason [fear of depopulation] they forbade women to suffer abortions and imposed a penalty upon those who disobeyed; for this reason they forbade them to use contraceptives on themselves and to prevent pregnancy, and for this reason they gave to both husband and wife a reward for large families and set a penalty upon childlessness.[135]

This garbled account of Augustus' legislation in fact described the law not as it existed, but as Musonius Rufus wished it to be. Hierocles, a Stoic of the second century, probably came closer to contemporary opinion in only going so far as to assert that nature desired families to raise 'all, or at least most children'.[136]

Paul Veyne has suggested that it was increasingly good form for a man to be a Stoic; to hide his concubine from the children. Marcus Aurelius (AD 161–80) would be the new sort of emperor who congratulated himself on his sexual self-control. This is not to say there was any necessary change in the practices of the elite, but styles changed and asceticism and conjugality came into vogue. Tacitus' famous description of German women, which contained an attack on contraception, was a classic example of this moralizing stance:

> So their life is one of fenced in chastity. There is no arena with its seductions, no dinner-tables with their provocations to corrupt them . . . so they take one husband only, just as one body and one life, in order that there may be no second thoughts, no belated fancies: in order that their desire may not be for the man, but for marriages; to limit the number of their children, to make away with any of the later children is held abominable, and good habits have more force with them than good laws elsewhere.[137]

The emergence of this new morality was sustained by doctors. Sexual pleasures were, like other excesses, increasingly presented as dangerous. Pliny the Elder could exclaim, 'Heaven knows, the less indulgence in this respect the better.'[138] The healthiness of virginity was lauded while masturbation, thought to accelerate sexual maturity, was attacked.

Why did this shift occur? Veyne suggests family roles changed as the warriors of the city states became the citizens of an empire, as a military aristocracy became a service aristocracy. With political compromise replacing fighting as a means of resolving conflicts, attempts necessarily had to be made to elaborate a new protective morality. It manifested itself in shifting the weight of public approval from bisexuality to heterosexuality; from concubinage to married life.[139] Marriage, which was once strictly private, became a public rite. It was even made accessible to the poor to serve as a prop to personal relationships and indirectly to social order.

Stoicism preached this new morality of the couple: the purpose of sex as ever was to have legitimate children, but the wife was now a friend. New demands were advanced for the reasonable use of marriage. It was instituted to provide citizens stated Antipater of Tarsus, for procreation argued Musonius Rufus, to avoid adultery which was theft claimed Epictetus, to instill equal moral obligations asserted Seneca. Musonius and Athenagoras began to speak of non-procreative sex as bad. Philo described parents who exposed their children as beasts that copulated for pleasure.[140] Pliny the Elder lamented the avarice spawned by civilization that resulted in 'lack of children'.[141]

Stoicism was not the only cause. Indeed, one would have expected that Stoicism, which preached personal autarchy, would have provided a critique of the sentimental family instead of being coopted by it.[142] And certainly Stoicism was not the same as Christianity. The philosophy had a functionalist side to it. Why, it asked, sleep together if not to procreate? Such an approach implied not so much a desire for asceticism as for a rational use of time and resources. There was no particular sexual practice or activity – not masturbation nor abortion nor homosexuality – that especially aroused the concerns of the Romans; rather it was the idea of 'excess' that preoccupied them. This concern for a victory over the powers of the flesh preceded Christianity and should not be confused with it; the goal was hygiene, not holiness. Christians and pagans appeared to say much the same thing – especially about non-procreative sexuality – but for distinctly different reasons.

Notes

1 Suzanne Dixon, *The Roman Mother* (Croom Helm, London, 1988) p. 91; Karl Galinsky, 'Augustus' Legislation on Morals and Marriage', *Philologus*, 125 (1981), pp. 126–44; Pal Csillag, *The Augustan Laws on Family Relations* (Akademiai Kirdo, Budapest, 1976); L. F. Raditsa, 'Augustus' Legislation Concerning Marriage, Procreation, Love Affairs, and Adultery', *Aufstieg und Niedergang der Romischen Welt*, II, 13 (1980), 278–339.

2 P. A. Brunt, *Italian Manpower, 225 BC–AD 14* (Oxford University Press, Oxford, 1971), p. 151; Richard Duncan Jones, *The Economy of the Roman Empire: Quantitative Studies* (Cambridge University Press, Cambridge, 1974), p. 295.

3 W. V. Harris, 'The Roman Father's Power of Life and Death', in *Studies in Roman Law in Memory of A. Arthur Schiller*, eds R. S. Bagnall and W. V. Harris (Dordrecht, Leiden, 1986), pp. 87–93.

4 Aline Rousselle, 'Gestes et signes de la famille dans l'Empire Romain', in *Histoire de la famille*, eds André Burguière, C. Klapische-Zuber and M. Segalen (Colin, Paris, 1986), vol. I, pp. 231–72; Saara Lilja, 'Homosexuality in Republican and Augustan Rome', *Societas, Scientiarum Fennica: Commentationes Humanarum Litterarum*, 74 (1982), pp. 82–134.

5 J. A. Crook, 'Patria Potestas', *Classical Quarterly*, 17 (1967), pp. 113–22; Richard P. Saller, 'Patria Potestas and the Stereotype of the Roman Family', *Continuity and Change*, 1 (1986), pp. 7–22; Richard P. Saller, 'Men's Age of Marriage and its Consequences in the Roman Family', *Classical Philology*, 82 (1987), pp. 32–3.

6 Richard Saller, 'Familia, Domus and the Roman Conception of Family', Phoenix, 38 (1984), pp. 336–55; Keith R. Bradley, 'Child Care in Rome: The Role of Men', Historical Reflections/Réflexions historiques, 12 (1985), pp. 485–516.

7 Beryl Rawson, ed., The Family in Ancient Rome: New Perspectives (Croom Helm, London, 1986); Paul Veyne, 'L'Empire romain', in Histoire de la vie privée, eds Philippe Ariès and Georges Duby (Seuil, Paris, 1985), vol. I, pp. 23–196.

8 Naphtali Lewis, Life in Egypt under Roman Rule (Clarendon, Oxford, 1983), p. 44.

9 M. K. Hopkins, 'The Age of Roman Girls at Marriage', Population Studies, 18 (1965), pp. 309–27; N. M. Kay, Martial: Book XI: A Commentary (Duckworth, London, 1985), p. 237.

10 Brent D. Shaw, 'The Age of Roman Girls at Marriage: Some Reconsiderations', The Journal of Roman Studies, 77 (1987), pp. 30–46; Gillian Clark, 'Roman Women', Greece and Rome, 28 (1981), pp. 193–212.

11 Martial, Epigrams, tr. Walter C. A. Kerr (Harvard University Press, Cambridge, Mass., 1930), 6.7. Seneca, On Benefits, in Moral Essays, tr. John W. Basore (Harvard University Press, Cambridge, Mass., 1935), 3.16.2.

12 Paul Veyne, L'élégie érotique romaine: L'amour, la poésie et l'occident (Seuil, Paris, 1983).

13 P. E. Corbett, The Roman Law of Marriage (Clarendon, Oxford, 1930); Susan Treggiari, 'Contubernales in CIL 6', Phoenix, 35 (1981), p. 43.

14 M. I. Finley, 'The Silent Women of Rome', in Finley, Aspects of Antiquity (Viking, New York, 1968), pp. 129–42.

15 A. J. Gratwick, 'Free or Not So Free? Wives and Daughters in the Late Roman Republic', in Marriage and Property, ed. Elizabeth M. Craik (Aberdeen University Press, Aberdeen, 1984), pp. 43–4.

16 Judith P. Hallett, Fathers and Daughters in Roman Society: Women and the Elite Family (Princeton University Press, Princeton, NJ, 1984), pp. 79–81; Susan Treggiari, 'Digna Condicio: Betrothals in the Roman Upper Class', Classical Views, 3 (1984), pp. 419–51

17 Suzanne Dixon, 'The Marriage Alliance in the Roman Elite', Journal of Family History, 10 (1985), 353–78. The point that high mortality rates resulted in emotional insecurity for children and serial marriages for adults is made in K. R. Bradley, 'Dislocation in the Roman Family', Historical Reflections/Réflexions historiques, 14 (1987), pp. 33–62.

18 Pliny, Natural History, tr. A. Rackham (Harvard University Press, Cambridge, Mass., 1940), 28.70–1.

19 Bruce Frier, 'Roman Life Expectancy: The Pannonian Evidence', Phoenix, 37 (1983), pp. 328–44.

20 Soranus, Gynecology, tr. Oswei Temkin (Johns Hopkins University Press, Baltimore, 1956), 1.9.34.

21 *The Attic Nights of Aulus Gellius*, tr. John C. Rolfe (Heinemann, London, 1920), 4.3.

22 Keith R. Bradley, 'Child Labor in the Roman World', *Historical Reflections/ Réflexions historiques*, 12 (1985), pp. 311–25.

23 Plutarch, 'Cato the Younger', in *Plutarch's Lives*, tr. Bernadotte Perrin (Harvard University Press, Cambridge, Mass., 1919), 25.5; 52.3–4.

24 Yan Thomas, 'À Rome, pères citoyens et cité des pères', in Burguière et al., *Histoire de la famille*, vol. I, pp. 218–19.

25 Augustine, 'The Good of Marriage' ('De bono conjugali'), in *Treatises on Marriage and Other Subjects*, tr. Charles Wilcox (Fathers of the Church, New York, 1955), 15.17.

26 Eva Cantarella, *Pandora's Daughters*, tr. Maureen B. Fant (Johns Hopkins University Press, Baltimore, 1987), p. 149.

27 Jack Goody, 'Adoption in Cross-Cultural Perspective', *Comparative Studies in Society and History*, 11 (1969), p. 60.

28 Seneca, *Ad Lucilium epistulae morales*, tr. R. M. Gummere (Harvard University Press, Cambridge, Mass., 1925), 95.18–19; Plutarch, 'De tuenda sanitate praecepta', in *Plutarch's Moralia*, tr. F. C. Babbitt (Harvard University Press, Cambridge, Mass., 1928), 126.8–134.22.

29 Soranus, *Gynecology*, 1.11.42, and see also 1.4.23, 1.7.32.

30 Monica Helen Green, 'The Transmission of Ancient Theories of Female Physiology and Disease Through the Early Middle Ages', unpublished Princeton University PhD, 1985, pp. 23–36.

31 Galen, *On the Natural Faculties*, tr. A. J. Brock (Heinemann, London, 1928), 2.3.

32 Galen, *On the Usefulness of the Parts of the Body*, tr. Margaret Tallmadge May (Cornell University Press, Ithaca, NY, 1968), 14.2.265–336; Anthony Preus, 'Galen's Criticism of Aristotle's Conception Theory', *Journal of the History of Biology*, 10 (1977), pp. 65–85; Michael Boylan, 'Galen's Conception Theory', *Journal of the History of Biology*, 19 (1986), pp. 47–78.

33 See also *The Extant Works of Aretaeus the Cappadocian*, tr. Francis Adams (Sydenham Society, London, 1856), 'Acute Diseases', 2.11; 'Chronic Diseases', 2.11; 'Therapeutics of Acute Diseases', 2.10.

34 Galen, *Oeuvres anatomiques, physiologiques et médicales*, tr. Dr Ch. Daremberg (Baillière, Paris, 1856), 14, 15. Galen's vitalist and teleological interpretation of embryological development asserted that innate 'faculties' induced development. As experimentation declined, such all-encompassing theorizing proved popular. His works were copied by the encyclopedist Oribasius (AD 326–403) and the Byzantine compilers Aetius of Amida (AD 527–67), and Paulus Aegineta (AD 610–41).

35 Galen, *On the Affected Parts*, tr. Rudolph E. Siegel (S. Karger, New York, 1976), 6.5.

36 Soranus, *Gynecology*, 1.3.8, 1.11.35. Masters had an obvious interest in encouraging slave fertility; see Keith Bradley, *Slaves and Masters*

in the Roman Empire: A Study in Social Control (Oxford University Press, Oxford, 1987), p. 51.

37 Artemidorus, *Oneirocritica: The Interpretation of Dreams*, tr. Robert J. White (Noyes, Park Ridge, NJ, 1975), p. 63.

38 Paulus Aegineta, *The Seven Books of Paulus Aegineta*, tr. Francis Adams (Sydenham Society, London, 1844–7), 1.35; and see also *Oeuvres de Rufus d'Ephèse*, tr. Charles Daremberg (L'imprimerie nationale, Paris, 1879), 3.8.

39 J. N. Adams, *The Latin Sexual Vocabulary* (Duckworth, London, 1982).

40 Pliny, *Natural History*, 10.83; Lucretius, *De rerum natura*, tr. W. H. D. Rouse (Harvard University Press, Cambridge, Mass., 1935), 4.1190–270.

41 Soranus, *Gynecology*, 1.3.10.

42 Pliny, *Natural History*, 24.11; 28.30, 80; 20.263.

43 *Ovid's Amores*, tr. Guy Lee (Viking, New York, 1968), 1.14.39; 3.7.27; and see also Horace, *Satires*, tr. Rushton Fairclough (Harvard University Press, Cambridge, Mass., 1936), 1.8.30–2; Horace, *Odes and Epodes*, tr. C. E. Bennett (Harvard University Press, Cambridge, Mass., 1914), 1.13; 4.25.

44 Pliny, *Natural History*, 28.64.

45 Plutarch, 'Advice to Bride and Groom', in *Plutarch's Moralia*, 140.8; and see also *The Fasti of Ovid*, tr. Sir James George Fraser (Macmillan, London, 1929), 2.425–6.

46 Pliny, *Natural History*, 28.34, 60.

47 Pliny, *Natural History*, 25.114. On the use of astrology to ensure conceptions, predict defective births and determine sex see *Ptolemy's Tetrabiblos*, ed. J. M. Ashmond (Foulsham, London, 1917), 3.2, 3.7, 3.9–10.

48 *The Poems of Propertius*, tr. Constance Carrier (Indiana University Press, Bloomington, Indiana, 1913), 2.7.

49 Pliny the Younger, *Letters*, tr. William Melmoth (Harvard University Press, Cambridge, Mass., 1952), 4.15; and see also Aulus Gellius, *Attic Nights*, 2.13; Plutarch, 'Cato the Younger', in *Plutarch's Lives*, 25.3.

50 Seneca, *On Benefits*, 3.33.4; Seneca, 'Ad Marciam', in *Dialogues*, tr. A. Bourgery (Les belles lettres, Paris, 1961), 19.2.

51 Petronius, *Satyricon*, 116; see also Martial, *Epigrams*, 6.63; Horace, *Satires*, 2.5, Juvenal, *Satires*, 1.37–9.

52 L. P. Wilkinson, *Classical Attitudes to Modern Issues* (Kimber, London, 1979), p. 28; and see Seneca, *On Benefits*, 3.11.1.

53 In Egypt under Roman rule the census data revealed households of two to five children, and every fourth house with a slave or two. Lewis, *Life in Egypt under Roman Rule*, p. 53; Deborah Hobson, 'House and Household in Roman Egypt', *Yale Classical Studies*, 28 (1985), pp. 211–29.

54 Keith Hopkins, *Death and Renewal: Sociological Studies in Roman*

History (Cambridge University Press, Cambridge, 1984), vol. II, pp. 70–88.

55 Mark Golden, 'Did the Ancients Care When their Children Died?', *Greece and Rome*, 35 (1988), pp. 152–63.

56 Brent D. Shaw, 'The Family in Late Antiquity: The Experience of Augustine', *Past and Present*, 115 (1987), p. 46.

57 Longus, *Daphnis and Chloe*, tr. Paul Turner (Penguin, London, 1956), 4.35; see also Plautus' plays *Cistellaria* and *Casina*. The fullest account of abandonment is provided by John Boswell, *The Kindness of Strangers: The Abandonment of Children in Western Europe from Late Antiquity to the Renaissance* (Pantheon, New York, 1988).

58 Tacitus, *The Histories*, tr. Clifford H. Moore (Harvard University Press, Cambridge, Mass., 1962), 5.5.

59 Lewis, *Life in Egypt under Roman Rule*, 54.

60 Soranus, *Gynecology*, 2.5.10.

61 Seneca, 'De ira', in *Dialogues*, 1.15.2.

62 Seneca, *Ad Lucilium*, 66.26–8.

63 William Harris, 'The Theoretical Possibility of Extensive Infanticide in the Graeco-Roman World', *Classical Quarterly*, 32 (1982), p. 116.

64 Philo, *De specialibus legibus*, 3.114–15, cited in Jane F. Gardener, *Women in Roman Law and Society* (Croom Helm, London, 1986), p. 155.

65 H. S. Nielsen, 'Alumnus: A Term of Relation Denoting Quasi-Adoption', *Classica et Mediaevalia*, 38 (1987), pp. 141–88.

66 John Garret Winter, *Life and Letters in the Papyri* (University of Michigan Press, Ann Arbor, 1933), p. 31.

67 Ovid, *Metamorphoses*, tr. Mary Innes (Penguin, London, 1950), 9.666ff; and see also Apuleius, *Metamorphoses*, tr. Robert Graves (Penguin, London, 1950), 10.23; Terence, *The Self-Tormenter*, tr. John Sargeaunt (Harvard University Press, Cambridge, Mass., 1983), 637–42.

68 Jérôme Carcopino, *Daily Life in Ancient Rome* (Routledge, London, 1941), pp. 42, 77; W. den Boer, 'Demography in Roman History', *Mnemosyne*, 26 (1973), pp. 29–46.

69 Emiel Eyben, 'Family Planning in Graeco-Roman Antiquity', *Ancient Society*, 11–12 (1980–1), p. 26.

70 Boswell, *Kindness of Strangers*, pp. 69–73; William Langer, 'Infanticide: A Historical Survey', *History of Childhood Quarterly*, 1 (1974), p. 355.

71 The literary accounts frequently presented the mother seeking to save the daughter. See Ovid, *Metamorphoses*, 9.666ff; Apuleius, *Metamorphoses*, 10.23.

72 Dio Chrysostom, *Discourses*, 15.8, cited in Eyben, 'Family Planning', p. 77.

73 Cited in Danielle Gourevitch, *Le mal d'être femme: la femme et la médecine à Rome* (Les belles lettres, Paris, 1984), p. 133.

74 Aline Rousselle, 'Gestes et signes de la famille dans l'Empire Romain', in Burguière et al., *Histoire*, vol. I, p. 253.
75 Paulus Aegineta, *The Seven Books*, 1.38, 3.66; Soranus, *Gynecology*, 3.12.46.
76 Rufus d'Ephèse, *Oeuvres*, 3.8.
77 Caelius Aurelianus, *On Acute Diseases and on Chronic Diseases*, tr. I. E. Drabkin (University of Chicago Press, Chicago, 1950), 'Acute Diseases', 2.13.87, 3.5.48; 'Chronic Diseases', 1.17, 1.127, 1.147, 1.178, 2.79, 2.182.
78 Celsus, *De Medicina*, tr. W. G. Spencer (Harvard University Press, Cambridge, Mass., 1935), 1.1.
79 Aline Rousselle, *Porneia: On Desire and the Body in Antiquity*, tr. Felicia Pheasant (Blackwell, Oxford, 1988), p. 20.
80 Paulus Aegineta, *The Seven Books*, 1.5.
81 Tacitus, *Germania*, tr. W. Peterson (Harvard University Press, Cambridge, Mass., 1914), 20.
82 Dixon, *The Roman Mother*, pp. 61–2.
83 Keith Bradley, 'Wet Nursing in Rome', in Rawson, *The Family in Ancient Rome*, pp. 216–20.
84 Plutarch, 'Advice to Bride and Groom', 140.16.
85 Kay, *Martial*, p. 222.
86 Paul Veyne, 'L'Homosexualité à Rome', *Communications*, 35 (1982), 26–33; John Boswell, *Christianity, Social Tolerance and Homosexuality: Gay People in Western Europe from the Beginning of the Christian Era to the Fourteenth Century* (University of Chicago Press, Chicago, 1980), pp. 28–64.
87 Lucretius, *De rerum natura*, 4.1274–8.
88 Keith Bradley, 'Sexual Regulations in Wet Nursing Contracts from Roman Egypt', *Klio*, 62 (1980), pp. 321–5; Bradley, *Slaves and Masters*, p. 70.
89 John T. Noonan Jr, *Contraception: A History of its Treatment by Catholic Theologians and Canonists* (Harvard University Press, Cambridge, Mass., 1965), pp. 20, 50.
90 Some male slaves were castrated. Paulus Aegineta stated that doctors opposed such operations, 'But since we are sometimes compelled against our will by persons of high rank to perform the operation, we shall briefly describe the mode of doing it'; *The Seven Books*, 6.68. Martial claimed women preferred the company of eunuchs; *Epigrams*, 6.67.
91 Seneca, *Ad Lucilium*, 66.26–8.
92 Juvenal, *Satires*, 6.595–7. The assumption that women necessarily interested themselves in such matters led to one of the more popular medical treatises that dealt both with aids to fecundity and with abortifacients and contraceptives – the *Gynaecia Cleopatra* – being attributed to the Egyptian queen. No modern edition is available, but see *Gynaeciorum, hoc est, de mulierum tum aliis*, ed. H. K. Wolf (Thomas Guarinum, Basel, 1566), pp. 91–4, and Green, 'The Transmission of Ancient Theories', pp. 156–9.

93 Gardener, *Women in Roman Law*, p. 1.
94 Soranus, *Gynecology*, 1.10.36.
95 Keith Hopkins, 'Contraception in the Roman Empire', *Comparative Studies in Society and History*, 8 (1965–6), p. 140; Ann Ellis Hanson, 'The Eighth Month's Child and the Etiquette of Birth: *Obsit Omen!*', *Bulletin of the History of Medicine*, 61 (1987), pp. 589–602.
96 Lucretius, *De rerum natura*, 4.1270–4.
97 Soranus, *Gynecology*, 1.19.61.
98 Pliny, *Natural History*, 16.110.
99 Pliny, *Natural History*, 24.72.
100 Soranus, *Gynecology*, 64–5.
101 For the argument that some of these herbal potions were effective see John M. Riddle, *Dioscorides on Pharmacy and Medicine* (University of Texas Press, Austin, 1985), pp. 59–63, and Marie-Thérèse Fontanille, *Avortement et contraception dans la médecine Gréco-Romaine* (Laboratoires Searle, Paris, 1977).
102 Pliny, *Natural History*, 24.18.
103 Robert T. Gunther, *The Greek Herbal of Dioscorides* (University of Texas Press, Austin, 1985), 2.189; 3.146, 5.123.
104 Hopkins, 'Contraception in the Roman Empire', p. 167.
105 Soranus, *Gynecology*, 1.19.61.
106 Kay, *Martial*, p. 117; and see Martial, *Epigrams*, 2.1; 6.69.
107 Ovid, *Amores*, 3.90–6, and see Paul Veyne, 'La famille et l'amour sous l'Haut-Empire Romain', *Annales ESC*, 33 (1978), p. 46.
108 Hopkins, 'Contraception in the Roman Empire', p. 132.
109 Eyben, 'Family Planning', p. 9.
110 Pliny, *Natural History*, 29.45.
111 Soranus, *Gynecology*, 1.19.60.
112 Cantarella, *Pandora's Daughters*, p. 149.
113 Ovid, *The Fasti*, 1.622–9.
114 Ammianus Marcellinus, *History*, tr. John C. Rolfe (Heinemann, London, 1935–9), 16.10.18–19.
115 Seneca, 'Ad Helviam matrem', in *Dialogues*, 16.3.
116 Plutarch, *De tuenda sanitate praecepta*, 22.134.
117 Pliny, *Natural History*, 10.172.
118 W. J. Watt, 'Ovid, the Law and Roman Society on Abortion', *Acta Classica*, 16 (1973), pp. 89–101.
119 An exception was Suetonius' depiction of Domitian forcing his niece Julia – with whom he had an affair – to abort. Suetonius, *The Lives of the Caesars*, tr. J. C. Rolfe (Harvard University Press, Cambridge, Mass., 1929), Dom. 22.2.
120 Porphyre, 'À Gauros. Sur la manière dont l'embryon reçoit l'âme', in A. M. Fustugière, *La révélation d'Hermès Trismegiste* (Lecoffre, Paris, 1953), vol. II, pp. 268–76.
121 Soranus, *Gynecology*, 1.19.60.
122 Soranus, *Gynecology*, 1.19.63.
123 Pliny, *Natural History*, 14.29; 27.16, 55. Pliny also claimed that menstrual fluid could magically cause abortions.

124 Paulus Aegineta, *The Seven Books*, 3.61
125 R. Etienne, 'La conscience médicale antique et la vie des enfants', *Annales de démographie historique* (1973), pp. 15–29.
126 Aretaeus, *The Extant Works*, 2.11.
127 Soranus, *Gynecology*, 3.1.12.
128 Gourevitch, *Le mal d'être femme*, p. 224; Natalie Kampen, *Image and Status: Roman Working Women in Ostia* (Gebr. Mann Verlag, Berlin, 1981), pp. 35, 69, 116.
129 *Juvenal's Satires*, tr. John Warrington (Dent, London, 1954), 6.595–7. In Epistle 19 of *The Love Epistles of Aristaenetus*, tr. N. B. Halked and R. B. Sheridan (Wilkie, London, 1783), p. 126, an abortionist gave her account of the services rendered a courtesan:

> She was splendidly kept – but was highly afraid
> Lest breeding should spoil so important a trade.
> Among the old gossips, she learn'd to divine
> Whene'er she conceived, by infallible sign.
> So when the case happen'd, she told her old dame:
> And to me for advice, as more knowing, they came.
> I gave my opinion, and added a drug,
> Which demolish'd her fears, expeditious and snug.

130 Enzo Nardi, *Procurato aborto nel mundo Greco Romano* (Giuffre, Milan, 1971), pp. 367–79.
131 Digest 47.11.4, cited in Dixon, *The Roman Mother*, p. 102, ft. 37. See also Cicero, 'In Defense of Cluentius', in *The Speeches*, tr. H. G. Hodge (Harvard University Press, Cambridge, Mass., 1927), 11.32.
132 Brunt, *Italian Manpower*, p. 147.
133 Eyben, 'Family Planning', p. 29.
134 Cora E. Lutz, 'Musonius Rufus, "The Roman Socrates"', *Yale Classical Studies*, 10 (1977), pp. 87–101; Michel Foucault, *The Care of the Self*, tr. Robert Hurley (Pantheon, New York, 1986), pp. 180–2.
135 Musonius Rufus cited in Eyben, 'Family Planning', p. 41; and see also Keith Hopkins, 'A Textual Emendation in a Fragment of Musonius Rufus', *Classical Quarterly*, 15 (1965), pp. 72–4.
136 Eyben, 'Family Planning', p. 43.
137 Tacitus, *Germania*, 19.
138 Pliny, *Natural History*, 28.58.
139 Veyne, 'La famille et l'amour sous l'Haut-Empire Romain', pp. 35–63.
140 A. Cameron, 'The Exposure of Children and Greek Ethics', *Classical Review*, 46 (1932), p. 112.
141 Pliny, *Natural History*, 14.5.
142 Veyne, 'L'Empire romain', pp. 54–5.

3

Abortion and Contraception in the Christian West

'Use which is against nature'
St Augustine (*c*.400 BC), *The Good of Marriage*

The historian attempting to investigate the relationship of changing family forms and fertility restriction in Greek and Roman times finds the apparent silence of women a major problem. But when one turns to the Christian era an additional barrier is encountered. The sources no longer provide simple descriptions of family limitation methods; such acts were now only noted in order to be ferociously condemned. Is it reasonable to hope that such a prescriptive literature, generated increasingly by celibate churchmen and often clearly formulaic in nature, could tell us anything about actual practices? If stop signs imply the existence of traffic, the clergy's on-going condemnations of abortion and contraception can at the very least be taken as evidence of the continued employment of such practices. But an analysis of the copious religious writings of the first six centuries of this era offers additional insights. The early church fathers, fixated as they were on the evils of sexuality, often revealed themselves to be more prepared than their pagan counterparts to recognize the very real problems posed by procreation. Indeed, their preaching of marital continence may ironically have had the unintended consequence of legitimating women's attempts to limit childbearing.

Augustine (AD 354–430), a member of the North African Roman elite and later bishop of Hippo, was the most influential formulator of early Christian attitudes towards fertility control. He knew of what he spoke. From the age of eighteen to twenty-nine he was a novice or 'auditor' in the Manichean sect. The Manichees had in the third and fourth centuries renewed the attack on procreation originally launched by the Gnostics in the first century. Dualists who hated matter and sought to protect the 'light' by maintaining bodily purity, they rejected procreation as an evil act which resulted in entrapping souls in bodies. Orthodox Christians accused them of going beyond the heretical extreme of condemning marriage as sinful. Some, claimed the Christians, were not foregoing sexual intercourse, but indulging in it while employing contraceptive practices to thwart its results.

Augustine was aware of such practices; he probably employed them himself. In his youth he was allowed, since not yet a member of the Manichean 'elect' who had to forego all sexual relations, but still a simple auditor, to take a concubine. He did so, like many other male members of the Roman elite, with the idea of postponing the question of marriage until he reached his thirties. Augustine fathered one son in the first year of this relationship; the remaining thirteen years were barren.[1] After converting to Christianity and abandoning his mistress, he accused the Manichees of instructing the married on how to avoid conceptions:

> Is it not you who regard the begetting of children, by which souls are bound up in flesh, to be a more serious sin than sexual union? Is it not you who used to urge us to observe, to the extent that it was possible, the time when a woman after her menstruation is likely to conceive, and to abstain from intercourse at that time for fear that a soul might become entangled in flesh?[2]

Such a misplaced belief in conception being most likely to take place near menstruation was widespread in the ancient world. Augustine was presumably thinking of the more effective protective measures employed by his concubine when, in *Against Secundinus*, he referred to prostitutes who 'take steps not to conceive'.[3] And elsewhere, in one of the earliest attacks on coitus interruptus, he accused the Manicheans of withdrawing before orgasm, by which seed with 'a shameful slip is poured out'.[4]

What exactly did such Christian condemnations signify? There is a danger in simply accepting the claim of Augustine and his fellow church fathers that they were revolutionizing morality. Easily lost sight of is the fact that the early Christians did not make a dramatic break from most contemporary ethical attitudes. Indeed, their proselytizing successes were based in large part on providing answers to problems already being wrestled with in late antiquity, in particular the fear that the empire's decline was somehow related to moral degeneration.

In the latter half of the second century the Romans' confident defence of their culture of hedonistic puritanism waned. The accompanying shift in attitudes towards sexuality was associated with, rather than caused by, the rise of Christianity. A more important factor was the ruralization of the empire. The manpower shortages that accompanied the decline of slavery and the interruption of trade due to foreign pressures on the German and Persian borders disabled the economy. The barbarians did not descend on Rome; they were sucked into the empire by its inherent weaknesses. The empire, defending itself more and more with foreign levies and moving its capital to Milan and finally Ravenna, continued to call itself 'Roman' but in reality had become something quite different.

The expense of dealing with unrest on the borders proved crippling. From the third century on the tottering regime had to extort from the cities ever increasing taxes and services. Their urban, educated style of life was destroyed and their exhausted civic elite replaced in power by the army and the provincial magnates. Symbolic of the change in social climate was the replacement of the republican ruling class's simple toga with the new hierarchically organized society's heraldic devices. The complex middling social stratum of freedmen was liquidated. The rural masses – or at least those who did not find barbarian rule preferable – were reduced to poverty and bound as labourers to the *latifundia* or great estates.[5]

Placed under increased pressure, the empire exalted the need for order and discipline and turned philosophy to the purposes of social control. Responding to the rise of self-doubt, new magical and mystery cults emerged; once sceptical westerners now took an anxious interest in the spiritual philosophies of the east. In times so insecure that individuals had to beg the protection of an oppressive and bureaucratic state or submit the control of their movements and even their occupations to local warlords, the self-denial and austerity preached by Christians and Stoics appeared to provide some solace. Christianity attracted educated Romans like Augustine in presenting itself as both a rational and supra-rational creed. The emperor Constantine's Edict of Milan of AD 314 guaranteed its toleration; Theodosius (AD 379–85) declared Christianity the state religion.

This turning inward was complemented by a shifting of attention from the public to the private. The family was extolled as a key social building block and its order and concord accordingly stressed. Respectable family life was, by the third century, the norm and in the west replaced urban life in importance. 'Privacy' emerged as the 'state' declined. The rational, optimistic approach to sexuality was eclipsed by more fearful views. Sexual excesses were increasingly condemned as weakening; in artistic portrayals nudes were replaced with clothed figures.

Christians did not so much create this new morality as act as its conduit. Already the Stoics had put in place a 'puritanical' creed, and the metaphysics of the neo-Platonists and mystery cults had popularized an otherworldliness. The passions were suspect; sexuality was regarded as necessarily pitted against reason. The attacks on the old style of life launched by the Stoics were simply continued by Christian converts. John Chrysostom (AD 347–407), bishop of Constantinople, was preceded in his opposition to public baths and nudity by pagan moralists. Seneca had condemned adultery because of the trouble and disorder it caused; Jerome (AD 347–420) attacked it as immoral and dangerous. Musonius Rufus' and Seneca's critiques of the pursuit of sexual pleasure were followed by those of Jerome, Origen and Clement.[6]

Most Christian virtues had been anticipated by the ancients. But Christians were not simply philosophers; they also formed a social movement; they practised and preached.[7] Especially striking was the vigour with which they listed and attacked a vast range of vices. They carried over the Jewish abhorrence of sexual perversions and prided themselves on 'avoiding porneia', which as catalogued in the *Didache* or *Teachings of the Twelve Apostles* (c.AD 100), a Syrian statement of Christian teachings, included abortion, infanticide, magic and homosexuality. The second-century *Book of Barnabas*, in drawing on Hellenic natural history, likened the adulterer to the hyena which changed sex each year, the fellator to the weasel which conceived through the mouth, and the corrupter of children to the hare which 'increases unduly its discharge each year, and thus has as many holes as it is years old'.[8] The more extreme Christian thinkers ultimately objected to almost every manifestation of sexuality from abortion, contraception, divorce and adultery to the wearing of wigs and the use of make-up.[9] The purported intent of condemning such acts was to end debauchery. Similar concerns had been voiced by the pagans, but a new shift in emphasis was evident. What had been primarily proprietary concerns were made ethical issues. The ancients sought to police sexuality for the conservative purpose of subjecting every individual to a family patriarch; the church for the radical purpose of freeing Christians from the entangling world of secular ambitions and family squabbles.

Where the church was truly innovative was in making sexuality the symbol of the difference between Christians and pagans and the key indicator of individual morality. The married and the celibate, the rich and the poor all had held up to them as a new moral common denominator the importance of controlling sexual urges. An enormous ethical burden was now borne by acts heretofore considered hardly more significant than eating or drinking. The pagans had not been unthinking hedonists, but the idea of viewing mundane sexual practices as the privileged indicators of one's spiritual condition had previously been unthinkable. The Christians made a difference in nuance the basis for a fundamental cultural cleavage.[10]

This odd Christian fixation on sexuality resulted from the inherent tension posed by the question of how to reconcile the warring demands of the spirit and the body. The New Testament was coloured by a clear eschatological tone in which marriage and all family concerns were disparaged. Its tenor bore the imprint of both the pessimism of the Stoics and the puritanism of radical Judaism. The Essenes, an austere Jewish cult described by the historian Josephus (AD 37–93), perhaps provided the initial inspiration for this turning away from the world.[11] Certainly Philo (30 BC–AD 45), a Jewish scholar working in the Greek milieu of first-century Alexandria, developed something close to Christian views in his attacks on divorce, incest, adultery, pederasty and the marriage of the sterile.[12] Noonan correctly suggests that the revulsion against the body was an idea 'in the air' in the first centuries after Christ.[13] Christianity did not create this milieu, but it was certainly to thrive in it.

The Stoics had been pessimistic about the body; even gloomier were the eastern, Gnostic Christians who developed the idea that man's 'fall' was somehow a direct result of sins of the flesh.

Salvation accordingly required the extinguishing of the sexual passions, directed by a Christian hierarchy practising obligatory celibacy. The androgynous, non-procreative ideal advanced by such ascetics clearly had a powerful attraction. Tertullian (AD 155–220) confessed himself unclear as to why intercourse was permitted; Gregory of Nyssa, John Chrysostom, Ambrose and Jerome all declared virginity superior to marriage.

Virginity had traditionally been esteemed in women, but Christian celibacy shored up male power and was associated with a violent misogyny which spread, particularly in the east, in the fourth century. Origen (AD 185–255) declared it a sin to pray in the marriage bed, defiled as it would necessarily be; monks openly asked if the married could ever be saved, involved as they were in 'that beastly copulation, that shameless coition, that foulness of stinking and uncomely deed'.[14] These were extreme views, in part coloured by eschatological beliefs. The recluses of the desert – some so convinced of their indifference to sexuality as to countenance even the mingling of monks and virgins – were viewed by the laity as distinctly bizarre. Nevertheless, the desert morality of monasticism percolated into the west. The literature on spiritual guidance was in demand and fasting widely undertaken to subdue the flesh.[15] But the reality was that the clergy was slow to embrace celibacy; clerical concubinage was to be tenaciously maintained. Only from the fourth century onward were attempts made to end it.

Where did lay marriage fit in all of this? For traditional Jews marriage was a religious duty; Christians were ambivalent. Marriage had been defended by Paul as only better than burning. 'God has allowed us', stated Origen, presbyter of Alexandria, 'to marry wives, because not everybody is capable of the superior condition which is to be absolutely pure.'[16] Ambrose, the fourth-century bishop of Milan, not able to see how sex could even be part of God's plan, equated virginity with paradise. But while orthodox Christians stressed the moral superiority of virginity, they recognized the public scandal created by the Gnostic opposition to all procreation. Clement of Alexandria (AD 150–215) attacked those who 'blasphemed by their continence both the creation and the Holy Creator . . . and teach that one must reject marriage and begetting of children.'[17]

The church fell back on the Stoic–Jewish argument that the need to procreate provided a rational reason for marriage. Clement was representative: he narrowly supported marriage inasmuch as it could produce children, but asserted that a chaste marriage was superior to a prolific one. In the fourth century John Chrysostom agreed that marriage served a purpose in that procreation raised the shadow of eternity.[18] Ambrose accordingly opposed the unfruitful intercourse of the old and pregnant as unnatural. Pleasure in and of itself was wrong; its pursuit in marriage had to be curbed. Jerome, in beginning from such a premise, was quite logical when he concluded that 'An adulterer is he who is too ardent a lover of his wife.'[19]

Augustine's importance lay in his crystallizing the doctrine that would have such a long life in Christian thought – that marriage could be defended if it produced offspring, fidelity and continence. He did not mention mutual love. 'Love' was viewed by Christians, as it had been by pagans, as a subversive and destructive passion and therefore dangerous in marriage. The church was more interested in assuring 'caritas conjugalis' – amity, charity, and fidelity. Augustine contrasted a respectable marriage 'contracted for the sake of issue, and the compact of a lustful love'.[20] Sex continued to symbolize the fall from grace and the coming of disorder. Impotency, frigidity and erections were, asserted Augustine, all uncontrolled; all demonstrated man's enslavement to lust. Marriage was good, but celibacy was better.

Adam and Eve might have had intercourse in paradise, Augustine asserted, yet their organs would have been governed by reason: 'For as there were no groans of pain in childbirth, but an impulse at maturity relaxed the female organs, so for gestation and conception there was no lustful appetite, but voluntary exercise united in both natures.'[21] Augustine was not as misogynistic as the monks who castigated women for exhausting men; he saw men equally enslaved by the body.[22] But he did lament the fact that 'many matrons, . . . although they are not adulteresses, force their husbands, who often desire to be continent, to pay the debt of the flesh, not with any hope of progeny, but through an intemperate use of their right under the ardour of concupiscence.'[23] Augustine, like other early church fathers, was not desirous of large families. He hoped that if Christians had to marry they would have one or two children and then mutually agree to lead a life of continence.

Peter Brown has pertinently remarked that Augustine was

'lyrical' in his defence of virginity; merely conscientious in his defence of the married state.[24] If with hindsight his arguments look half-hearted, their importance should not be discounted. He and other orthodox Christians were aware they were charting a tricky course between the extremes of Gnostic hostility to the flesh and pagan indulgence in it.[25] Augustine played a key role in elaborating the subtle Christian argument that evil lay not in copulation *per se*, but in the lust that accompanied it. His thesis combined the old Roman concern for the danger of irrational passions with the new monastic distrust of pleasure. Procreation was made the obligatory price of marriage. Sexual intercourse undertaken for pleasure – even with one's spouse – was declared a venial sin. To employ purposefully any means to prevent conception Augustine judged a sign of cruel lust.

Christians condemned any method of fertility control that permitted pleasure, but prevented children.[26] It was the perversity of seeking an 'empty and sterile pleasure' rather than the specific means employed that was the focus of attack.[27] What threat did such practices pose the church? Catholic historians tend to assume that the church countered such practices in the first centuries for much the same reasons as it would in the twentieth century. But such an approach – in seeking to trace clear, consistent continuities – takes the issue out of context.

To restore the context, it first should be noted that population concerns played little part in such teachings. Many converts, convinced that they lived in the last days, were indifferent to the issue of producing heirs. In later centuries the command 'increase and multiply' would be brandished as an indication of God's desire for large families; the early Christians interpreted it as an injunction to grow in reason. Spiritual descendants were more important than children; perfection was to be sought in virginity rather than in the married state. 'Virginity does not cause the human race to dry up', claimed John Chrysostom, 'but sin and unnatural intercourse do, which was proven in Noah's time when men, their flocks, and everything else living on the earth was destroyed.'[28] Tertullian sounded equally 'Malthusian' in claiming that increased numbers were not needed:

The strongest witness is the vast population of the earth to which we are a burden and she scarcely can provide for our needs; as our demands grow greater our complaints against nature's inadequacy are heard by all. The scourges of pestilence, famine, wars, and earthquakes have come to be regarded as a blessing to overcrowded nations, since they serve to prune away the luxuriant growth of the human race.[29]

The same note was struck by Jerome's complaint, 'A field is sown with seeds so that it may be harvested. The world is already filled; the earth is too small for us.'[30] John Chrysostom asserted that 'the earth and sea and all the world has been inhabited'.[31]

Christians placed in doubt the value of the family. Tertullian asked in *To His Wife* why one would want children who were only encumbrances 'perilous to the faith' in this 'most wicked world'.[32] Caesarius, bishop of Arles (AD 503–43), provided an equally gloomy view of paternity in asserting that when 'sons reach manhood it is difficult for most of them not to desire the death of their parents'.[33] It was in this context that Constantine, the first Christian emperor, revoked the laws put in place by Augustus to penalize childlessness. Ironically the church preached continence at the very time when the demographic decline of the late empire was forcing it to accept the threatening assistance of barbarian migrants.

Most Christians were not opposed to children. Indeed, the church boasted that it alone opposed exposure and infanticide. Clement of Alexandria raised the spectre of the incest that resulted when the abandoned, raised as prostitutes by procurers, were sold unwittingly to kin.[34] Tertullian, denying the claim of pagan detractors that Christians killed and ate children as part of their religious ceremonies, flung back the taunt, 'You expose them to the cold and hunger and to wild beasts, or else get rid of them by the slower death of drowning.'[35] But such practices were mainly the last recourse of the desperate, and hostility to such acts was already widespread. Philo, the Jewish scholar, was only one of the more notable opponents of such inhumane undertakings. If a child was protected in the womb, he reasoned, there was all the more reason to protect it once outside.[36] The emperor Constantine had infanticide treated as murder, but there is no evidence that his decree had any marked effect. Indeed, Lecky later suggested that Christian prudery, in making it more imperative to hide the evidence of illegitimate affairs, might well have led to an increase in exposure and infanticide.[37]

'Christians marry, as do all [others]', declared the author of the *Epistle to Diognetus*; 'they beget children; but they do not destroy foetuses.'[38] Were Christians particularly concerned by the need to protect fetal life? Catholic historians such as John Noonan, who defend contraception but oppose abortion, have argued that early Christians, like their twentieth-century counterparts, condemned abortion because it entailed the killing of a live fetus. But this was not quite the case. Early abortion and contraception were regarded by some early Christians not as different but as very much the same thing – attempts to enjoy sexual pleasures without bearing children.

It is true that Tertullian attacked the abortions of the pagans, in *Ad nationes*, as the shedding of the blood of the future.[39] The Christian apologist Athenagoras, in his *Legatio* (AD 176–80), similarly advanced the Christians' condemnation of abortion as a sign of their superior morality. 'Again, what sense does it make to think of us as murderers when we say that women who practice abortion are murderers and will render an account to God for abortion?'[40]

But such condemnations were not based on a concept of fetal vitality. In Roman law the fetus was referred to, not as *homo* (human being) or *infans* (child), but as *spes animantis* (that which has hopes of living or being ensouled). Until its birth it was considered part of the mother and warranted no special consideration. Christian concerns for fetal life can be traced back to the translation into Greek of the Old Testament (the Septuagint) in the third century BC. Exodus 21:22–3 called for the punishment of accidental abortion by fines.[41] Compensation, determined by the stage of fetal development, was to be paid by the party who accidently caused the miscarriage. If the mother died the punishment was death. The Greek translation produced by the Hellenic Jews shifted the focus of concern from the mother to the fetus.[42] The destruction of a formed fetus was now declared to be murder. Philo of Alexandria followed the Aristotelian argument in seeing vitality occurring at forty and eighty days, and the Stoics in declaring that a fetus was until birth part of the woman.[43] But at the same time he moved beyond biblical injunctions to condemn violently exposure, infanticide and abortion of a formed fetus.

Christians like Jerome argued along the same lines that protection was due the formed fetus.

Augustine, like his pagan contemporaries, did not believe a fetus was fully formed at the moment of conception. He referred to stages of development when describing those who 'extinguish and destroy the fetus in some way in the womb, preferring that their offspring die before it lives, or if it was already alive in the womb to kill it before it was born'.[44] He held that the woman who aborted was guilty, not of homicide, but of perversion. 'Because it is not yet possible to speak of a soul living in a body destitute of sensation if such a kind is not formed in flesh, it is therefore not endowed with sensation.'[45] John Chrysostom was equally confused about how to deal with abortion: 'something even worse than murder for I have no name to give it, since it does not take off the thing born, but prevents its being born'.[46]

Tertullian likened late abortion to infanticide: 'To forbid birth is only quicker murder. It makes no difference whether one takes away the life once born or destroys it as it comes to birth. He is a man who is to be a man; the fruit is always present in the seed.'[47] But Tertullian, like Augustine, followed the ancient doctors in agreeing that one could not talk of a fetus until after quite some time – 'while yet the mother's blood is still being drawn on to form the human being' – and that an abortion was justified if required to save the mother's life.[48]

A harder line was advanced by some. Basil, the defender of Greek monasticism, in a letter of 374, instructed Amphilochius, recently appointed to the see of Iconium, that he should ignore such subtleties: 'She who has deliberately destroyed a fetus has to pay the penalty of murder. And there is no exact inquiry among us as to whether the fetus was formed or unformed.'[49] The penance of ten years, the same as for attempted suicide, had to be levied. Caesarius of Arles similarly asserted,

As many as they kill after they are conceived or born, before the tribunal of the eternal Judge they will be held guilty of so many murders. If women attempt to kill the children within them by evil medicines, and themselves die in the act, they become guilty of three crimes on their own: suicide, spiritual adultery, and murder of the unborn child.[50]

In the Councils of Elvira (AD 305) and Ancyra (AD 314) and the Synods of Lerida (AD 546) and Trulla (AD 629) – all local rather than ecumenical gatherings – the distinctions concerning the stage of fetal development were ignored and abortion lumped in with infanticide. 'And we pay no attention', declared the bishop of the last conclave, 'to the subtle distinction as to whether the foetus is formed or unformed.'[51] But in fact canon law followed Augustine in holding that the embryo was 'besouled' in the second month and 'besexed' in the fourth. What even the writings of the more conservative made clear is that they had no way of basing their condemnations of abortion on the concept of animation at the point of conception. Their condemnations were based rather on the more general argument that it was a non-procreative act.

In the twentieth century the western defenders of contraception have usually sought to draw a clear line between birth control and abortion. In late antiquity such demarcations were rarely made. Given the fact that the same medicines were employed as both contraceptives and abortifacients, it was quite natural that Christians should feel no great need to discriminate one from the other. Thus contraception in the form of 'medicine' was attacked in the *Didache* as employed by the 'killers of offspring, corrupters of the mold of God'.[52] Marcus Minucius Felix, in *Octavius* (second century AD), contrasted the decent Christian matrons with the pagan 'women who, by the use of medical potions, destroy the nascent life in their wombs, and murder the child before they bring it forth'.[53] Caesarius of Arles cautioned 'that no woman may take a potion so that she is unable to conceive or condemns in herself the nature which God willed to be fecund'.[54] Augustine, in *Marriage and Concupiscence*, presented the classic formulation of Christian hostility to contraception, which linked it with magic and abortion. The sinful, he asserted, were those

for the sake of lust obstructing their procreation by an evil prayer or an evil deed . . . Sometimes this lustful cruelty, or cruel lust, comes to this, that they even procure poisons of sterility, and, if these do not work, extinguish and destroy the fetus in some way in the womb, preferring that their offspring die before it lives, or if it was already alive in the womb to kill it before it was born.[55]

To employ such devices, he charged, made a wife a harlot and a husband an adulterer.

John Chrysostom also referred to couples having recourse to libations, incantations and love potions. The wife, he declared, became in this the subject of activities used by whores. 'For sorceries are applied not to the womb that is prostituted, but to the injured wife, and there are plottings without number, and invocations of devils, and necromanciers; and daily wars, and truceless fightings, and home-cherished jealousies.'[56] Clement of Alexandria referred to women who 'keep up old wives' whisperings over their cups, learning charms and incantations from soothsayers, to the ruin of nuptial bonds'.[57] Caesarius attacked the Gallo-Romans' use of herbs, amulets and 'diabolical marks'. He opposed, in referring to the use of an 'impious drug' to cure barrenness, all such attempts to regulate fertility.[58]

> Therefore, those to whom God is unwilling to grant children should not try to have them by means of herbs or magic signs or evil charms . . . Just as women whom God wants to bear more children should not take medicines to prevent their conception, so those whom God wishes to remain sterile should desire and seek this gift from God alone.[59]

But in fact Christians had their own rituals to promote fecundity. Augustine mocked the pagan belief in gods protecting the various stages of procreation – Janus opening the womb, Saturn protecting the seed, Mena presiding over the menstrual flow and so on – but in Christian lands saints were appealed to and pilgrimages made to overcome barrenness.[60]

The Christian condemnations of fertility control were aimed particularly at women. Little was said of male contraceptive practices. But Christian scholars showed themselves as preoccupied as the pagans by the loss of male seed. Clement of Alexandria argued, 'Because of its divine institution for the propagation of man, the seed is not to be vainly ejaculated, nor is it to be damaged, nor is it to be wasted.'[61] He really echoed Plato when he declared, 'Moses taught: "Do not sow seeds on rocks and stones, on which they will never take root."' Although he was apparently attacking homosexuality, such an injunction could also have been levelled against 'unnatural' heterosexual acts. Not only was the 'scattering of seed' wrong; so too were sexual encounters during menstruation, nursing and pregnancy, because the womb 'refuses seed when intercourse is contrary to nature'.[62]

Augustine, as we saw, accused the Manicheans of withdrawing before orgasm, by which seed with 'a shameful slip is poured out'. Epiphanius, a fourth-century Cypriot bishop, was the first of the patristic writers to focus on the story in Genesis of Onan to condemn such acts.[63] Onan was killed by God for refusing to have children by his dead brother's wife and for 'casting his seed on the ground'. Jewish scholars stressed the general disobedience of Onan as being the cause of his punishment; Christians narrowed it to the specific act of ejaculating *ex utero*. Jerome's translation of Genesis played a key role in the Christian condemnations of the practice. According to his version Onan was killed because he did a 'detestable thing'; the original passage simply read that Onan 'did not please God'.[64] The early Christian references to coitus interruptus were rare; only Epiphanius, Jerome and Augustine clearly condemned the practice.

Christians might call contraception 'murder' and likewise refer to homosexuals as murderers, yet they knew that the seed did not have a rational soul. Clearly they were using the terms in a moral rather than legal way. Jewish scholars continued to argue that Onan's disobedience was of greater significance than the specific act that symbolized it. Accordingly there were some rabbis such as R. Eliezer (AD 80–100) and R. Meir (AD 150) who held that withdrawal should be employed to protect a nursing mother from a subsequent conception. 'During the twenty-four months [that the mother nurses her child] he must thresh inside and winnow outside.'[65] The good spouse was to be not only fertile but in addition prudent and charitable. No Christian defences were ever offered of such practices.

As their references to Plato, Aristotle, Hippocrates and Soranus made clear, the church fathers, though they opposed fertility control, did not reject the medical texts in which so much of it had been discussed. Indeed, the fear and denigration of women that was expressed by many patristic writers was shored up by references to writings by ancient doctors.[66]

Patristic writers such as Origen and Ambrose condemned contraceptives that could be employed by women, but searched the herbals for drugs such as the willow and the chaste tree that could help in ensuring continence. Methodius cited Homer in describing the willow's ability to extinguish 'every inclination to the begetting of children'.[67] Clement likewise repeated Theophrastus' belief that beans could cause barrenness.[68] The monks carefully avoided the foods – meat, wine and flatulent vegetables – that the pagan authors recommended for the production of seed. The ancients feared that loss of semen endangered health; the monks were alarmed that it threatened virtue.

Lactantius (AD 250–317) provided, in 'The Workmanship of God', the fullest early Christian account of embryology. He drew on Aristotle, Varro, Cicero and Lucretius to argue that procreation provided evidence of God's masterful plan. The two semens, drawn from both sexes, mixed, congealed, coagulated, and were finally 'consummated' on the fortieth day. The child's sex was determined by which semen was stronger; character was determined by whether the mixed seed adhered to the right/male or the left/female horn of the womb.[69] A more Aristotelian idea of conception with the emphasis on male seed was maintained by Augustine, Clement and Jerome. Whereas Lactantius noted that the 'excitement of pleasure' was needed for procreation, the fear that intercourse endangered men was expressed by Clement, who cited Democritus in likening orgasm to 'a minor epilepsy'. 'A whole man is torn out', he warned, 'when the seed is lost in intercourse . . . Certainly we can see at a glance that the nerves are strained by it as on a loom and, in the intense feeling aroused by intercourse, are stretched to the breaking point. It spreads a mist over the senses and tires the muscles.'[70] Macrobius (fl. 400), who it is assumed was a Christian apologist, provided in his *Saturnalia* an account of women's weaker, wetter physiology that was equally true to the humoral teachings of the classics.[71] By the sixth century, Greek medical works were becoming rare in the west, but a few condensed and abbreviated editions of Soranus, Hippocrates and Galen continued to circulate. Ironically, much of their detailed gynaecological information was to be compiled and passed on by celibate monks.

What was the relevance of the Christian discussion of fertility control to the status of women? It was once thought that the church held a special appeal for the oppressed, in particular slaves and women. In fact it clearly directed its attention at converting the urban male elite.[72] Moreover, the most ascetic church fathers viewed women with fear and loathing; their greatest concern was to shield young men from their seductions. The celebration of celibacy was accompanied by a denigration of women's reproductive power. The misogyny of even moderate Christians was quite striking. 'If it is not to generate children that the woman was given to the man as a helpmate', asked Augustine, 'in what could she be a help for him?'[73]

But the early church fathers were often ambivalent in their attitudes towards women. Jerome and John Chrysostom described the evil nature of females in general, but some of their best friends were women.[74] In the early years of persecution, Christian scholars such as Tertullian and Clement made special appeals to them. Women for their part seemed to ignore the misogyny in Christianity and root out arguments in the scriptures that could be used to defy husbands and fathers.

What was there in the Christian message that could appeal to women? The Christian defence of the celibate, contemplative life, which clearly had a powerful spiritual appeal, presented the option of avoiding marriage and childbearing altogether. Women who were attracted to such a life were not motivated by mere masochism. A genuine desire to overcome and redefine sex roles can be detected in such a choice. Marriage and the bearing of children had traditionally been policed by men to serve their purposes. Now women at least had a legitimate alternative.[75]

What of the married? The Christian condemnations of infanticide and exposure would presumably have resulted in fewer mothers having to envisage the sacrifice of their infants. Similarly, the church's attack on the institutions that supported the sexual double standard – prostitution, slavery, adultery, divorce – may have served women's interests.[76] The ancient world had been primarily a monogamous society, but forms of polygamy had been tolerated for the purpose of providing heirs. Christians 'radicalized' monogamy in condemning concubinage and divorce.[77] Since procreation was, in the church's view, no longer essential, the stratagems devised to sustain it were not needed. Augustine would not sanction, as the Romans did, a divorce simply because a wife was barren. Christians did envisage marriages ending in separation if adultery took place, but they would not tolerate the idea of a subsequent remarriage.[78] Athenagoras equated even the second marriages of widows with adulterous unions.

How did women fare from the church's condemnation of fertility control? Churchmen were aware of how preoccupying childbearing was to women. John Chrysostom noted the inevitable round of 'labor pains, childbirth and children'. Courtship and the settling of the dower posed hurdles, he noted, 'Yet, once that anxiety is eased, the fear of childlessness straightaway replaces it. In addition, there is the conflicting worry of too many children.'[79] A woman was always fearful that her husband would be angry if she was either too fertile or not fertile enough. Jerome concurred that the wealthy woman's hectic round of pleasing her husband, educating her children, greeting guests, computing expenses and directing a staff of weavers, cooks and servants was tiring, but that she only became her own person when 'no longer subject to the anxieties and pain of childbirth'.[80] In defending the virtues of continence, suggests Aline Rousselle, Christianity directly appealed to such women.[81]

No doubt there were many like Paula, of whom Jerome wrote that she continued 'to fulfil a wife's duty, but that she only complied with her husband's longing to have male offspring'.[82] Wives who found themselves in forced, early unions were attracted to the asceticism and equality preached by Christians. Roman matrons, rendered hysterical by repugnantly unhappy marriages, found consolation in its message. The church's most important innovation was its stress on the continence of the married couple, for life or after the childbearing years of marriage. There is evidence that, following conversion, some couples decided to live lives of what Tertullian described as 'freedom'. In the first instance this option may not have been that onerous, inasmuch as it was chiefly chosen by the elderly and particularly widows.

For younger couples the church hoped to restrict intercourse solely to procreation. 'For as the husbandman throwing the seed into the ground awaits the harvest, not throwing more upon it', claimed Athenagorus, 'so to us the procreation of children is the measure of our independence in appetite.'[83] Some women were attracted by such an ideal. Jerome and Ambrose opposed intercourse during menstruation and pregnancy as contaminating, and such interdictions increased over time. By the sixth century, Caesarius of Arles was arguing that a Christian at the very least should observe chastity for a few days before communion and during Lent. Indeed the hope was that he 'should never know his wife except from the desire for children'.[84] Children born from parents who indulged too frequently would be sickly. 'If those who are unwilling to control themselves plowed and sowed repeatedly their land which was already sowed, let us see in what kind of fruit they would rejoice.' Children conceived during menstruation, he warned, would 'be born as lepers, or epileptics, or perhaps even demoniacs'.[85] Caesarius' advice was to beat down the passions with fasting. But Augustine candidly doubted the possibility of complete success. 'Never', he reported, 'in friendly conversation have I heard anyone who is or who has been married say that he never had intercourse with his wife except when hoping for conception.'[86] Nevertheless, such an ideal provided new arguments that could be employed by women to ward off the excessive demands of men that led to more pregnancies.

Though the church acknowledged the burdens marriage and childbearing imposed on women, it did not condone their attempts to regulate fertility. On the contrary, churchmen insisted on holding wives almost solely responsible for such sinful undertakings. This attitude was maintained despite the fact that fertility control was, in the Christian world as in the pagan, primarily employed to protect the well-being of the entire household. Lactantius, tutor of Constantine's son, attacked pagans for indulging in a number of non-procreative practices ranging from oral intercourse to self-castration, but acknowledged that economic reasons made a limitation of family size understandable. His response was to assert that the only reason God gave man genitals was so he could reproduce; Christians would reject abortion, infanticide and exposure and in times of economic need adopt continence as the only permissible tactic.[87] Augustine likewise noted that fertility was usually curbed out of fear of impoverishing the family.

But church fathers tended to play down the economic argument – which would implicate men – and attribute most of the blame for fertility control to women, whom they portrayed as driven by avarice and lust. Ironically the first clear Christian attack on contraception was made when Pope Calixtus was charged with allowing Christian free women to consort with their slaves, while taking means to prevent conceptions. 'Hence, so-called faithful women began to try contraceptive drugs, and to bind themselves round in the hopes of aborting what they had conceived, because they did not want to have a child by a slave or a humble man on account of the family ties and their huge property.'[88] Ambrose, in the fourth century, likewise charged that rich women aborted while the poor simply abandoned their children. He described the continued use of contraceptive and abortifacient potions by the wealthy who, 'lest their patrimony be divided among several, deny their own fetus in their uterus and by a parricidal potion extinguish the pledges of their womb in their genital belly, and life is taken away before it is transmitted'.[89]

Caesarius of Arles similarly placed the blame for abortion on the greed of women. 'Does not the Devil clearly exercise his deceits still further, dearly beloved, when he persuades some women, after they have two or three children, to kill either any more or those already born, by taking an abortion draught? Apparently, such women fear that if they have more children they cannot become rich.'[90] Caesarius proceeded to ask why noble matrons, who saw the need of their slaves reproducing, sought to limit their own fertility:

> Moreover, women should not take diabolical draughts with the purpose of not being able to conceive children. A woman who does this ought to realize that she will be guilty of as many murders as the number of children she might have borne. I would like to know whether a woman of nobility who takes deadly drugs to prevent conception wants her maids or tenants to do so too.[91]

Her duty, concluded Caesarius, was to bear her own children and then nurse them or send them out to nurse.

Women's lusts were also cited as a cause of fertility restriction inasmuch as contraceptives were usually associated by Christians with prostitution, adultery, perversions and fornication. Moreover concubines, divorcees, widows and the remarried, because their children would enjoy only an ambiguous legal status, were especially suspected of avoiding pregnancies. Christians accordingly sought to break down the barrier that separated concubinage and marriage and establish one sexual standard. This had the curious effect of sexualizing marriage. Now wives who employed contraceptives were described as acting like whores, of seeking to hide evidence of fornication. Indeed, Augustine argued that since a wife was supposed to be impregnated, her 'use which is against nature' was a more damnable offence than that employed by a prostitute.[92] John Chrysostom likewise linked contraception to prostitution. He first asked the harlot, 'Why do you sow where the field is eager to destroy the fruit? Where there are medicines of sterility? Where there is murder before birth? . . . Indeed it is something worse than murder and I do not know what to call it; for she does not kill what is formed but prevents its formation.' Then wives and husbands were made the target of his wrath: 'In this indifference of the married men there is greater filth; for then poisons are prepared, not against the womb of a prostitute, but against your injured wife.'[93] Martin of Braga (died AD 579) similarly lumped together those who 'take steps so that [they] may not conceive in either adultery or legitimate marriage'.[94]

The woman thus bore the full brunt of the church's hostility to fertility control. In the *Didache* she was warned of the sinfulness of using abortifacients; in the *Apocalypse of Peter* a pit of torment was described in which women were thrown 'who have caused their children to be born untimely and have corrupted the work of God who created them'.[95] Tertullian asked how they could deny the vitality of the fetus they carried. Jerome denounced those who 'drink sterility and kill a man not yet born'.[96] Ambrose condemned cruel mothers who took 'away life before it was transmitted'.[97] St Basil seemed to refer to women assisting each other when he thundered, 'Moreover, those, too, who give drugs causing abortion are murderers themselves, as well as those receiving the poison which kills the fetus.'[98] The Council of Elvira in 305 excommunicated women who committed abortion after adultery. The Council of Ancyra in 314 denounced such women and condemned them to ten years' penance. Medieval monks would continue to accuse women of employing potions and *'maleficia'* to sterilize themselves.

The idea that the use of a contraceptive might be a lesser evil in offering protection from the dangers of a pregnancy was never voiced by the early Christians. But such speculations were made by others. Reference was made in the *Tosephta* (AD 230) by rabbis to the use of sponges. 'There are three women that must co-habit with a sponge; a minor, a pregnant woman, and one that nurses her child – a minor, because she might become pregnant and die; a pregnant woman, because the foetus might become a *foetus compressus* (or papyraceus); one that nurses her child, because she might kill her child.'[99] The last concern reflected the belief that a mother's milk could be spoilt if she conceived; similarly, a concern to protect the already conceived child from 'flattening' was voiced in the fear of superfetation. Though rabbis highly esteemed procreation, they could envisage situations in which pregnancies should be avoided. God had directed man to multiply; woman might have her own needs to consider. Christians, in contrast, placed the responsibility for procreation primarily on the woman.

So far we have been dealing mainly with the prescriptive literature. Most of the Christian ideas discussed were normative and repressive – as expressed in laws and teachings. But others, such as those contained in sermons and letters, are more evocative inasmuch as they actually appear to have dealt with reality. The question remains – did the masses in fact accept these teachings? And if they did, was it because they were prepared to by other causes?

In the eastern half of the Roman empire, marital relations appear to not have changed all that much. Separations were still allowed and concubines common.[100] Women continued to be segregated and secluded and married off early to protect their virtue. Family tactics remained important. But there was a new concern for male 'virginity'. Growing restrictions were called for on sexual intercourse – during menstruation and pregnancy – though doctors still stressed the necessity of pleasure for procreation.[101] The practice of abstinence appears to have grown; population growth was not sought. Such concerns were linked to heretical groups such as Gnostics and later the Bogomils.[102] But excess children, if not married or castrated, could now be sent to a monastery or convent.

In the west, by the sixth century, the imperial administration had disappeared. The cities, if not destroyed, were in decline and depopulated. The owners of the *latifundia* were the new elite of the manorial system which was emerging. Constantine laid the legal basis for the Christian empire. Infanticide was treated as murder, divorce restricted and adultery punished. Augustus' laws punishing the childless were revoked; abduction and concubinage outlawed.[103] The church did not institute new forms of marriage, but simply took over old ones. Although consent was all that was needed, nevertheless by the fourth century the church began to draw up rules and marriages were now blessed. But marriage did not become a sacrament until the Middle Ages. Though in the ancient world there were no Christian marriages in the formal sense, there were marriages of Christians.

The ancients often did not marry but – because of the spouses' differing social statuses – lived in concubinage. Under Christian influence, bigamy was made a crime and the line between concubinage and marriage dissolved. By the fifth century, conjugality had replaced consanguinity as the central principle of social relations. Exogamy rose and endogamy fell as new incest laws required a new reckoning of kin.[104] The conjugal family was more than ever the crucial unit of production and reproduction. The Roman 'rape marriage' was replaced with the fiction of conjugal equality. The church insisted on regularized unions; whether they were more equitable and companionate is a moot point. Some figures suggest that Christian wives were closer in age to their spouses, but this could have been a result of either their lower social status or a general raising of the age of marriage. In Christian as in classical culture, the submission of woman to man was still stressed.

It was obviously more than coincidental that the control of fertility had been openly discussed in the Hellenic period and the early empire when women enjoyed a good deal of freedom. They had some access to education, assisted in various religious cults and actively participated in the arts and medicine. Many must have in turn been initially attracted to Christianity by its preaching of the equality of the sexes. But by AD 200 the church swung round to support social and political order.[105] It emerged as a male-dominated, hierarchical institution calling in increasingly conservative terms for women's return to their 'natural', silent and subordinate role.[106] Only the Gnostic and Manichean heretics remained sensitive to women's concerns, allowing them to preach and prophesy.[107] Irenaeus (AD 120–200), Tertullian and Augustine charged that such heresies even went so far as to condone abortion and contraception.[108] The most interesting aspect of such claims is not their truth or falsehood – which cannot be established – but their authors' clear expectations of such a linkage of religious ideas and social practices.

Though Christianity became the established religion, it is difficult to determine the effect of its condemnations of fertility control. If a decline in recourse to contraception and abortion occurred, it probably took place because the urbanized style of life in which large families were regarded as a burden was swept away. But though the economic reasons for the sort of dynastic Malthusianism practised by the Romans disappeared, women's desire to continue to control their bodies was maintained. The church's censures make it clear that this 'womanly question' would not go away. Caesarius of Arles reported that Gallo-Roman women argued that they could take what potions they liked: 'They maintain that the poison which has been transmitted through their drinking is unconnected with them.'[109] Jerome was equally unsuccessful in inculcating in Roman matrons his views on such evils. In response to his attacks on abortion he was shocked to hear them retort, 'All things are clean to the clean. The approval of my conscience is enough for me.'[110]

Notes

1 Brent D. Shaw, 'The Family in Late Antiquity: The Experience of Augustine', *Past and Present*, 115 (1987), pp. 45–6.
2 St Augustine, 'The Way of Life of the Manichaeans', in *The Catholic and Manichaean Ways of Life* (Catholic University of America Press, Washington, DC, 1966), 18.65. The classic account of the early Christian response to fertility control, on which this chapter relies heavily, is John T. Noonan Jr., *Contraception: A History of its Treatment by Catholic Theologians and Canonists* (Harvard University Press, Cambridge, Mass., 1965).
3 Noonan, *Contraception: A History*, p. 122; for a contemporary North African reference to the woman who as a prostitute made efforts not to have children, but as a wife sought to have them, see Quodvultdeus, *Livre des promesses et des prédictions de dieu*, tr. René Braun (Cerf, Paris, 1964), 2.15.28.
4 Augustine, *Against Faustus*, cited in Noonan, *Contraception: A History*, p. 121. See also Samuel N. C. Lieu, *Manichaeism in the Later Roman Empire and Medieval China: A Historical Survey* (Manchester University Press, Manchester, 1985), pp. 117–53.
5 Geza Alfoldy, *The Social History of Rome*, tr. David Braund and Frank Pollock (Croom Helm, London, 1985), p. 157.
6 See also Lactantius, *The Divine Institutes*, tr. Mary F. MacDonald (Catholic University of America Press, Washington, DC, 1964), 1.17, 6.20; Marcia L. Colish, *The Stoic Tradition from Antiquity to the Early Middle Ages* (Brill, Leiden, 1985), vol. II.
7 Peter Brown, 'Antiquité tardive', in *Histoire de la vie privée*, eds Philippe Ariès and Georges Duby (Seuil, Paris, 1985), vol. I, pp.

286–95; Ramsay MacMullen, *Christianizing the Roman Empire (AD 100–400)* (Yale University Press, New Haven, 1984), pp. 10–79.

8 *Didache*, 2.2; *Barnabas*, 10.6–8, in Robert A. Kraft, *The Apostolic Fathers*, vol. III (Nelson, New York, 1965).

9 See, for example, Tertullian, *On the Apparel of Women*, in *The Ante-Nicene Fathers*, tr. R. Arbesmann (Christian Literature Publishing Co., Buffalo, 1885), 2.1.

10 Wayne A. Meeks, *The First Urban Christians: The Social World of the Apostle Paul* (Yale University Press, New Haven, 1983). Consecrated virgins and celibate priests, sibyls and seers were, of course, also found in some pagan cults.

11 Josephus, *The Jewish Wars* (Zondervan, Grand Rapids, 1982), 2.8.120–1.

12 Philo, *On the Special Laws (De specialibus legibus)* tr. F. H. Colman (Harvard University Press, Cambridge, Mass., 1937); and see also D. M. Feldman, *Birth Control in Jewish Law* (New York University Press, New York, 1968), p. 65.

13 Noonan, *Contraception: A History*, pp. 52–4.

14 Eusebius declared that such was Origen's fear of sexuality that he castrated himself; see Gerard E. Caspary, *Politics and Exegesis: Origen and the Two Swords* (University of California Press, Berkeley, Cal., 1979), pp. 60–2.

15 Aline Rousselle, *Porneia: On Desire and the Body in Antiquity*, tr. Felicia Pheasant (Blackwell, Oxford, 1988), pp. 156–76.

16 Origen, *Contra Celsum*, 8.55 cited in Darrel Amundsen, 'Medicine and Faith in Early Christianity', *Bulletin of the History of Medicine*, 56 (1982), p. 388.

17 Clement of Alexandria, 'On Marriage', in *Alexandrian Christianity*, eds John E. L. Oulton and Henry Chadwick (Westminster, Philadelphia, 1954), 7.57; and see also Willy Rordorf, 'Marriage in the New Testament and in the Early Church', *Journal of Ecclesiastical History*, 29 (1969), pp. 193–99.

18 Eric Osborn, *Ethical Patterns in Early Christian Thought* (Cambridge University Press, Cambridge, 1976), pp. 53–8, 119–28.

19 Noonan, *Contraception: A History*, p. 80.

20 Augustine, *Confessions*, in *Basic Writings of St. Augustine*, ed. Whitney Jones (Random House, New York, 1948), 4.2.

21 Augustine, *City of God*, 14.26, cited in John Bugge, *Virginitas: An Essay in the History of a Medieval Ideal* (Martinus Nijhoff, The Hague, 1975), p. 25. Especially useful for the understanding of the Christian view of sexuality are Elaine Pagels, *Adam, Eve, and the Serpent* (Random House, New York, 1988); Peter Brown, *The Body and Society: Men, Women and Sexual Renunciation in Early Christianity* (Columbia University Press, New York, 1988).

22 For the idea that marriage was a sort of punishment meted out to men for Adam's disobedience, see John Chrysostom, *On Virginity:*

Against Remarriage, tr. Sally Shore (Edwin Mellen, New York, 1983), 17.5.

23 Augustine, 'The Good of Marriage', in *Treatises on Marriage and Other Subjects*, tr. Charles T. Wilcox (Fathers of the Church, New York, 1955), 5.

24 Peter Brown, *Augustine of Hippo: A Biography* (University of California Press, Berkeley, Cal., 1967), pp. 388–90.

25 The Gnostics who opposed marriage and even practised self-castration were condemned in AD 325 by the Council of Nicea. They became the symbolic antithesis of Christians in purportedly employing contraceptives rather than self-control.

26 On the stress placed on procreation by monotheistic religions see Carol Delaney, 'The Meaning of Paternity and the Virgin Birth Debate', *Man*, 21 (1986), p. 502.

27 Lactantius, 'The Workmanship of God', in *The Minor Works*, tr. M. F. McDougal (Catholic University of America, Washington, DC, 1965), 12.

28 John Chrysostom, *On Virginity: Against Remarriage*, 18.1; see also St Cyprian, 'The Dress of Virgins', in *Treatises*, tr. Roy J. Deferrari (Fathers of the Church, New York, 1958), 23.

29 Tertullian, *On the Soul*, tr. R. Arbesmann (Fathers of the Church, New York, 1950), 30.4

30 Jerome, 'On the Perpetual Virginity of the Blessed Mary Against Helvidius', in *Dogmatic and Polemical Works*, tr. J. N. Hritzu (Catholic University of America Press, Washington, DC, 1965), 21.

31 John Chrysostom, *On Virginity: Against Remarriage*, 19.1.

32 Tertullian, *To His Wife*, in *The Ante-Nicene Fathers*, 3.5.

33 St Caesarius of Arles, *Sermons*, tr. M. M. Mueller (Fathers of the Church, New York, 1956), 51.3.

34 Clement of Alexandria, 'The Instructor' ('Paedagogus'), in *The Ante-Nicene Fathers*, tr. B. P. Pratten (Erdmans, Grand Rapids, 1951), 3.2.

35 Tertullian, *Ad nationes*, in *The Writings of Tertullian*, ed. A. Roberts and J. Donaldson (Clark, Edinburgh, 1869), 15; and on child sacrifices see *Apologetics*, tr. T. R. Glover (Harvard University Press, Cambridge, Mass., 1931), 9.

36 Philo, *De specialibus legibus*, 3.110–16.

37 William E. Lecky, *History of European Morals* (Longman, London, 1880), vol. 2, p. 24.

38 *Epistle to Diognetus*, 5.6, in *The Apostolic Fathers*, tr. Kirsopp Lake (Harvard University Press, Cambridge, Mass., 1912).

39 Tertullian, *Ad nationes*, 15; and see also *To His Wife*, 5.

40 William R. Schoedel, *Athenagoras: Legatio and De Resurrectione* (Clarendon, Oxford, 1972), p. 85.

41 Noonan, *Contraception: A History*, pp. 86ff; and for a recent overview see Norman M. Ford, *When Did I Begin?* (Cambridge University Press, Cambridge, 1988).

42 John Boswell, *Christianity, Social Tolerance and Homosexuality: Gay People in Western Europe from the Beginning of the Christian Era to the Fourteenth Century* (University of Chicago Press, Chicago, 1980), p. 99.
43 Philo, *De specialibus legibus*, 3.108–9, 117.
44 Augustine, *Marriage and Concupiscence*, cited in Noonan, *Contraception: A History*, p. 136.
45 Daniel A. Dombrowski, 'St. Augustine, Abortion, and Libido Crudelis', *Journal of the History of Ideas*, 49 (1988), p. 156.
46 St John Chrysostom, *The Homilies of St. John Chrysostom* (Parker, Oxford, 1841), 24.413.
47 Tertullian, *Apologetics*, 9.8.
48 Emiel Eyben, 'Family Planning in Graeco-Roman Antiquity', *Ancient Society*, 11–12 (1980–1), p. 69. But Noonan disagrees; see 'An Almost Absolute Value in History', in *The Morality of Abortion: Legal and Historical Perspectives*, ed. John T. Noonan (Harvard University Press, Cambridge, Mass., 1970), p. 15.
49 St Basil, *Letters*, tr. A.C. Way (Fathers of the Church, New York, 1955), 188.
50 Caesarius, *Sermons*, 51.4.
51 Joseph Needham, *A History of Embryology* (Cambridge University Press, Cambridge, 1934), pp. 58–9.
52 *Didache*, 5.1, and see Noonan, 'An Almost Absolute Value in History', p. 10.
53 Minucius Felix, *Octavius*, tr. R. Arbesmann (Fathers of the Church, Washington, DC, 1950), 30.2
54 Caesarius, *Sermons*, 1.12.
55 Augustine, *Marriage and Concupiscence*, cited in Noonan, *Contraception: A History*, p. 136.
56 St John Chrysostom, *The Homilies*, 24.414.
57 Clement of Alexandria, 'The Instructor', 3.4.
58 Caesarius, *Sermons*, 51.1.
59 Caesarius, *Sermons*, 51.4.
60 St Augustine, *The City of God Against the Pagans* (Harvard University Press, Cambridge, Mass., 1963), 7.2.3
61 Clement of Alexandria, 'The Instructor', 2.10.91.
62 Clement of Alexandria, 'The Instructor', 2.10.89.
63 Epiphanius accused Gnostic women of receiving the male emission in their hands and eating it as a sort of communion.

But though they copulate they forbid procreation. Their eager pursuit of seduction is for enjoyment, not procreation, since the devil mocks people like these, and makes fun of the creature fashioned by God. They come to climax but absorb the seeds in their dirt – not by implanting them for procreation, but by eating the dirt themselves.

Epiphanius, *The Panerion (or Medicine Chest) of Epiphanius of Salamis*, tr. Frank Williams (Brill, Leiden, 1987), 5.2–3, 11.10. The reference to the murder of a child 'by destruction/corruption' in *Barnabas*, 19.5, may also refer to Onanism. See Kraft, *The Apostolic Fathers*, vol. III, p. 144.

64 Noonan, *Contraception: A History*, p. 100.
65 Norman E. Himes, *A Medical History of Contraception* (Williams and Wilkins, Baltimore, 1936), p. 71.
66 Amundsen, 'Medicine and Faith in Early Christianity', pp. 326–50.
67 Methodius, 'The Banquet of the Ten Virgins', in *The Ante-Nicene Fathers* (Erdmans, Grand Rapids, 1951), 4.7.
68 Clement of Alexandria, 'On Marriage', 7.
69 Lactantius, 'The Workmanship of God', 12. Lactantius stated that human embryological development supposedly began in the heart, but that one saw that in birds' eggs the eyes were the first organs to appear. This suggests he carried out actual observations.
70 Clement of Alexandria, 'The Instructor', 2.10.94.
71 Macrobius, *The Saturnalia*, tr. P. V. Davies (Columbia University Press, New York, 1969), 7.6.11–13.
72 Dimitris J. Kyrtatas, *The Social Structure of the Early Christian Community* (Verso, London, 1987).
73 Augustine, *The City of God*, 14.22.
74 Rosemary Rader, *Breaking Boundaries: Male–Female Friendships in Early Christian Communities* (Paulist Press, New York, 1983).
75 Jo-Ann McNamara, 'Cornelia's Daughters: Paula and Eustochium', *Women's Studies*, 11 (1984), pp. 9–27.
76 Aline Rousselle, 'Gestes et signes de la famille dans l'Empire Romain', in *Histoire de la famille*, eds André Burguière, C. Klapische-Zuber and M. Segalen (Colin, Paris, 1986), p. 268.
77 Wayne A. Meeks, *The First Urban Christians: The Social World of the Apostle Paul* (Yale University Press, New Haven, 1983), p. 101.
78 Augustine, 'The Good of Marriage', 3.
79 John Chrysostom, *On Virginity: Against Remarriage*, 47.4.
80 Jerome, 'Against Helvidius', 19.
81 Rousselle, *Porneia*, p. 193.
82 Jerome, 'To Eustochium', in *Early Latin Theology*, tr. S. L. Greenslade (SCH, London, 1956), 4.
83 Athenagoras, 'A Plea for Christians', tr. B. P. Patten in *The Ante-Nicene Fathers* (Christian Literature Publishing Co., Buffalo, 1885), 2.33.
84 Caesarius, *Sermons*, 44.3.
85 Caesarius, *Sermons*, 44.4–7.
86 Augustine, 'The Good of Marriage', 13.14.
87 Lactantius, *Divine Institutes*, 5.9.17; and book 6. See also Minucius Felix, *Octavius*, 28.
88 Hippolytus, 'Refutation of All Heresies', 9.12.25, in Catherine

Osborne, *Rethinking Early Greek Philosophy: Hippolytus of Rome and the Presocratics* (Duckworth, London, 1987), p. 347.

89 St Ambrose, *Hexameron*, 5.18.58, cited in Noonan, *Contraception: A History*, p. 99.

90 Caesarius, *Sermons*, 52.4.

91 Caesarius, *Sermons*, 44.2

92 Augustine, 'The Good of Marriage', 10.

93 St John Chrysostom, *The Homilies*, 24.413–14.

94 Martin, *Opera*, 142, cited in Noonan, *Contraception: A History*, p. 149.

95 Noonan, 'An Almost Absolute Value in History', p. 10.

96 Tertullian, *On the Soul*, 25; Jerome, *To Eustochium*, 22.13.

97 Ambrose, *Hexameron*, 5.18.58.

98 St Basil, *Letters*, 188.

99 Himes, *Contraception*, p. 72.

100 Evelyne Patlagean, 'Byzance: Xe–XIe siècles', in Ariès and Duby, *Histoire de la vie privée*, pp. 574–95.

101 Brown, 'Antiquité tardive', p. 290.

102 Evelyne Patlagean, 'Sur la limitation de la fecondité dans la haute époque byzantine', *Annales ESC*, 24 (1969), pp. 1353–69.

103 J.H.W.G. Liebeschuetz, *Continuity and Change in Roman Religion* (Clarendon, Oxford, 1979), p. 295. See also T. D. Barnes, *Constantine and Eusebius* (Harvard University Press, Cambridge, Mass., 1981), pp. 52, 219–20.

104 Jack Goody, *The Development of the Family and Marriage in Europe* (Cambridge University Press, Cambridge, 1983).

105 On attempts to curb the active public life of early Christian women see St Cyprian, 'The Dress of Virgins'.

106 Elaine Pagels, 'Adam and Eve, Christ and the Church: A Survey of Second Century Controversies', in *The New Testament and Gnosis: Essays in Honour of Robert McL. Wilson*, eds A. H. B. Logan and A. J. M. Wedderburn (Clark, Edinburgh, 1983), pp. 146–75; Jean Laporte, *The Role of Women in Early Christianity* (Mellen, New York, 1982).

107 Elaine Pagels, *The Gnostic Gospels* (Random House, New York, 1979), pp. 59–65.

108 Irenaeus, 'Against Heresies', tr. A. Roberts and J. Donaldson (Ante-Nicene Christian Library, Edinburgh, 1867), 1.6.2–3.

109 Caesarius, *Sermons*, 52.4.

110 Jerome, *To Eustochium*, 22.13.3.

4

Procreation in the Middle Ages

'Moore for delit than world to multiplye'
Chaucer (1390), *Nun's Priest's Tale*

The decline of the cities of western Europe – where contemporaries assumed fertility control was widely employed – was by the year 600 well advanced. Much of the sophisticated medical knowledge of the Greeks was lost and illiteracy widespread. Under the full onslaught of the Germanic tribes, the unity of the Mediterranean world was broken and the west cut off from the culture of the eastern empire that lingered on in Constantinople. A formal break was finally made in 751 when the fall of Ravenna forced the popes to turn reluctantly to the Franks as the new protectors of Latin Christendom.

The western barbarian states had begun to emerge in the fifth century. These were violent, pagan and Arian Christian societies marked by endogamy, bad diet and poor stature, in which fears of rape, kidnappings and incest were the paramount sexual concerns.[1] The German tribes based their law on the collective responsibility of the kindred and reciprocal revenge. Theirs was a rural world of roaming bands of unmarried young men who, unlike their Roman counterparts, were considered independent once they came of age. Gone was the Europe based on urban culture and long-distance commerce. In its stead stood a smaller, more rural civilization. Plagues swept across the continent between AD 542 and 750, cutting the population in half; it only crept back to its previous high of thirty-two million around the year 1000. Rapid growth then took place until another disastrous pandemic – the famous Black Death – descended in the fourteenth century.[2]

Some idea of a person's life chances in the early Middle Ages has been provided by Luc Buchet in a demographic reconstitution study of a Norman village. It reveals a 45 per cent infant mortality rate and an average life expectancy of thirty.[3] Over half the population was under twenty-five; three-quarters were women and children. Brides were married off as early as thirteen; only about one-half lived through twenty years of childbearing. Since infant survival rates through much of the Middle Ages were so remarkably low, family size could not be other than modest. The gift-givers to the great abbeys had on average only 2.6 descendants; close to half had no children at all.[4]

Most historians have concluded that in the 'Dark Ages' the limitation of pregnancies would not have been practised. Norman Himes in a few pages of his classic account, *A Medical History of Contraception*, dismissed the period as of no interest to the historian of birth control. Subsequent researchers tended to agree; was it not a brutal, superstitious age in which reason held little sway, women's needs were ignored and hordes of children were welcomed as a source of cheap labour? The medieval mind set, it was decided, was one which could envisage neither the need nor the means of controlling procreation.[5]

But was it that simple? Clearly the sophisticated discussion of reproduction begun by the Greeks and Romans was not sustained. The church, as custodian of what western culture remained, condemned all unnatural sexual practices. Yet between the sixth and fourteenth centuries, the idea of controlling fertility was never completely lost. What did disappear was the old Roman-style family. New symmetrical households slowly emerged as a result of changing material circumstances, ideological pressures and the force of cultural norms. The most important material change was the decline of slavery. The use of slave labour on farms had never been terribly efficient; with the fall of the empire, both the supply of slaves and their policing were jeopardized. In the future landowners could only hope to exploit their properties fully by settling on them families of tenured serfs. The huge *latifundia* with their gangs of slave labourers were slowly replaced by multiple family manors. The creation of new family forms necessarily resulted in a reappraisal of traditional reproductive strategies.

Tacitus lauded the Germans for their monogamous, hard-working wives who did not employ contraceptives and nursed their numerous children.[6] In fact monogamy was slow to emerge fully in northern Europe. The Gallo-Romans employed concubinage with slaves and also secondary marriages – 'friedlehe' – to shore up family alliances. Charlemagne had four successive official wives and six concubines. Barbarian chiefs frequently took concubines because any resulting children could make no claim on the family fortune. Caesarius attacked this double standard that tolerated the man who 'wallows in the sewer of lust with many maids'.[7] Endogamy was also employed to strengthen the family and only declined among the Carolingians after the Council of Mainz (829). Women tended to gravitate toward powerful males. Marriage was sealed by a property exchange and sexual intercourse; the wife henceforth belonged to the husband. The decree in 614 of Clotaire III which stated that women had to agree to marriage was a dead letter. They had little say in such unions; polygamy was accepted and 'rapt' or abduction common. It is not clear if the Franks had divorce, but the Burgundians could send back a wife for adultery, 'malefice' (the use of drugs to carry out abortion) and being raped.[8] Women were everywhere subjected to male power; adulteresses risked being strangled, burnt alive or subjected to the water test.

Christianity provided Germans and Romans with a means of communication, but only really exercised influence on the Franks after 751, when Pepin ended the Merovingian line. From the time of Louis the Pious (814–40), the church severely denounced polygamy and concubinage. The church also attacked incest resulting from relations of either blood or affinity. The elite was slow to give up the use of either concubinage to limit legitimate heirs or endogamy to protect property. The aristocracy took it as given that it had to produce male heirs and accordingly abandon barren wives. Hincmar's and Nicolas I's prevention of the divorce of Lothar II in the ninth century proved to be a turning point. As a compromise, the church henceforth allowed separations and remarriages only if incest were used as a reason for ending the first marriage.[9] By the tenth century the theory of the monogamous and indissoluble marriage was finally anchored; first in the south, later in the north.

Marriage was restricted by the need for property – a dowry. The Greeks and Romans gave their daughters dowries, but the emperor Marjorian expressed alarm in 458 that the inflation of grooms' counter-dowries was delaying marriages and lowering the birth rate. Some evidence suggests that in late antiquity the age of brides did increase somewhat and that of grooms declined. The Romans were especially concerned by the emergence of the spinster; she had been a rare being in the ancient world, given the assumption that every woman would eventually marry. In the more turbulent German society men traditionally 'bought' women with bridewealth. Though the 614 decree of Clotaire III stated that the woman had to agree to marriage, the family still arranged it and a bride price was given by the groom's relatives. The husband provided the 'morning gift' as payment for the bride's virginity, a sum given back to the woman by her kin to serve as her dower.

It has been argued that in the early Middle Ages women enjoyed greater powers than their Roman counterparts, powers that were lost by the thirteenth century. Although there are dangers in searching for the 'good old days' for women, it does appear that Frankish women did enjoy some freedoms.[10] They were not considered legal minors and could act as guardians of their children. The Germans, who reckoned kinship bilineally, left inheritances to both sons and daughters. The matrilineal line was important; the mother's brother often served as the protector of her children. Queens wielded real power, as did widows. Feudal relations, based as they were on kinship, provided aristocratic women with effective leverage.

Women also turned to the church to protect their interests. They were often its first recruits, attracted as they were by its defence of spiritual equality, monogamy, forgiveness of adultery and hostility to divorce.[11] The church, in advancing the importance of individual consent in marriage, unintentionally became a champion of 'love'. Moreover, the clergy, in part because of its search for alms, defended the right of women to make wills, and set itself up as defender of widows and orphans. Rich widows in turn aided the church, many ultimately retiring to convents. Although attacks on clerics' wives and women who preached were common, religion offered women a legitimate refuge from married life that the pagans lacked.

Jack Goody has suggested that the Christian church played a key role in establishing a new European family form. The church recognized that by taking over control of marriage, it could undermine paganism: 'Since religion was embedded in the domestic domain, conversion implied the control of family life.'[12] But more was at stake. Goody claims that in condemning as sinful close marriage, concubinage and adoption – the traditional family strategies employed by the Romans to produce heirs, continue the family line and consolidate family property – the church found a way of building up its own economic power base. With the old strategies of heirship blocked, many individuals had no choice but to cede their land to the local parish. Similar effects were obtained when the church defended women's rights and testamentary freedom. Widows, whose rights to their dowers were supported but whose remarriages were blocked by priests, were also likely to leave their wealth to the church. In short, Goody suggests that the church had its own good reasons for opening up kinship and defending the autonomy of the nuclear family.[13]

In the twelfth and thirteenth centuries the church's employment of the theme of 'Christ as mother', argues Carolyn Walker Bynum, also provided a more positive evaluation of marriage and motherhood. Concern for children was evident in the miraculous cures reported of ill infants and in the new emotionalism manifested in the icons of the nativity. But the status of real women actually appears to have declined by the fourteenth century. Mother devotion could often be accompanied by misogyny.[14] Women's drift towards spirituality in the later Middle Ages and the spread of convents may well have been due to a closing down of other options.

The German tribes reckoned kin bilineally, but by the end of the ninth century the European family was becoming more 'vertical', with a decline in the wife's right to property. Over time the bride price diminished in importance, as the once small trousseau given to the bride ballooned to reemerge in the peaceful and prosperous eleventh century as a dowry. The groom's morning gift, given in return for the bride's virginity and the basis of the association of conjugal goods, also grew, but was now pegged as a portion of the estate, the concern being to guard it from the widow. The estate was also increasingly protected from daughters, their dowry in effect being a premortem inheritance that ended any other claims they might have on the estate.[15] The reemergence of the dowry was a sign of a skewed marriage market. All daughters were pressured to marry, but only the eldest son. Women had to compete against each other; at the same time they found marriage all the more important as they were shut out of the new regime of male institutions – the army, the state bureaucracy and the guilds.[16]

Among the elite a primarily patrilineal system emerged in which the woman's relatives were increasingly discounted. Bilaterality did not disappear, but served new functions. Duby sees an important shift in aristocratic family structure occurring around the year 1000. The elite lineages pruned their collateral branches by discouraging the marriages of younger sons and sending them into the church or off on crusades. Primogeniture was now employed to pass on the major portion of the estate to a single male heir. The patronymic – the use by all family members of the father's name – emerged with the seigneurial system and the feudal revolution. There were, of course, regional differences. It was in open country, where the larger, prosperous farms could be efficiently exploited, that the number of heirs tended to be limited; in woodlands, where more intensive labour was required, there were more likely to be partible inheritances divided between the children.

Age of marriage shifted. It appears that barbarian males married earlier than the Romans. Devroy thought their women still married as early as fourteen or fifteen; Zerner suggests a later age. The Carolingians clearly started to postpone marriage. By the high Middle Ages marriage took place rather late in England. Hajnal concluded that England, like Bulgaria and Rumania, experienced early marriage in the Middle Ages and shifted to a later age in early modern times. The west European marriage system that eventually emerged would be marked by both the late age of marriage of the bride and a small gap of a few years between her age and that of the groom. But age of marriage during the Middle Ages seems to have been quite variable.[17] David Herlihy found that in Italy it could dip into the teens in good times but be held back to the twenties in poor times. Property structures, patriarchal controls and sex ratios all played a role. In fourteenth-century Florence, men normally married after twenty-seven and women before twenty-two. Male age of marriage was everywhere driven up to the late twenties in the disastrous fourteenth century.[18] Many never married. Large households frequently represented not growth but children who could not marry. Spinsters sought refuge in religious foundations, convents and the 'beguinage' or lay sisterhoods. In England, convents were closed to peasant girls and marriage remained the only option.

This emergence in the Middle Ages of a particular family form unique to western Europe continues to fascinate social theorists. It is a moot point whether or not it encouraged, as its enthusiastic defenders claim, mobility, individualism and love. What is clear is that it differed from non-western family structures in that it was bilineal, consisted of a strong conjugal pair and weak kin, embraced an exogamous marriage pattern in which women circulated, and encouraged not the seclusion, but the public activity of women. Its demographic peculiarity, first signalled by Hajnal, was its late average age of marriage and the sizable portion never marrying. On the whole, fewer late medieval women married and those who did so tended to be older than their Roman counterparts. The later age of marriage of west European women has been taken as evidence that they enjoyed some economic independence, an independence that might also have manifested itself in a desire to control their own bodies.[19]

The west European family structure that eventually emerged placed a good deal of emphasis on independence.[20] In England and northern France, simple conjugal families were most common. Clearly there existed a great desire for separate households; even where partible inheritance occurred, common joint households were rare. Enormous efforts were made to establish sons and daughters on their own, and when parents retired they sought by contracts with their children to maintain as much independence as possible. Northern and western Europe thus increasingly distinguished itself from southern Europe, where a different pattern was discernible. Along the Mediterranean littoral, kinship was determined simply through the male line; in northern Europe through both parents' families. And in the south one continued to encounter more multiple households, a greater age disparity between couples, greater male dominance and less public life accessible to women.

Even in north-western Europe one should not claim too early a victory for the nuclear family. The likelihood is that the peasant father dreamt of the luxury of a joint family which only his own poverty or early death prevented. Moreover, there still existed throughout Europe a wide age gap between spouses, a sexual double standard, the likelihood of the early death of one or both parents and the necessity of the survivors' relying at some point on the aid of kin. The conclusion has to be that there was no simple evolution from an extended to a nuclear family. It was a more complex process depending on changing economic fortunes. Individual families were freer in the high Middle Ages, but as a result of the disasters of the fourteenth century retreated to the protection of extended patrilineal forms. Indeed, whenever troubles arose – such as the death of a breadwinner – the extended family, if living in close proximity, could be expected to intervene.[21]

Duby makes the point that there existed two models of marriage in the eleventh century – the profane and the religious. In the profane, the idea was to employ whatever tactics necessary to protect the patrimony and ensure the continuation of the family line. The religious model was advanced by the church, which waged war on endogamy and divorce. It viewed marriage itself with suspicion, but eventually employed it as a weapon against lust and made it a sacrament. Duby notes suggestively that although we only have church accounts of marriage, it is clear from the opposition it met that other models were present:

> The resistance did not arise, as the priests pretended to believe, out of deliberate disobedience or unruliness. It derived from a different quarter altogether, from another set of rules and principles that, instead of being imported, like Christianity, were time-honored and indigenous. We know nothing about them except what we learn from the resistance they offered, for they were preserved not in writing but in people's memories and revealed themselves only in ceremonial customs, words, and fleeting gestures.[22]

Did the church encounter similar resistance to its teachings on procreation? Duby and Goody have led scholars in researching the ways the church sought to limit aristocratic men's attempts – by divorce, remarriage, polygamy, concubinage and adoption – to produce heirs. But little has been said of the church's attempt to stop women from employing traditional means to restrict births. The church eventually compromised with the aristocracy over the need to produce heirs. Is there any trace of a similar compromise with women over the need to limit pregnancies?

Duby does not address the problem; he states that prolific marriages were the 'point on which ecclesiastical and lay morality most nearly converged'.[23] It was indeed striking that, whereas the early church fathers had viewed marriage and childbearing with disinterest if not distaste, the medieval church came to share the northern tribes' fervour for fruitful families. Given the barbarians' reportedly large broods of children, it might well be supposed that any church injunction to 'go forth and multiply' would have been superfluous. Isidore of Seville was not alone in thinking that the 'Germans' derived their name from the fact that they were so apt at generating children.[24]

The dynastic Malthusianism of the ancient world was no longer defended. The barbarians clearly did not have the same interest as the Romans in limiting the number of their offspring for the reason that they did not invest in their education. Children were seen as a precious commodity, and procreation accordingly became an obsession. The fines levied by the Germans on the person responsible in cases of violent death gave an indication of the importance they attributed to reproduction: for the death of an old woman 200 sous, for a childbearing woman 400 sous, for a pregnant woman 700 sous and for an abortion ensuing on an attack 100 sous.[25] If natural offspring could not be obtained, replacements were seized on raids and turned to work as slaves. Many were given to monasteries that served, as the Venerable Bede made clear, as veritable nurseries. At times when numbers were particularly needed, as during the reconquest of the Iberian peninsula from the Muslims, fertility was especially praised.

Though they rarely gave birth until their twenties, many medieval queens married between ten and fourteen. Blanche of Castile, for example, married Louis VIII at twelve, had her first child at nineteen and twelve more before she was forty.[26] The 'good' wife was the fertile wife. Some, recognizing the 'political value of conspicuous pregnancy', adopted a policy of flaunting their bellies. Barbara, wife of Ludovico Gonzaga, who bore eleven children in twenty-two years, wrote, 'I believe there are few wives who do such honor to their husbands as I do and especially being pregnant at this age as I am.'[27] For the commoners there were similar concerns. In fourteenth-century Italy, women married on average at fourteen and men at thirty. Rapid procreation was undertaken once married, especially amongst the elite; up to a quarter of first births took place before nine months of marriage.

The double entendres of the French *fabliaux* and the ninth-century Anglo-Saxon riddle songs provide evidence of a popular, bawdy naturalness that lauded such reproduction. In one riddle the question was asked what was 'stiff, strong, bold, brassy and pierced in front'.[28] The obvious hope was that a more interesting answer than 'key' would be elicited. The idea that the 'marital debt' had to be fulfilled was taken so seriously that in 1068 William the Conqueror allowed troops to return to Normandy after they petitioned for satisfaction.[29] And doctors for their part continued to assert the old argument that coitus was essential for good health.

The public applauded vigorous marital sexuality. Obscenities were shouted at the marriage ceremony to promote the passions. The kin took the wedding couple to their marriage bed and exposed their sheets the next day. One consequence of such community surveillance was that though premarital sex was common, illegitimacy rates were low. There were, of course, important regional variations. The folklore of southern Europe placed a much greater stress on the importance of virginity, marriage at puberty and endogamy than did English culture.

Curiously enough this desire for children did not manifest itself in adoptions. For the ancients, rearing had been as important as bearing children, and adoption had been widely employed. As a result the concepts of maternity and paternity were diluted and diffused. Fostering and wet-nursing were criticized by the church, but it aggressively sought to end adoption and ultimately succeeded. Why? Because of fear of incest? Because adoption was associated with ancestor worship? Because fictive heirs were associated with plural marriages? All these concerns no doubt played a role, but Christians put the greatest stress on the notion that heirs were not as important as spiritual offspring. Godparenthood emerged as an increasingly important institution.[30] Ironically, such attacks on adoption resulted in Christians' placing an unprecedented emphasis – similar to that of the barbarians – on the biological nature of procreation.

With the intent of abetting conceptions, recourse was made by couples to a variety of medical and magical methods. The Anglo-Saxon leech books contained information on how potions and prayers could be employed to excite or abate passion, facilitate and secure pregnancy, prevent miscarriage, determine the child's sex, ensure safe delivery and assure an adequate milk supply.[31] Across Europe traditional pagan fertility rites were maintained with their appeals to sacred wells, groves and stones.

Classical humoral theories were also exploited. For example, in the *Merchant's Tale* Chaucer referred to the means a man might take to assure his potency or 'courage': 'He drynketh ypocras,

clarree, and vernage / Of spices hoote, t'encreessen his corage.'[32]
Such information on the promoting of conceptions was popularized
in tracts including *De secretis mulierum*, attributed to Albertus
Magnus (1206–80), and John XXI's *The Treasury of Healthe*
(1276). In the latter work, of one hundred and sixteen prescriptions
thirty-four were for aphrodisiacs, twenty-seven were for anaphrodisiacs, fifty-six to ensure fertility and twenty-six for contraception.
Instructions were also given on dealing with 'inflamation of the
yard', 'swelling of the coddes' and 'withholding of the floures'.[33]
In the fifteenth century, Antonius Guainerius' *Treatise on the
Womb* described doctors lecturing midwives on how to respond to
patients' queries regarding sterility, wandering wombs and retained
menses. Warming plasters and pessaries were advised to ensure
conception. To combat excessive heat that resulted in randiness,
cooling diets and fasting were suggested.[34] One read in such
medical texts that a 'sucking' feeling on the penis implied a
successful union and that pregnancy could be tested by having a
woman drink honey and water; if colic resulted she was declared to
be with child. Cravings and titillation of the womb were also
determined to be propitious signs. To test for sterility urine was
added to bran; its sprouting indicated fecundity.[35]

The church turned a blind eye to attempts made by magic to
determine sex and promote fecundity.[36] Indeed, Guibert of
Nogent (1053–1124) referred approvingly to a case in which magic
was employed to end impotence. A man asserted that his
misfortune was obviously caused by black magic because 'to sleep
with a former concubine for pleasure was possible, and with his
legally chosen wife impossible'. Eventually 'churchly medicine'
restored his potency.[37] Philip II of France suffered a similar
complaint.[38] Therapeutic 'white magic' was not condemned by the
church. The first church involvements in marriage – the blessing of
the bed, and so on – were in fact forms of exorcism. Pilgrimages
and prayers, made to seek cures for barrenness, were common.

Duby suggests that the medieval tradition of hypergamy –
aristocratic men marrying women of a superior status – underlay
fears of impotence and led to projection of defilement. But one also
has to recognize that men's concern for, but also fear of, women's
reproductive power fuelled much of the pronounced misogyny of
the Middle Ages. The irony was that though women's health and
well-being were threatened by marriage and the subsequent

problems posed by pregnancy, the church chose to present female sexuality as dangerous. Ordinary intercourse was said to have ruined men's health and driven some to retire exhausted to monasteries. Guibert referred to one such noble 'advanced in years and worn out in body, having – what is deadly for such men – a wife with more vigor for married life'.[39] Moreover, the menses were declared by priests to be polluting and the idea was propounded that men could, unlike women, contract leprosy as a result of intercourse.[40]

The old idea of women's sexual insatiability was maintained. Male masturbation was determined to be worth ten days' penance; female masturbation, since it allowed women to avoid their duties to both men and procreation, was subjected to one year's penance. Burchard of Worms, the noted canonist, was equally indulgent to men who fornicated with a *'femme vacante'*. It was a worse sin to be over-zealous with one's wife, since marriage was supposed to be a curb on lust.[41] Such antifeminist currents, found in John of Salisbury and Walter Map, could be traced back to Theophrastus and St Jerome. In these writings women were all likened to adulteresses, gluttons and whores. Burchard's *Decretum* dwelt on their recourse to lesbianism, dildos and bestiality as well as on their employment of abortion and contraception.

Marriage and the responsibilities it entailed were commonly disparaged in popular humour: 'The man's an ass pricked on by spur / To feed the brats produced by her.' Attacks on immodesty in marriage usually assumed that the woman was the instigator, that is, interested in sex for reasons other than procreation. Accordingly, calls were made for her to be trained in submissiveness:

> To help their mates were wives designed,
> To keep the seed of humankind.
> Apart from this a wife's a pain
> But rules the roost in his domain.[42]

The rites of marriage and homage became remarkably similar, both stressing the need for hierarchy and order. The church thus sought to protect men from female domination. Its elaboration in the twelfth century of the doctrine of the immaculate conception of Mary highlighted the gulf that separated real, sexually dangerous women and the female paragon.[43]

Despite all the attempts to enforce female submissiveness and all the medical and magical methods employed to promote fertility, family size in the Middle Ages was modest. Economic constraints played a major role. The reality was that the men and women of the Middle Ages were living in an overwhelmingly rural society. Small farms meant that it was unlikely that there could be anything else but relatively small families. Their size was determined in the main by late marriage. Since land was the pre-eminent source of wealth, sons usually had to wait for a father's death or retirement to gain the economic independence that would permit the establishment of a new household. Moreover, a large portion never married. For those who did marry, short life expectancy combined with late age of marriage resulted in unions lasting only about fifteen to seventeen years and consequently low reproductive capacity. In addition, the high infant mortality rate depleted the number of children born; in Sicily only 1.7 children survived per family, compared to over four in Quercy.[44] Across Europe only about a half of the population reached age twenty. Most households were small. In the Carolingian world the average household had two to three children in Provence and Champagne; three to four further north.[45] In the England of the thirteenth century there were about five residents per household; in the early fifteenth century the number dipped to four.[46]

Many noble families proved to have real difficulty in reproducing. The Carolingian line died out in 987, the Ottonian in 1002 and the Rudolphian of Burgundy in 1032. Because brotherly rivalries often proved the greatest threat to family harmony, attempts were made to have no more than one son. The Bosonids Bobo and Hugh each had only one legitimate son and then as a 'conscious choice' turned to concubines.[47] As long as partible inheritance dominated – as it did in most of Europe until the eleventh century – propertied families which did not want to see their lands divided had an interest in limiting heirs. The emergence in the eleventh century of primogeniture, which allowed the passing on of the estate intact to the eldest son, eased such pressures.

The relatively low numbers of children in the medieval family have been attributed primarily to late marriage and high infant mortality. But limitation of pregnancies could also have played a role. Leyser, in broaching the subject of the birthing careers of nobles in Ottonian Saxony, noted that it was striking 'that the children of the Ottonian rulers in the tenth century were born in quick succession to one another and that the child-bearing ceased altogether before the mother even reached the age of thirty'.[48] Similar evidence has been collected by Herlihy which indicates that family size in fourteenth-century Tuscany was controlled. Women who married young did not produce larger numbers of children than those who married later; from age twenty-seven on their fertility dropped. Moreover, the women of Florence – in particular lower- and middle-class women – stopped having children sooner than country women. At age thirty-five, one-half of urban wives were barren but only one-third of the rural. St Bernardino, the great fifteenth-century Sienese preacher, clearly knew what was going on when he lamented, 'Oh, in how many unspeakable and unbelievable ways do husbands abuse their wives. Who could ever state them with decency?'[49]

Findings such as Herlihy's have been viewed by traditionalists with suspicion. It has been suggested that the people of the Middle Ages, not being able to envisage the separation of procreation from pleasure, did not have a 'contraceptive mentality'. But since there existed a dominant set of family practices aimed at producing children, it is only to be expected that there would have been a parallel oppositional set to limit their number. Obviously contemporaries did not believe that procreation was the only purpose of intercourse. It is suggestive that in the courtly love stories of the mid-twelfth century, births did not result from seductions. Those who bedded 'moore for delit than world to multiplye' were the target of Chaucer's ire in the *Nun's Priest's Tale*.[50] Bartholomaeus Anglicus likewise noted in the thirteenth century that some used their sexual members not to have children 'but to foule lust and likynge of lecherye'.[51] The French popular literature of the fifteenth century similarly made it clear that pregnancies were often regretted.[52] Some cultural differences cropped up in such reports. In French folklore, complaints were frequently made about numerous pregnancies. An additional child – particularly from the thirteenth century onwards – was often described as a catastrophe. Such laments were much less common in English tales.

Attempts to control procreation were attributed mainly to women. St Bernardino chided husbands for using means 'against nature and against the proper mode of matrimony', but reserved his harshest comments for wives:

And I say this to the women who are the cause that the children that they have conceived are destroyed; worse, who also are among those who arrange that they cannot conceive; and if they have conceived, they destroy them in the body. You (to whom this touches, I speak) are more evil than murderers . . . O cursed by God, when will you do penance? Do you not see that you, like the Sodomite, are cause for the shrinking of the world; between you and him there is no difference.[53]

Fertility regulation was dealt with by the church as a 'womanly question' because it was assumed that it was undertaken at her initiative. The penitentials made it clear that only the woman was believed to be responsible for abortions and contraception.

Why were attempts made to control fertility? Churchmen recognized that economic pressures underlay the desire of both men and women to limit pregnancies. Hostiensis (Henry of Susa) charged, 'Let the offspring be gratefully received whether it be a boy or girl; give thanks to the Creator and do not murmur even in the face of exceeding poverty.' Peter de Palude noted in the fourteenth century that coitus interruptus was employed by the husband to avoid 'having more children than he can feed'. These views were reiterated in the fifteenth century by John Nider and Trovamala.[54]

But women were thought to have additional reasons for seeking to limit pregnancies. The first would be to protect their health. A clear idea of the physical costs of childbearing was conveyed by a thirteenth-century Provençal poetess: 'A husband would please me though / But to bear children I believe is a great penance / Since the breasts fall down and the belly becomes heavy and burdening.'[55] The hagiographic literature carried the same message. St Catherine's sister was depicted as dying in childbirth. St Peter Damian's mother was described as 'worn out by childbearing'. After her brother attacked her for producing so many children, she rejected her new baby and the servants were forced to intervene.[56] Whether or not women relished the mystical view that regarded them as being torn apart, like food, in order to give life, they certainly were aware that pregnancy was life threatening.[57]

Misogynists countered that women were motivated by frivolous concerns. They were frequently accused of limiting their pregnancies merely to protect their beauty or reputation. Thomas of Chobham, author of a popular thirteenth-century confessor's manual, asserted that they had recourse to means to hide the evidence of illegitimate affairs and spare themselves the dangers of childbirth.[58]

Women were presumed to have not only their own reasons for restricting fertility, but secret knowledge to achieve it. In 1150 the monk Hermann de Tournai wrote that Clemence, wife of Robert II, count of Flanders, having had three children in three years decided not to have any more and succeeded by '*arte muliebri*'.[59] Such arts were purportedly described in the anonymously authored *De secretis mulierum*. Women obviously did know more about reproduction than men. The Dominican theologian Albertus Magnus, while following like a good scholastic the physiological teachings of Galen and Aristotle, declared 'much belief should be given to trustworthy women who have borne many children'.[60]

The easiest way for women to avoid large families was no secret; it was simply necessary to avoid intercourse. Periodic continence was encouraged by the church and may have played some role in the slow population growth that took place in Europe prior to the tenth century. As one passage from an Irish penitential indicates, the church placed numerous restrictions on times of intercourse.

> Anyone that lives in lawful wedlock, these are his rules of conduct: continence during the three Lents of the year, and on Fridays, Wednesdays and Sundays, and between the two Christmases and between the two Easters, if he goes to the Sacrament on Christmas Day and Easter Day and Whitsun Day. Also they are bound to observe continence at the time of their wives' monthly sickness, and at the time of pregnancy, and for thirty nights after the birth of a daughter, twenty nights after the birth of a son.[61]

The main thrust of the penitentials was to regulate the timing of intercourse. It was forbidden in specific stages of the woman's physiological cycle – during menses, pregnancy, birth and nursing – and in specific stages of the liturgical cycle – Sunday, Wednesday, Friday, Lent, Advent and Pentecost as well as during feast days and vigils and before and after communion. The intent of such instructions was not to limit fertility, but to prevent immorality. Nevertheless, some have wondered if a scrupulous couple would have been able to follow such a calendar and still reproduce. Jean-Louis Flandrin has determined that it was mathematically possible.[62]

But what, one further wonders, were the psychological effects of teachings that condemned all intercourse that did not take place at night, when partly clothed, and in the missionary position? Even in the later saints' lives marital sensuality was castigated. St Francesca Romana de'Ponziani (died 1440) was said to have vomited every time she was forced to have intercourse with her husband.[63] Church artists only illustrated monstrous couplings and the *Hali Meidenhad* referred to marriage as that 'indecent burning of the flesh, that same flaming itch of carnal lust, before that loathsome act, that beastly copulation, that shameless coition, that foulness of stinking ordure and uncomely deed'.[64] Flandrin argues that such teachings were effective in creating a sober, guilt-ridden peasantry. But how was such personal behaviour policed? There is much evidence of the masses' indifference to or ignorance of the church's views. And it appears that the peasantry had its own ideas about favourable and unfavourable periods for conception. Evidence suggests that attempts were made to avoid having children in the summer, when women would be hard at work in the fields. It is likely that seasonal variations in conceptions were thus not so much a result of Christian teachings as a response to the demands of the rural economy. And women like Margery Kemp, who in fact found the 'debt of matrimony . . . abominable', could in addition seek to use church doctrine to win periods of continence if not completely chaste marriages.[65]

Couples often chose to be continent while the wife was nursing. Extended lactation itself offered a margin of contraceptive protection, but it is not clear if this was fully appreciated. When Favorinus of Arles asked the women of Gaul to nurse their children, he was presumably most concerned with the welfare not of the mothers, but of their offspring.[66] His request did highlight the fact that nursing was a culturally determined practice and not carried out by all Germans as Tacitus implied. Breastfeeding, when it was resorted to, was often prolonged from eighteen to twenty-four months and postponed a subsequent birth on average by about eleven months. Three-year cycles between births were accordingly common.

Various post-partum taboos against a mother's resumption of intercourse were noted in the penitentials, usually longer if a girl were born. Some parents refrained from intercourse until the first child was weaned. The church preferred couples to abstain, but did not enforce such a restriction. Historians seem to be unaware of the health protection offered women and children by extended nursing and the associated taboo against intercourse. 'Well-to-do women', writes James Brundage, 'could avoid this prohibition, however, since they usually entrusted their infants to wet nurses shortly after birth.'[67] Indeed, in fifteenth-century Tuscany the wealthiest women were the most fecund; they sent out their children to nurse and quickly conceived again. But it was the husband who was likely to have the greater interest in immediately resuming conjugal intercourse, since, at no risk to his health, it brought the promise of additional heirs.

If wives sought, for whatever reason, to refrain from intercourse, it was not expected that their husbands would necessarily follow suit. They might have recourse to prostitutes, who were recognized as providing a necessary safety valve for the release of male sexual passion. A sexual double standard was explicitly accepted; the penitentials, though they attacked lust and adultery, did not refer to prostitutes. Indeed, prostitution was theologically defended in the late Middle Ages. The elite moved from a toleration of, to an active interest in, prostitutes. Brothels were established by cities to support marriage and combat adultery and homosexuality.[68] They were provided with royal and municipal protection in Spain and southern France, where their noble or bourgeois owners 'farmed' them out to keepers.

Prostitutes had few children. William of Conches believed that their barrenness was simply due to sexual excess: 'Prostitutes after frequent acts of coitus have their womb clogged with dirt [oblimata] and the villosities in which the semen should be retained are covered over; that is why, like greased marble, the womb immediately rejects what it receives.'[69] Others believed prostitutes were skilled in preventing or ending pregnancies. Clearly marital and extra-marital intercourse differed; there was more motivation to avoid pregnancy in the latter case. Prostitutes, procuresses and midwives were all traditionally thought to have access to arcane sexual knowledge. In Venice, for example, prostitutes were reported to have secret herbal remedies.[70] Although it is important not to exaggerate its significance, it is likely that the rebirth of the urban world from the twelfth century onwards and the accompanying growth of brothels could have played a role in the transmission of such fertility-regulating lore.

What sort of birth-control techniques were known in the Middle Ages? In the *Parson's Tale*, Chaucer provided an impressively full account. He spoke of a woman taking potions, 'drynkynge venenouse herbes thurgh which she may not conceive'; of using pessaries and suppositories, by putting 'certeine material thynges in hire secree places to slee the child'; unnatural intercourse, 'by which man or womman shedeth hire nature in manere or place ther as a child may not be conceived'; and finally abortion.[71] In other works, changes in the reportage of methods can be detected. The Germans and Celts seem to have been prone to employ potions to control fertility. The Greek and Roman texts which were reintroduced to Europe in the Middle Ages via Arab translations stressed the use of pessaries and suppositories. But from the thirteenth to fifteenth centuries there appears to have been a shift. More condemnations were made against 'sins of nature' and fewer against the use of 'poisons of sterility'. This suggests a decline in the use of herbal potions – for contraceptive purposes at least – and a rise in coitus interruptus.

Whether or not coitus interruptus is a self-evident or a learned technique of contraception, it is clear that in the Middle Ages it was believed that some positions could either inhibit or aid conception. The point was amusingly made in a German verse story in which a servant told his naive master, who had just had intercourse for the first time, that a child was born to whomever was underneath. '"Woe is me", thought the monk, who was starting to realize the extent of his misfortune. "Ah", he said to himself, "whatever can I do? What a disaster! I was the one underneath. I'm going to have a baby!"'[72] The church condemned the woman mounting the man, as it did oral and anal sex, as unnatural acts that frustrated procreation.

Coitus interruptus was not noted in the penitentials, but Theodolphus, Visigothic bishop of Orleans, in diocesan legislation of 813 referred to it as 'Irrational Fornication'. 'Not to have relations with a woman in a natural way is called uncleanness or a detestable sin, whence we read that Onan, the son of Juda, was struck by God, after entering into his wife and spilling his seed on the ground.'[73] Although Onan's sin was to be confused by some with masturbation, the twelfth-century French glosses on the Bible made it clear that God's displeasure was provoked by the contraceptive practice of coitus interruptus.[74] John of Gaddesden, physician to Edward II, warned that women should avoid the sin of 'jumping backwards or too sudden a motion after coitus'.[75]

There is evidence that implies coitus interruptus was particularly employed in incestuous relationships. A man confessed to defiling his bride's mother by 'external pollution' that could possibly have been withdrawal. Yves of Chartres declared that in this case a divorce was not necessary since 'a couple becomes one flesh in the mingling of sperm'.[76] In Montaillou the injunction, 'With a second cousin, plunge it in her all the way!' suggests that full penetration was not always attempted.[77]

Both the heretical Cathars and the troubadours were believed to have popularized contraceptive techniques such as coitus interruptus. But the two movements were quite different and should not be confused. Catharism in its most rigorous form, a latter-day Manicheanism, opposed even the touching of the opposite sex; courtly love envisaged ultimate sexual possession. Cathars were active in southern France from the early eleventh century and came to public attention in the 1140s. 'If they indulge in married intercourse', Eckbert of Schonau declared, 'they nevertheless avoid conception and generation by whatever means they know.'[78] Innocent III appealed in 1215 for a crusade to crush the heretics; the Inquisition was launched against them by Gregory IX in 1233. Courtly love was the art of arousal. It possibly led to the employment of coitus interruptus, since the lover would not want to impregnate his mistress. Andreas Capellanus' *De Amore*, originally written in Latin in 1170 and translated into French in 1290, has been interpreted in this way.[79]

Although the church condemned coitus interruptus, St. Antoninus of Florence in the fifteenth century sanctioned coitus reservatus – that is, penetration without emission. 'For no one is obligated to have more children than one can support.'[80] This line was set by Huguccio and Peter de Palude and cautiously followed by Trovamala and John Nider. The church had earlier been remarkably explicit about which coital positions were sinful; from the eleventh century onward it became more discreet and simply condemned 'unnatural acts'. The populace increasingly viewed with indignation meddlesome priests prying into marital affairs.[81]

The church was alarmed that some nonprocreative practices

were not only 'unnatural', but diabolical. Women were frequently accused of employing magic to prevent either their own or their enemies' conceptions. The chronicles are full of references to princes who were victims of female intrigues and spells conjured in the women's quarters. St Godelive was strangled on her husband's orders while on her way to a sorceress to obtain a magic potion for marriage.[82] Duke Colman's divorced wife was reported as having used incantations to murder the offspring of his new wife.[83]

Burchard referred to women's magic employed to 'change from hate to love or vice versa the passions of the man'.[84] The desperate mistress was condemned for using magic to incite love. Successes were claimed to have been accomplished by her serving a man bread she had kneaded with her buttocks or a fish she had previously inserted in her vagina.[85] Sterilizing spells were purportedly turned to malicious purposes. Guibert, in his early twelfth-century *Memoirs*, stated that magic was commonly employed by the laity and certainly believed to be the cause of unconsummated marriages. His own father's impotence, which lasted for seven years, was only ended by the 'aid of a certain old woman'.[86] These crimes were mentioned frequently in the penitentials. The tying of knots was believed an effective way in which sympathetic magic could cause the impotence of enemies. Joannes Andreae (1270–1348) and Nicholas de'Tudeschi (died 1453) expressed the common fear that discarded concubines and prostitutes could thus revenge themselves.

The church attacked as unholy such recourse to magic, but used similar tactics; saints not infrequently cursed their enemies and their seed. Such a scene was depicted in the Salamanca Codex, in which St Kiernan was described as having rescued a nun from kidnappers: 'When the man of God returned with the girl to the monastery, the girl confessed that she had conceived in the womb. Then the man of God, prompted by zeal for justice, not wishing that the seed of vipers should quicken, making the sign of the cross on the womb, caused it to empty.'[87] This interesting idea that the church might sanction some actions taken after conception but prior to quickening or ensoulment is an issue to which we will return.

Women also used magic to protect themselves from pregnancies. Magical potions, amulets and drinks of willow were employed in the hopes of causing barrenness. In the revision of the Salic law of the Franks under Guntram (567–593), it was declared in title 19, section 4, 'If a woman has committed maleficium so that she cannot have infants, she will be judged liable to a fine of sixty-two gold semis.'[88] It was presumably a magical amulet that Beatrice de Plainisolles described as used by her Cathar lover:

> When Pierre Clergue wanted to know me carnally, he used to wear this herb wrapped up in a piece of linen, about an ounce long and wide, or about the size of the first joint of my little finger. And he had a long cord which he used to put round my neck while we made love; and this thing or herb at the end of the cord used to hang down between my breasts, as far as the opening of my stomach.[89]

The early medieval texts said little of the pessaries and suppositories mentioned by the ancients. Western Europeans were largely reintroduced to the barrier methods of fertility control of Greek medicine via translations from the Arabic in Salerno and Montpellier from the eleventh century onward. In the west some Latin medical texts had survived, but were so pruned down to practical matters that European biology was theoretically impoverished. Much of Aristotle's and Galen's works had in effect to be rediscovered. Particularly important were the translations of Constantine the African, Michael Scot and Gerard of Cremona.[90]

Avicenna's *Canon* was translated by Gerard of Cremona in the mid-twelfth century. This enormously important compendium of ancient medicine referred to a variety of birth-control devices, including cedar oil spermicides, mint pessaries, potions of rennet, sweet basil and iron filings, suppositories of cedar oil, pomegranate, alum, willow, pepper and cabbage, and talismans of sowbread and saxifrage. From Soranus, Avicenna cited the classic references to jumping backward and sneezing and from Aristotle the use of cedar oil on the penis.[91] To combat lust he listed such classic anaphrodisiacs as black and white henbane, melon, lead, lettuce seed, lily, coriander, chaste tree, rue and camphor.[92]

Albertus Magnus followed Aristotle on embryology but drew on Avicenna's commentary for the idea that women also produced semen.[93] The two-seed and pleasure theory was pursued by Bernard of Gordon, John of Gaddesden, Michael Savonarola and Jacques Despars, though opposed by Giles of Rome.[94] Albertus

Magnus believed and reported the idea that conception could be prevented if the woman was on top or urinated immediately after intercourse. In Book IV of *On Vegetables and Plants*, he listed recipes that could inhibit or assist conception. The widely read *Secreta mulierum*, published in Augsburg in 1491 and attributed to Albert, contained two contraceptive potions.

Similar classical references to contraceptives were included in many medieval compendia. The curious work of John XXI, *The Treasury of Healthe*, listed twenty-six recipes for contraception. The Catalan physician Arnold of Villanova likewise described anaphrodisiacs, fumigations and potions drawn from Dioscorides.[95] To restrain sexual intercourse the works of Trotula suggested a number of 'cooling' herbs: camphor, willow, poplar, vervain, columbine, lettuce seed, henbane, colewort, rue and St John's Wort.[96] References were made to similar herbs used by the Cathars.[97] John of Gaddesden provided, in *The English Rose*, a medley of recipes for potions and talismans. Magnino of Milan, in his *Regimen of Health* (1300), discussed the way in which stones and talismans – heart of a deer, rennet of a hare, matrix of a mule – could be employed by women to achieve or prevent pregnancy. Suppositories – possibly for abortion – were also noted. The idea that young or weak women might have to avoid pregnancy was recognized by William of Saliceto. He passed on the recommendation of jumping to cause abortion and the use of oils for contraception.[98]

Sexuality was treated with surprising candour in such medieval texts. Avicenna's stress on the delights of conception, for example, was faithfully reported.[99] And despite the church's condemnations of contraception, the clerical scholars usually noted the ancients' references to such practices with neither approbation nor hostility. Vincent of Beauvais, who ignored Avicenna's references to contraception and abortion, was unusually reticent. Such clerical compilations as drew on Arab astronomy and Aristotelian science reflected an encyclopedic curiosity.[100] There was, however, a difference in tone. Avicenna advanced women's fear of death in pregnancy as an argument in favour of a variety of methods of fertility control, including therapeutic abortion. His clerical followers – with the exception of William of Saliceto – passed over such reasoning in silence.[101] The clergy attempted to reconcile the teachings of the Bible with the scientific findings of the ancients and the Arabs. The result was the rise of natural philosophy.

Clerics were soon arguing that semen was intended by 'nature' to produce children; therefore any frustration of such intent was more than a mere sin; it was a violation of natural law.

By the late thirteenth century, expositions of reproduction were produced in the vulgar tongue.[102] No one would argue that these texts were read or that their recipes were acted upon by the masses. They were written by and primarily for clerics. Nevertheless, the interest taken in them implies that they represented more than the mere reiteration of old ideas. They were produced in response to demands for enlightenment by a literate laity who had no Latin. Contemporary events and concerns, in particular the continuation of the desire of ordinary people to limit their fertility, clearly explained the care with which clerics prepared such texts.

Should the various potions, positions and suppositories have failed to prevent a conception, a woman might have recourse to abortion. Hanawalt cites one coroner's inquest:

> On 12 Dec. 1503 Joan Wynspere of Basford, 'singlewoman,' being pregnant, at Basford drank divers poisoned and dangerous draughts to destroy the child in her womb, of which she immediately died. Thus she feloniously slew and poisoned herself as a suicide and also the child in her womb.[103]

It was assumed that seduced, single women would be more likely than the married to brave such risks. But the practice was not simply a resort of the unmarried. The clear intent of spacing pregnancies was suggested in the report that the mother of St Germain of Paris tried to abort him 'because she had conceived in a short space of time after another pregnancy'.[104]

Abortion was frequently associated with sterilizing potions and incantations. In the Iberian peninsula, the Second Council of Braga of 572 accused women of aborting and recourse to magic. Such reports were continued through the ninth and eleventh centuries in the penitentials' references to 'the little cup' – the use of magical potions for contraception and abortion.[105] Such brews were sometimes provided by accomplices. In 1285 the Synod of Riez in Cathar country imposed excommunication on whoever 'sells or gives poisons or deadly herbs for death and abortion'.[106] What seems to be a similar reference to abortionists appears in the

Confessional of St Antoninus, which included the question of whether doctors provided therapeutic abortion and whether ointment sellers 'teach or sell what procures abortion . . . or if they sell poisons to those who they believe will abuse them'.[107]

The Galenic humoral theories reintroduced to Europe from the eleventh century were employed for regulation of the menses. A number of recipes for herbal potions were included in the work of John XXI. In the fourteenth century, the flood of translations from Latin into the vernacular made available to a wider audience the classical fertility-regulating recommendations. The works of Trotula, translated into English, contained a typical recipe for an abortifacient pessary of iris, savin, white wine, ivy and honey:

> Also the root of iris put into the womb or fumigated underneath makes a woman lose her child, for iris roots are hot and dry and have the virtue of opening, heating, consuming and wasting. For when woman is feeble and the child cannot come out, then it is better that the child be killed than the mother of the child also die.[108]

If potions and pessaries did not work, more violent methods might be employed. The popular preacher Gerson referred to abortions being caused by 'clothes, dancing, blows, potions, or otherwise'.[109]

Early abortion enjoyed an ambiguous moral status. As the quote from Trotula suggested, some doctors followed the classical authorities in assuming that therapeutic abortions should be provided. In Byzantium canon law continued, as in Roman times, to treat abortion not as murder but as a fault committed against the husband; he could in the ninth century divorce a wife who aborted.[110] Anglo-Saxon and Visigothic law referred only to abortion, not contraception. King Gontran inflicted a fine of 62½ sous for giving abortifacient information.[111]

But in the Middle Ages it was the church, not any government, that policed morality. Flandrin asserts that in the thirteenth and fourteenth centuries abortion was condemned whether animation took place or not. It was made clear by the repeated arguments of the clergy, however, that lay people were slow to accept the immorality of such acts. The ambiguity of the concept of animation or ensoulment muddied the waters. A particularly detailed account of generation, entitled the *Anatomia Ricardi*

Anglici, asserted that at seven days there was merely a frothy foam, at twelve the blood flowed, at thirty formation was complete, but only at sixty to seventy days was vitality detected. 'Everything which has been said about the time of formation', boasted the author, 'has been gained by observation of abortions at different times, in which successive stages of formation appeared to the view of the ancient physicians.'[112] Augustine was quoted in the collection of canons made by Gratian to the effect that there was 'no soul before the form'. Similarly, Thomas Aquinas followed Albertus Magnus in accepting Aristotle's theory that the rational soul was only provided the fetus once a certain level of development was achieved. Animation was said to occur at forty days and quickening at one hundred and twenty days. This view of a succession of souls, which was also depicted in Dante's *Divine Comedy*, could be employed to legitimate early abortion.[113] Abortion prior to ensoulment was certainly not considered by the church as homicide and would not be until 1917.[114]

In the early thirteenth century, Bracton and the anonymous compiler of the law treatise known as *Fleta* were the first English legal commentators to write on abortion. In *Fleta* (1.23) it was apparent that the confusion over animation had also spilled over into the legal treatises:

> He, too, in strictness is a homicide who has pressed upon a pregnant woman or has given her poison or has struck her in order to procure an abortion or to prevent conception, if the foetus was already formed and quickened, and similarly he who has given or accepted poison with the intention of preventing procreation or conception. A woman also commits homicide if, by potion or the like, she destroys a quickened child in the womb.[115]

In other words, it was illogically argued that only abortion after ensoulment was as serious a crime as contraception. Only the fact that the law was acted upon so rarely allowed such confusions to lie undetected.

The medieval church, with the intent of providing an alternative to both abortion and infanticide, provided refuge for children left at monasteries. In German as in Roman society, the child was not considered part of the family until it was formally accepted. In

Scandinavia it continued to be the right of fathers to expose deformed children. The father of St Odila, we are told, wanted to kill her since she was born blind.[116] But it was unlikely, given the fines levied by the Alamanni and other tribes for injuring women and babies, that infanticide was employed all that much.

Historians who follow Ariès' view that children were not cherished in the Middle Ages risk misunderstanding the period.[117] Coleman has suggested that in medieval as in ancient times a sex imbalance resulted from the infanticide of girl babies. There is little doubt that boys were more warmly welcomed, but the theory that large numbers of females were sacrificed has been discounted.[118] The fact that infanticide was always presented as a horrible tragedy suggests that it was only a resort of the desperate.[119] Infanticide was noted by Gregory of Tours, but there were only rare references to the crime in church and court records. In such records its perpetration was almost always attributed to women.[120] The penitentials dealt with one form of infanticide, 'overlaying' or the smothering of the child, fairly liberally, imposing only a penance of three years. And in France and England it was not until the sixteenth century that the law made it quite clear that a woman was culpable for the death of her child.

But if the killing of children was rare, their exposure by poor and desperate parents was, until at least the eleventh century, a common occurrence. In the Middle Ages as in the ancient world, children were abandoned with the hopes they would be taken in. John Boswell has noted that the church in effect 'institutionalized' the abandonment of children as an alternative to infanticide by allowing stepchildren, the deformed and the offspring of illegitimate and incestuous relationships to be given as an 'oblation' or offering to a monastery. Indeed, Boswell argues that abandonment was probably the 'primary means that ancient and medieval families had for regulating family size'.[121] It provided parents with a safety valve in times of economic hardship along with the hopes that all contact with the child would not be lost.

Churchmen always harboured the suspicion that some simply abandoned their children in order to protect the family estate. From the fourteenth century on, they began to impose age restrictions to protect both monasteries from the disruptions caused by the influx of children and the children from having a religious vocation forced on them. Boswell makes the case that oblation allowed parents to be both flexible in their attitude towards optimum family size and true to church teachings. Although it is difficult to determine how many children were taken in, it is clear that the ending of the practice forced women to look for other alternatives. But what Boswell tends to play down are the psychic costs of abandonment. Many women no doubt preferred to take the risks run in employing dangerous contraceptive and abortive brews before envisaging such a step.

A new need was probably felt for family limitation by 1300 because of over-population and the accompanying shortage of land. Although the Middle Ages ended with the great plague of 1347–8 that reduced the European population by from one-half to two-thirds, it followed several centuries of demographic advance. Between the twelfth and the early fourteenth centuries, the population of England moved from something like one to four million; France from five to nine million and Italy from four to eight million. Europeans had more money and more confidence. From the thirteenth century onwards, the accompanying optimism laid the basis for the emergence of a civilized way of living. Urban life reappeared and with it a new age of 'courtoisie', in which troubadours and the fabliaux satirized cuckolds, prostitutes and seducers, Boccaccio lauded sensuality, and some humanists like Lorenzo Valla found in the classics fresh arguments in defence of the passions. But the prosperity of the times entailed certain social costs; there was evidence of a loss of community feeling. Families replaced lineages in importance in France. In England by the fifteenth century there was both a clear decline in pledging and community policing and a rise in accusations of trespassing. As centralized royal authority established itself, a more individualistic society was created.

That this spirit of individualism was regarded as inimical to the growth of large families might explain why, as Biller notes, a campaign against coitus interruptus occurred in the early fourteenth century. He cites the condemnations of the practice by the confessors William of Pagula, John Bromyard, Nicholas of Lyra, Peter de Palude and Alvarus Pelagius.[122] Moreover, we know that many communities did not breed up to the Malthusian maximum.[123] Dante's assertion in his *Paradiso* (1318–21) that Florence's corrupted morals resulted in empty houses, and St Catherine of Siena's declaration that coitus interruptus was the most common sin committed by the married, have to be viewed in this light.[124]

The rebirth of the west was not simply a secular phenomenon; it also entailed the reform of the church begun by popes Leo IX (1048–84) and Gregory VII (1073–85). These reforms included new canon law compilations rigorously opposed to sexual deviancy and clerical marriage. In the tenth century Regino of Prüm had invented an Augustine text, *Si aliquis*, which held, 'If someone to satisfy his lust or in deliberate hatred does something to a man or woman so that no children be born of him or her, or gives them to drink, so that he cannot generate or she conceive, let it be held as homicide.'[125] *Si aliquis* emerged from the penitentials, was used by confessors and was included in papal decretals in 1230. Similar condemnations followed; in 1230 Raymond de Peñafort condemned abortion; in 1272 Richard de Middleton assimilated birth control and murder; and in 1227–34 Pope Gregory IX's decretal *Si conditiones* declared null and void the marriages of those whose intention it was not to have children.[126] But the church's arguments were more frightening than coherent. While on the one hand it condemned contraception as homicide, on the other it asserted that only abortion *after* formation could be likened to murder. Innocent III declared that a monk who had aborted his mistress before the fetus had been vivified was not irregular.[127]

According to Noonan, the Catholic church's renewed denunciations of contraception were due to two concerns: first, its traditional hostility to sensuality, which was reinvigorated in the high Middle Ages by a rebirth of Augustinianism, and second, the need to respond to a new twelfth-century heresy perceived as opposed to procreation – Catharism. That Innocent III regarded all marital sex as suspect was made obvious in his question, 'Who does not know that conjugal intercourse is never committed without itching of the flesh, and heat and foul concupiscence, when the conceived seeds are befouled and corrupted?'[128] Heretics who purportedly opposed procreation were therefore doubly damned. Like Augustine before them, the twelfth- and thirteenth-century churchmen responded to such sects by defending childbearing as the only justification of marriage. At the same time they hammered out explicit condemnations of contraception. That this entailed some division within the clergy itself was implied by Peter Cantor, a twelfth-century Paris master of disputation, in arguing against 'some' anonymous combatants who asserted that a woman endangered by pregnancy could legitimately procure a poison of sterility.

Why did the late medieval church renew its efforts to counter fertility control? Although it is true that churchmen were not as dismissive of marriage as the early church fathers had been, it should not be thought they had swung round to a pro-natalist position. Throughout the Middle Ages the church was more concerned with the pleasure that resulted from unnatural acts than their contraceptive effect. Peter Abelard was the only scholastic to deny the idea of the intrinsic sinfulness of sexuality. For others, because of what they took to be the innate dangers of intercourse, excesses in the forms of undue passion, unnatural positions and number of couplings were all condemned. But contraception *per se*, as Brundage points out, was viewed as a minor moral problem. It was certainly not subjected, as sodomy was from the thirteenth century, to savage punishments. The church's condemnation of fertility control was simply part of its general campaign to remake marriage, and is best understood in the context of the growth of marriage liturgy, the expansion of the confessional as an instrument for the closer policing of morals, and the attempted imposition of Christian codes on those still largely true to older sexual customs.

Notes

1　Michel Rouche, 'Haut Moyen Age Occidental', in *Histoire de la vie privée*, eds Philippe Ariès and Georges Duby (Seuil, Paris, 1985), vol. I, pp. 439–46.

2　Josiah Cox Russell, *The Control of Late Ancient and Medieval Populations* (American Philosophical Society, Philadelphia, 1985), p. 169.

3　Luc Buchet, 'La nécropole gallo-romaine et mérovingienne de Frénouille (Calvados), étude anthropologique', *Archéologie médiévale* (1978), pp. 5–53. On infant mortality see also Michel Mollat, *The Poor in the Middle Ages*, tr. Arthur Goldhammer (Yale University Press, New Haven, 1986), p. 6.

4　Pierre Guichard and J. P. Cuvillier, 'L'Europe barbare', in *Histoire de la famille*, eds A. Burguière, C. Klapische-Zuber and M. Segalen (Colin, Paris, 1986), vol. I, p. 311. Such figures could be skewed by offerings made by clerics and unmarried minors.

5　Philippe Ariès, 'Interprétation pour une histoire des mentalités', in

La prévention des naissances dans la famille, ed. Hélène Bergues (Institut national d'études démographiques, Travaux et documents, 35, Paris 1960), pp. 311–27.

6 On the dominance of small families among the elite in Gaul see André Pelletier, *La femme dans la société gallo-romaine* (Picard, Paris, 1984), pp. 31–2; on Favorinus' injunctions to nurse see Ludovic Legré, *Favorin d'Arles* (Aubertin, Marseilles, 1900), pp. 213–20.

7 St Caesarius of Arles, *Sermons*, tr. M. M. Mueller (Fathers of the Church, New York, 1956), 42.3.

8 Rouche, 'Haut Moyen Age Occidental', p. 456.

9 Georges Duby, *Medieval Marriage: Two Models from Twelfth Century France*, tr. Elborg Forster (Johns Hopkins University Press, Baltimore, 1978).

10 Judith M. Bennett, *Women in the Medieval English Countryside: Gender and Household in Brigstock Before the Plague* (Oxford University Press, New York, 1987), pp. 4–5.

11 Suzanne Fonay Wemple, *Women in Frankish Society: Marriage and the Cloister, 500–900* (University of Pennsylvania Press, Philadelphia, 1981).

12 Jack Goody, *The Development of the Family and Marriage in Europe* (Cambridge University Press, Cambridge, 1983), p. 42.

13 The preaching of chastity, virginity and continence could have worked against family strategies and led the childless to leave their estates to the church. On the other hand, the church protected family estates inasmuch as monasteries and convents provided repositories in which excess children were placed, the defence of monogamy strengthened the hand of patriarchs in removing confusions concerning the legitimacy of heirs, and the church's incest sanctions allowed chieftains to reject obligations to their kinsmen. There is also the danger of exaggerating the power of the clergy. Some aristocratic families willingly gave their land to the church for the very purpose of protecting it from the claims of kin. When, in the eleventh century, the church was strong enough to begin to free itself of secular exploitation, the chieftains turned to primogeniture as the means by which to protect their estates from competing claims. See Katherine Verdery, 'A Comment on Goody's *Development of the Family and Marriage in Europe*', *Journal of Family History*, 13 (1988), pp. 265–70, and Brent D. Shaw and Richard P. Saller, 'Close-Kin Marriage in Roman Society', *Man*, 19 (1984), pp. 432–49.

14 Carolyn Walker Bynum, *Jesus as Mother: Studies in the Spirituality of the High Middle Ages* (University of California Press, Berkeley, Cal., 1982), pp. 112–18, 142–3.

15 Diane Owen Hughes, 'From Brideprice to Dowry in Mediterranean Europe', in *The Marriage Bargain: Women and Dowries in European History*, ed. Marion A. Kaplan (Harrington Park Press, New York, 1985), pp. 13–58.

16 Widows were on occasion allowed to carry on their husband's

business to prevent the family losing its place in the merchant guild; some of the craft guilds were initially open to women.

17 J. Hajnal, 'European Marriage Patterns in Perspective', in *Population in History: Essays in Historical Demography*, eds D. V. Glass and D. E. C. Eversley (Edward Arnold, London, 1965), pp. 101–43.

18 David Herlihy, *Medieval Households* (Harvard University Press, Cambridge, Mass., 1985), p. 107; see also Anthony Molho, 'Deception and Marriage Strategy in Renaissance Florence: The Case of Women's Ages', *Renaissance Studies*, 61 (1988), pp. 193–217.

19 Judith M. Bennett, 'Medieval Peasant Marriages: An Examination of Marriage Licence Fines in *Liber Gersumarum*', in *Pathways to Peasants*, ed. T. Raftis (Pontifical Institute of Medieval Studies, Toronto, 1982), p. 214; Margaret W. Labarge, *Women in Medieval Life: A Small Sound of the Trumpet* (Beacon, Boston, 1986), pp. 159–60.

20 Alan Macfarlane, *The Origins of English Individualism: The Family, Property and Social Transition* (Blackwell, Oxford, 1978), pp. 134, 149, 158.

21 David Nicholas, *The Domestic Life of a Medieval City: Women, Children and the Family in Fourteenth Century Ghent* (University of Nebraska Press, Lincoln, Nebr., 1985), pp. 6–11.

22 Georges Duby, *The Knight, the Lady and the Priest: The Making of Modern Marriage in Medieval France*, tr. Barbara Bray (Pantheon, New York, 1983), p. 36.

23 Duby, *The Knight, the Lady and the Priest*, p. 129. Abandonment was a source of conflict; see Juha Pentikainen, *The Nordic Dead-Child Tradition*, tr. Antony Landon (Academia Scientiarum Fehnia, Helsinki, 1968), pp. 57–69.

24 Herlihy, *Medieval Households*, p. 28.

25 Rouche, 'Haut Moyen Age Occidental', p. 444.

26 Russell, *Late Ancient and Medieval Populations*, p. 143.

27 Elizabeth Ward Swain, 'My Excellent and Most Singular Lord: Marriage in a Noble Family of Fifteenth Century Italy', *Journal of Medieval and Renaissance Studies*, 16 (1982), p. 195.

28 Craig Williamson, *A Feast of Creatures: Anglo-Saxon Riddle Songs* (University of Pennsylvania Press, Philadelphia, 1982), p. 104; Edith Whitehurst Williams, 'What's So New About the Sexual Revolution?'; *Texas Quarterly*, 18 (1975), pp. 46–55; Robert Hellman and Richard O'Gorman, eds, *Fabliaux: Ribald Tales from the Old French* (Cromwell, New York, 1965), pp. 24–5.

29 James A. Brundage, *Law, Sex, and Christian Society in Medieval Europe* (University of Chicago Press, Chicago, 1987), p. 198.

30 Goody, *The Development of the Family*, pp. 68–72.

31 Wilfred Bonser, *The Medical Background of Anglo-Saxon England* (Wellcome, London, 1963), pp. 265ff; Dr G. Storms, *Anglo-Saxon Magic* (Martinus Nijhof, Hague, 1948), pp. 83, 196–205;

J.H.G. Grattan and Charles Singer, *Anglo-Saxon Magic and Medicine* (Princeton University Press, Princeton, NJ, 1952), pp. 189–191.

32 Geoffrey Chaucer, *The Canterbury Tales*, ed. J. Halverson (Bobbs-Merrill, New York, 1971), lines 1807–8. Chaucer condemned as lewd, however, Constantinus Africanus' *De Coitu*, with its lists of windy, warm and wet foods that provoked desire and its recipes for oils and ointments that would prolong it. See Paul Delaney, 'Constantinus Africanus' *De Coitu*: A Translation', *Chaucer Review*, 4 (1969), pp. 55–65.

33 Petrus Hispanus (John XXI), *The Treasury of Healthe*, tr. Humfre Lloyd (Lloyd, London, 1558), Di-ii, Pii-iii. The Spanish '*lapidarios*' – recipe books for the magical use of stones – referred to three that induced menses, nine that acted as aphrodisiacs and six as anaphrodisiacs, five that prevented miscarriage, five that prevented conception and four that guaranteed pregnancy; see J. Horace Nunemaker, 'Obstetrical and Genito-Urinary Remedies of Thirteenth-Century Spain', *Bulletin of the History of Medicine*, 15 (1944), pp. 162–79.

34 Helen Rodnite Lemay, 'Antonius Guainerius and Medical Gynecology', in *Women of the Medieval World: Essays in Honor of John H. Mundy*, eds Julius Kirshner and Suzanne F. Wemple (Blackwell, Oxford, 1985), pp. 323–31.

35 Helen Rodnite Lemay, 'Some Thirteenth and Fourteenth Century Lectures on Female Sexuality', *International Journal of Women's Studies*, 1 (1978), pp. 391–400.

36 Lucile B. Pinto, 'The Folk Practice of Gynecology and Obstetrics in the Middle Ages', *Bulletin of the History of Medicine*, 47 (1973), pp. 513–23; Grete Jacobsen, 'Pregnancy and Childbirth in the Medieval North: A Topology of Sources and a Preliminary Study', *Scandinavian Journal of History*, 9 (1984), 91–111.

37 Jane Bishop, 'Bishops as Marital Advisors', in Kirshner and Wemple, *Women*, p. 67. Hincmar of Rheims referred frequently to exorcism, prayers, tears and penance employed to counter impotence caused by magic. It says something of the medical knowledge of the time that he was not sure if an aborted woman could still be a virgin. See Jean Devisse, *Hincmar, archévêque de Reims, 845–882* (Droz, Geneva, 1975), vol. I, pp. 377–80, 400.

38 Duby, *The Knight, the Lady and the Priest*, pp. 142, 205. On impotence caused by spells, see also Guy of Chauliac (1300–1368), *Le Guidon en français, corrigé par maitre Canappe* (Hierosme, Paris, 1550), p. 264.

39 Guibert, *The Autobiography of Guibert, Abbot of Nogent-sous-Coucy*, tr. C.C. Swinton Bland (Routledge, London, 1960), p. 123.

40 Charles T. Wood, 'The Doctor's Dilemma: Sin, Salvation, and the Menstrual Cycle in Medieval Thought', *Speculum*, 56 (1981), pp. 710–27; Saul Nathaniel Brody, *The Disease of the Soul: Leprosy in Medieval Literature* (Cornell University Press, Ithaca, NY, 1977).

41 Duby, *The Knight, the Lady and the Priest*, p. 67.
42 A. G. Rigg, ed., *Gawain on Marriage: The De coniuge non ducenda* (Pontifical Institute of Medieval Studies, Toronto, 1986), pp. 73, 87–8.
43 Penny Schine Gold, *The Lady and the Virgin: Image, Attitude and Experience in Twelfth Century France* (University of Chicago Press, Chicago, 1985).
44 Henri Bresc, 'L'Europe des villes et des campagnes: XIIIe–XVe siècles', in Burguière et al., *Histoire de la famille*, vol. I, p. 410.
45 Pierre Toubert, 'Le moment carolingien', in Burguière et al., *Histoire de la famille*, vol. I, p. 340.
46 Barbara Hanawalt, *The Ties that Bound: Peasant Families in Medieval England* (Oxford University Press, Oxford, 1986), p. 67.
47 Constance B. Bouchard, 'The Bosonids or Rising to Power in the Late Carolingian Age', *French Historical Studies*, 15 (1988), p. 430.
48 K. J. Leyser, *Rule and Conflict in Early Medieval Society: Ottonian Saxony* (Edward Arnold, London, 1979), p. 55.
49 Herlihy, *Medieval Households*, p. 146.
50 Chaucer, *Nun's Priest's Tale*, line 3345; H. A. Kelly, *Love and Marriage in the Age of Chaucer* (Cornell University Press, Ithaca, NY, 1975), p. 285
51 *On the Properties of Things*, John Trevisa's translation of Bartholomaeus Anglicus' *De proprietatibus rerum* (Clarendon, Oxford, 1975), vol. I, p. 263.
52 Madeleine Jeay, 'Sexuality and Family in Fifteenth Century France: Are Literary Sources a Mask or Mirror?', *Journal of Family History*, 4 (1979), pp. 337–45.
53 David Herlihy and Christiane Klapische-Zuber, *Tuscans and their Families: A Study of the Florentine Catasto of 1427* (Yale University Press, New Haven, 1985), p. 251. For a fifteenth-century French preacher who similarly attacked women for recourse to abortion and infanticide, see Alexandre Samouillan, *Olivier Maillard: sa prédication et son temps* (Privat, Toulouse, 1891), pp. 316–27.
54 Hostiensis, *Golden Summa*, 4; Palude, *Sentences*, 4.31.3; Nider, *De morali lepra*; Trovamala, *Summa*; cited in Noonan, *Contraception: A History*, p. 220.
55 Etienne van Walle, 'Motivations and Technology in the Decline of French Fertility', in *Family and Sexuality in French History*, eds Tamara Hareven and Robert Wheaton (University of Pennsylvania Press, Philadelphia, 1980), p. 163.
56 Mary McLaughlin, 'Survivors and Surrogates: Children and Parents from the Ninth to the Thirteenth Centuries', *The History of Childhood*, ed. Lloyd de Mause (Psychohistory Press, New York, 1976), pp. 103–5.
57 Carolyn Walker Bynum, *Holy Feast and Holy Fast: The Religious Significance of Food to Medieval Women* (University of California, Berkeley, Cal., 1987), pp. 167, 226, 301.

58 P. P. A. Biller, 'Birth-Control in the West in the Thirteenth and Early Fourteenth Centuries', *Past and Present*, 44 (1982), p. 16.

59 Jean Verdon, 'Les sources de la femme en Occident aux Xe–XIIIe siècle', *Cahiers de civilization médiévale*, 20 (1977), p. 223.

60 *The Secrets of Albertus Magnus* (Jaggard, London, 1599); Luke Demaitre and Anthony A. Travill, 'Human Embryology and Development in the Works of Albertus Magnus', in *Albertus Magnus and the Sciences: Commemorative Essays 1980* (Pontifical Institute of Medieval Studies, Toronto, 1980), p. 412. Women, the traditional health givers, were shut out of the emerging thirteenth-century medical profession, but the memory of their competence and an implied unhappiness with male practitioners was maintained in the gynaecological texts attributed to 'Trotula', a woman who practised in twelfth-century Salerno. Though the evidence suggests that these gynaecological and obstetric works were written, read and employed by men, they nevertheless made the point that women's personal experiences were as important as scholastic wrangling. See John F. Benton, 'Trotula, Women's Problems, and the Professionalization of Medicine in the Middle Ages', *Bulletin of the History of Medicine*, 39 (1985), pp. 30–53; Monica H. Green, 'Essay Review: Toward a History of Women's Medical Practice and Medical Care in Medieval Europe', *Signs*, 14 (1989), pp. 434–73.

61 Ludwig Bieler, ed., *The Irish Penitentials* (Dublin Institute for Advanced Studies, Dublin, 1963), p. 205.

62 Jean-Louis Flandrin, *Un temps pour embrasser: Aux origines de la morale sexuelle occidentale (VIe–XIe siècle)* (Seuil, Paris, 1983), pp. 41–58

63 Herlihy, *Medieval Households*, p. 215. The most extreme devaluation of marriage was made in the twelfth century by Peter Damian, who praised the bee and vulture in the belief that they reproduced without coition. See Robert Bultot, *La doctrine du mépris du monde: Peter Damien* (Nauwelaerts, Louvain, 1963), pp. 25–6, 101–5.

64 *Hali Meidenhad*, ed. F. J. Furnivall (Early English Text Society, London, 1922), p. 12; see also John Bugge, *Virginitas: An Essay in the History of a Medieval Ideal* (Martinus Nijhoff, The Hague, 1975), pp. 88–90.

65 R. W. Chambers, ed., *The Book of Margery Kemp* (Devin-Adair, New York, 1944), p. 6. To ensure continence, recourse could be made to 'cooling' diets. The writings of John XXI and Arnold of Villanova (d. 1313) suggest that the medieval clergy was as concerned as the early church fathers with foods that restrained lust.

66 Jean Guyon, 'D'Auguste à Charlemagne: la montée des interdits', in *Le fruit défendu: les chrétiens et la sexualité de l'antiquité à nos jours*, ed. Marcel Bernos (Le Centurion, Paris, 1985), p. 27. See also Ole Jorgen Benedictow, 'The Milky Way in History: Breast Feeding, Antagonism Between the Sexes, and Infant Mortality in

Medieval Norway', *Scandinavian Journal of History*, 10 (1985), pp. 19–53.

67 James A. Brundage, *Law, Sex, and Christian Society in Medieval Europe* (University of Chicago Press, Chicago, 1987), p. 157.

68 Leah Lydia Otis, 'Prostitution and Repentance in Late Medieval Perpignan', in Kirshner and Wemple, *Women*, pp. 137–60; Leah Lydia Otis, *Prostitution in Medieval Society: The History of an Urban Institution in Languedoc* (University of Chicago Press, Chicago, 1985); Bronislaw Geremek, *The Margins of Society in Medieval Paris* (Cambridge University Press, Cambridge, 1987), pp. 211–41.

69 Danielle Jacquart and Claude Thomasset, *Sexuality and Medicine in the Middle Ages*, tr. Matthew Adamson (Polity Press, London, 1988), p. 25.

70 *Histoire de la famille*, vol. I, p. 410; and see also E. Pavan, 'Police des moeurs, société et politique à Venise à la fin du Moyen Age', *Revue historique*, 264 (1980), pp. 241–88.

71 Chaucer, *Parson's Tale*, lines 575–6.

72 Jacquart and Thomasset, *Sexuality*, p. 134.

73 Pierre J. Payer, *Sex and the Penitentials: The Development of a Sexual Code, 550–1150* (University of Toronto Press, Toronto, 1984), p. 57.

74 Biller, 'Birth-Control', pp. 5–6. On 'Onanism' as masturbation see Peter Damian, *Book of Gomorrah: An Eleventh Century Treatise Against Clerical Homosexual Practices*, tr. Pierre J. Payer (Wilfred Laurier University, Waterloo, Ontario, 1982), p. 33.

75 Noonan, *Contraception: A History*, p. 28.

76 Duby, *The Knight, the Lady and the Priest*, pp. 175, 206.

77 Frances and Joseph Gies, *Marriage and Family in the Middle Ages* (Harper and Row, New York, 1987), p. 327, ft. 77.

78 Noonan, *Contraception: A History*, p. 191.

79 Betsy Bowden, 'The Art of Courtly Copulation', *Medievalia et humanistica*, 9 (1979), pp. 67–85.

80 Herlihy and Klapische-Zuber, *Tuscans*, p. 253; Jacquart and Thomasset, *Sexuality*, p. 218.

81 James A. Brundage, 'Let Me Count the Ways: Canonists and Theologians Contemplate Coital Positions', *Journal of Medical History*, 10 (1984), pp. 81–93.

82 Duby, *The Knight, the Lady and the Priest*, p. 134.

83 Herlihy, *Medieval Households*, p. 39.

84 Duby, *The Knight, the Lady and the Priest*, p. 71.

85 John T. McNeil and Helena M. Gamer, *Medieval Handbooks of Penance* (Octagon, New York, 1965), pp. 119, 166, 197, 237, 291, 304, 330, 340.

86 Guibert, *The Autobiography*, pp. 40–4.

87 Herlihy, *Medieval Households*, pp. 31–2.

88 Noonan, *Contraception: A History*, p. 146.

89 E. Le Roy Ladurie, *Montaillou: Cathars and Catholics in a French Village, 1294–1324*, tr. Barbara Bray (Scolar Press, London, 1978), p. 173.

90 Brian Law, *The Salernitan Questions: An Introduction to the History of Medieval and Renaissance Problem Literature* (Clarendon, Oxford, 1963). St Hildegard (1098–1179), abbess of Rupertsberg, in following up on Aristotle's arguments, was the first western woman to write on embryology. See Bernard W. Scholz, 'Hildegard von Bingen', *American Benedictine Review*, 31 (1980), 361–83.

91 Ibn Sina, *Canon*, 2.3, cited in Noonan, *Contraception: A History*, pp. 201–2.

92 Islam was far more liberal than Christianity in its attitudes towards fertility control. Many Arab texts listed contraceptive potions, tampons and suppositories. Coitus interruptus was sanctioned or at least tolerated by the Prophet if employed to protect a family's property or a mother's health. Abortion performed prior to formation at one hundred days was defended. See B. F. Musallem, *Sex and Society in Islam: Birth Control Before the Nineteenth Century* (Cambridge University Press, Cambridge, 1983); Madeleine Farrah, *Marriage and Sexuality in Islam: A Translation of al-Ghazzali's Book on the Etiquette of Marriage from the Ihya'* (University of Utah Press, Salt Lake City, 1984).

93 Demaitre and Travill, 'Human Embryology', pp. 407–24; S. Belguedes, 'La collection hippocratique et l'embryologie coranique', *La collection hippocratique et son rôle dans l'histoire de la médecine* (Brill, Leiden, 1975), pp. 324–8.

94 Luke E. Demaitre, *Doctor Bernard de Gordon: Professor and Practitioner* (Pontifical Institute of Medieval Studies, Toronto, 1980), pp. 78–80; M. Antony Hewson, *Giles of Rome and the Medieval Theory of Conception* (Athlone Press, London, 1975), pp. 48–54.

95 Noonan, *Contraception: A History*, p. 207; on his humoral theories see also Arnaldus de Villa Nova, *Here is a New Boke, called the Defence of Age and Recovery of Youth*, tr. Jonas Drummond (Wyer, London, 1540).

96 Beryl Rowland, *Medieval Woman's Guide to Health: The First English Gynecological Handbook* (Kent State University Press, Kent, Ohio, 1981), pp. 157–9; see also Delaney, 'Constantinus Africanus' *De Coitu*', pp. 62–3.

97 R. Nelli, *La vie quotidienne des Cathars de Languedoc au 13e siècle* (Hachette, Paris, 1969), p. 62

98 Helen Rodnite Lemay, 'Human Sexuality in 12th to 15th Century Scientific Writings', in *Sexual Practices and the Medieval Church*, eds V. Bullough and J. Brundage (Prometheus Press, Buffalo, 1982), p. 200.

99 Lemay, 'Human Sexuality', pp. 187–205.

100 Helen Rodnite Lemay, 'The Stars and Human Sexuality: Some Medieval Scientific Views', *Isis*, 76 (1980), pp. 127–37.

101 Jews, like Muslems, believed that in cases where a woman's life was threatened a pregnancy could be legitimately ended. See Fred Rosner, *Medicine in the Mishneh Torah of Maimonides* (Ktav, New York, 1984), pp. 170–3. See also L. Rabinowitz, *The Social Life of the Jews of Northern France in the XII–XIV Centuries as Reflected in the Rabbinical Literature of the Period* (Goldston, London, 1938), pp. 150–1; S. D. Goitein, *A Mediterranean Society: The Jewish Communities of the Arab World as Portrayed in the Documents of the Cairo Geniza* (University of California Press, Berkeley, Cal., 1978), vol. III, pp. 168–70, 211, 230–1.

102 Claude Alexandre Thomasset, ed., *Placides et Timeo ou Li secres as philosophes* (Droz, Geneva, 1980); Claude Alexandre Thomasset, *Un vision du monde à la fin du XIIIe siècle: Commentaire du dialogue du Placides et Timeo* (Droz, Geneva, 1982). Medical knowledge was still primitive. Galen based his knowledge of anatomy on the dissection of monkeys; in medieval Salerno pigs served the same purpose. Human dissections only began in Padua in 1341, and old beliefs in the womb being divided into seven chambers and in the complementarity of male and female genitals lingered on. See George W. Corner, *Anatomical Texts of the Earlier Middle Ages* (Carnegie Institution, Washington, DC, 1927); M. C. Pouchelle, *Corps et chirurgie à l'apogée du moyen-âge* (Flammarion, Paris, 1983), pp. 134, 223–9.

103 Hanawalt, *The Ties that Bound*, p. 101; see also Y. B. Brissaud, 'L'Infanticide à la fin du moyen âge', *Revue historique de droit français et étranger*, 50 (1972), pp. 234–5.

104 Herlihy, *Medieval Households*, p. 53.

105 Heath Dillard, *Daughters of the Reconquest: Women in Castilian Town Society, 1100–1300* (Cambridge University Press, Cambridge, 1988), pp. 210–11.

106 Noonan, *Contraception: A History*, p. 218.

107 Noonan, *Contraception: A History*, p. 219.

108 Rowland, *Medieval Woman's Guide to Health*, p. 97. On humoral medicine, see also the work of Lanfranc (died 1306), *A Most Excellent and Learned Work of Chirurgie*, tr. John Halle (Marshe, London, 1565).

109 Gerson, *Opera*, 3, 1000, cited in Noonan, *Contraception: A History*, p. 273.

110 Joelle Beaucamp, 'La situation juridicaire de la femme à Byzance', *Cahiers de civilization médiévale*, 20 (1977), p. 164. On the possibility that abortions were performed in the *xenones* (hospitals) see Timothy Miller, *The Birth of the Hospital in the Byzantine Empire* (Johns Hopkins, Baltimore, 1985), p. 213.

111 Rouche, 'Haut Moyen Age Occidental', p. 444.

112 Corner, *Anatomical Texts*, pp. 105–6.

113 Dante Alighieri, *The Divine Comedy*, ed. Charles Singleton (Princeton University Press, Princeton, NJ, 1973), canto 25, 52–81,

vol. II, pp. 273, 610–16. Henri de Mondeville, surgeon of Philippe le Bel (1285–1314), wrote that at forty-five days the conceptus was perfected and at ninety quickened. Dr A. Bos, *La chirurgie de maître Henri de Mondeville* (Firmin, Paris, 1897), vol. I, pp. 114–15.

114 John T. Noonan, Jr, 'An Almost Absolute Value in History', in *The Morality of Abortion: Legal and Historical Perspectives*, ed. John T. Noonan (Harvard University Press, Cambridge, Mass., 1970), p. 20.

115 H. G. Richardson, ed., *Fleta* (Seldon Society, London, 1955), LXXII, 60–1.

116 Herlihy, *Medieval Households*, p. 53.

117 Barbara A. Hanawalt, 'Childrearing Among the Lower Classes of Late Medieval England', *Journal of Interdisciplinary History*, 8 (1977), pp. 1–22; Peter Biller, 'Childbirth in the Middle Ages', *History Today*, 36 (1986), pp. 42–9.

118 Emily Coleman, 'Infanticide in the Early Middle Ages', in *Women in Medieval Society*, ed., S. M. Stuard (University of Pennsylvania Press, Philadelphia, 1976), pp. 47–71. See also Barbara A. Kellum, 'Infanticide in England in the Later Middle Ages', *History of Childhood Quarterly*, 1 (1974), pp. 367–88.

119 Hanawalt, *The Ties that Bound*, pp. 101–2.

120 A. Porteau Bitker, 'Criminalité et délinquance féminine dans le droit pénal des XIIIe et XIVe siècles', *Revue historique de droit français et étranger*, 58 (1980), pp. 15, 34.

121 John Boswell, '*Expositio* and *Oblatio*; The Abandonment of Children and the Ancient and Medieval Family', *American Historical Review*, 89 (1984), pp. 10–33; John Boswell, *The Kindness of Strangers: The Abandonment of Children in Western Europe from Late Antiquity to the Renaissance* (Pantheon, New York, 1988), parts II–IV. Formal oblation – for those who ultimately would be ordained and whose parents provided a dowry – is not to be confused with the taking in of poor children who were to be raised as labourers.

122 Biller, 'Birth-Control', pp. 22–5.

123 London merchants produced strikingly small families. 'But it is unmistakeably clear that at no part of the period did the average number of heirs that a merchant left behind him in the direct male line reach two.' Sylvia L. Thrupp, *The Merchant Class of Medieval London* (University of Chicago Press, Chicago, 1948), pp. 199–200. For the countryside, see Bruce M. S. Campbell, 'Population Pressure, Inheritance and the Land Market in a Fourteenth-Century Community', in *Land, Kinship, and Life Cycle*, ed. R.M. Smith (Cambridge University Press, Cambridge, 1984), pp. 128–9. On the low fecundity of French merchants, see Arlette Higounet-Nadal, *Familles patriciennes de Périgueux à la fin du moyen âge* (CNRS, Paris, 1983), pp. 25, 134, 141–2.

124 Dante, *Paradiso*, xv, ii. 106–8; Noonan, *Contraception: A History*, p. 227, n. 47.
125 Noonan, *Contraception: A History*, p. 168.
126 Biller, 'Birth-Control', p. 16.
127 Noonan, *Contraception: A History*, pp. 299–300.
128 Noonan, *Contraception: A History*, p. 197.

5

Fertility Control in Early Modern Europe

In the early modern period the discussion of fertility, once dominated by the church, was 'secularized'. The state began to replace priests in policing motherhood by criminalizing infanticide and abortion, male obstetricians commenced their campaign to replace midwives in the delivery of babies, and writers of tracts on onanism and producers of condoms in effect launched the 'commercialization' of contraception. Childbearing was changing; by the eighteenth century the numbers of the married methodically limiting family size had grown to such an extent that the evidence of such practices was numerically significant. Europeans not only postponed and spaced births as they always had done; now they were beginning to prevent them altogether.[1]

Did the changing nature of contraceptive practices reflect a change in family forms? Researchers are divided as to the extent to which the western European family in the early modern period differed from that of the Middle Ages. In its quantitative aspects – late age of marriage, large numbers of never married and low fertility – it was very similar to what we saw in the previous chapter. Ordinary men and women continued to be enormously prudent in approaching both marriage and childbearing. The medieval injunction, 'no land, no marriage', was still largely honoured, though less so from the sixteenth century onward. Up to 20 per cent of the population remained single for life.[2] The young bloods of the village employed rough music or charivaris to censure unions that violated local custom. The church, of course, also had its say, but was beginning to be replaced in the policing of couples by the state. In 1556, the age of twenty-four was fixed for the term of London apprentices to check 'hastie maryages', and such restrictions soon spread to other towns.[3] The average marriage age of English peers rose between the sixteenth and eighteenth centuries from twenty-five to thirty for men and from twenty to twenty-three for women. Across north-western Europe, males married at twenty-nine to thirty and females at twenty-five to twenty-six. On the continent, the austere doctrine of late marriage and pre-conjugal chastity preached by counter-reformation priests complemented the concern of the laity that marriages were economically secured.[4]

The betrothal continued to be the vital step in laying the basis for a marriage which united not only two individuals, but two families; sexual intercourse frequently preceded the actual wedding. Something like a quarter of brides went to the altar pregnant, yet the fact that illegitimacy rates represented only about 2 per cent of births suggests the seriousness with which childbearing was taken. Whether such caution was due to an internalization of Christian ethics or a fear of social ostracism made little difference. Sexual self-control was clearly an ingrained form of rational behaviour.[5]

Late marriage, the wide spacing of births – a result of extended nursing possibly abetted by continence or contraception – and high infant mortality rates meant that until the mid-eighteenth century families had just enough children to sustain the population. In the small English village of Kibworth Harcourt, for example, women bore on average 4.87 children, of whom a sixth died before the age of twenty-one.[6] In North America, where there was neither the same shortage of land nor demographic pressure, families were larger. In the seventeenth-century Plymouth Colony, about eight children per family were produced.[7]

Households were, of course, not the same as families. The former tended to increase in size as one moved up the social hierarchy; the large household was a luxury the poor could not afford. An aristocrat might have up to forty persons under his roof while the average labourer had only three or four.[8] Artisans and crofters, not being able to keep their children for long, sent them out early in life as domestic servants or labourers. The wealthy appropriated such labour both to serve their economic needs and to demonstrate their social power, but with the rise of commerce they increasingly viewed servants as employees rather than as members of the 'family'.

This practice of leaving home when young to work in another household was not restricted to the poor. Being sent off to serve as a domestic or apprentice was a key feature of the life cycle of the western family, especially in Britain and Scandinavia. It was linked to late marriages and the ultimate establishment of independent households. Young men and women in service represented about 14 per cent of England's total population and 60 per cent of the fifteen to twenty-four age group.[9] Pre-industrial Europe was, with so many young people pursuing work away from home, a far more mobile society than is usually imagined. Their goal, however, was finally to settle down. Sending them away provided an answer to the problem of how they were to pass the ten or so potentially tension-ridden years they spent awaiting marriage. If their labour were well paid it meant that a new household could be established by a son before the death of his father. His bride would have either earned or inherited her marriage portion. The propertyless poor presumably had little to lose in marrying whenever and whomever they chose.

This practice of young people's working away from home, in lengthening adolescence, had an obvious impact on fertility. Kussmaul has described the servant stage of the life cycle as a sort of family planning strategy: 'The institution of service was a form of *ex post facto* family planning. Once the family knew that it had too many surviving children to be employed or maintained within the family, the surplus could be sent to the family that now knew that it had too few surviving children to help with the farm.'[10] Service, in delaying marriages and thus births, allowed a balancing of a community's supply and demand of labour. Moreover, as an initiation into a semi-independent life, it prepared young people to have some say in the choice of their marriage partner. The 'individualism' of west Europeans should not be exaggerated, however; John Gillis has pointed out that, despite demographic historians' stress on the 'nuclear' nature of the western family, couples knew they could only securely enter marriage when assured of the support of the community, friends and kin.[11]

In north-west Europe, kinship ties were relatively weak, brothers rarely shared land or households, and extended families were rare. In France and Germany, the 'stem family' was more in evidence: the eldest son took over from the retiring father while the younger sons left home or stayed on the family farm unmarried. Even here, because of relatively short life expectancies, there could only be a brief overlap of adult generations. Further south and east where the land was poorest and there existed the greatest need for family labour, the percentage of complex or multifamily households increased.

In southern and eastern Europe, life cycle service was, due partly to the absence of a labour market, uncommon. And when marriages did occur, the establishment of a new family did not always go together with the creation of a new household. In Italy, for example, extended families were the norm. Married sons brought their brides to their fathers' homes. Family solidarity rather than the independence found in the west was esteemed. It was a solidarity that exalted male dominance. In the extended households of Spain and Sicily, all women married and at an early age, usually between eighteen and twenty.[12] From the time of the Renaissance, Italian girls left their households either to enter convents as early as seven or for marriage at twelve. To grow out of a wedding dress was not thought shocking.[13] Wives tended to be viewed as guests in their husband's house and, when widowed, commonly returned to their 'own' family. The women of southern Europe were not as subservient as is often made out, but their margins of manoeuvre were clearly narrower than those of their counterparts in the west.

The marriage customs of the poor were regulated more by the community than by kin. A good deal of support was provided by workmates, and women in particular enjoyed a sexual solidarity. And though the economy dramatically improved from the sixteenth century onwards, the actual number of the poor increased. Western Europe shifted in the early modern period from subsistence to commercial farming; from small plots to enclosed estates. By the seventeenth century, many rural labourers were without land. Previously they would not have married; now waged labour not only allowed it, but on occasion provided an economic incentive both to marry and to have a large family. The smallholders, suggests Cicely Howell, concerned to prevent the division of lands amongst too many heirs, continued to have a 'preservative' instinct to limit fertility.[14] In eastern and southern Europe a 'refeudalization' occurred as the elite dispossessed the peasantry of their lands. Here too the peasants' attempts to augment their labour force by increasing family size only plunged them further into subservience.

Europe slowly recovered in the fifteenth and sixteenth centuries from the disastrous epidemics of the 1300s and in the eighteenth century experienced an unprecedented growth in population. This was once solely attributed by historians to declines in mortality occasioned by the diminution of the famines and diseases endemic to medieval Europe and by the increases made in agricultural productivity. Although such interpretations still appear to hold good for much of the continent, recent investigations have led to the conclusion that in England twice as much growth was due to rising fertility as to declining mortality. The country's population was governed, in the words of Wrigley and Schofield, by a 'fertility-dominated low pressure system'.[15] A lower age of marriage, an increased incidence of marriage, rising marital fertility and longer life expectancy combined to produce rising fertility rates. It was no coincidence that England, the first country to industrialize, should experience such changes. Much of the population growth was created, according to David Levine, by the proletarianization of labour. In the traditional community children were sent away into service, but the growth of domestic industry in the eighteenth century created a demand for child labour and provided wages that allowed earlier marriages. The demand for labour, in providing positive incentives to marry and bear children, elicited the 'prolific power' usually held in check by social controls.[16]

The darker side of all of this was that just as market prosperity sponsored early marriages, an economic downswing, in making such unions impossible, could produce high levels of illegitimacy. In the eighteenth century, pre-bridal pregnancies increased from something like 10 to 30 per cent and illegitimacy rates climbed from 2 to 8 per cent and in some places as high as 16 per cent.[17] The upper classes were periodically seized by moral panics in face of what they took to be the promiscuity and immorality of the poor; in fact high illegitimacy rates were due not to moral laxity, but to the frustration by economic dislocation of attempts at early marriage.

The real importance of the rise of the English birth rate, the discussion of which might seem out of place in a study of fertility control, is that it demonstrated that childbearing was not unchanging, but responsive to changing social forces. Both the Europeans who were raising and those who were lowering their fertility were demonstrating their desire to achieve an optimum family size.[18]

It might appear ironic, but the very fact that the European population was growing at an unprecedented pace played a role in widely extending fertility-control practices. Even those demographic historians who have been the most reluctant to accept the notion that past generations could or would have attempted to limit pregnancies have turned up 'hard evidence' that indicates that west Europeans were, from the seventeenth century onwards, not only attempting to but succeeding in limiting their fertility.

Wrigley found quantitative evidence in the parish records of the village of Colyton, Devon, of family limitation being employed as early as the seventeenth century. Large families were obviously not desired. Colyton women usually married from twenty-six to thirty; men often married brides older than themselves. Moreover, there was clear birth spacing, a marked decline in fertility in the later years of a woman's childbearing career and a long gap between the penultimate and last birth that suggested attempts made to stop. Those who married before thirty in the period 1647–1719 had their last child on average two years earlier than those who married between 1560 and 1646.[19] Wrigley subsequently discovered another curious phenomenon; across England births to the newly married and the already married tended to occur at the same times of year. This suggests means were taken to avoid them at inappropriate occasions.[20] Colyton's fertility returned to higher levels after 1720.

A similar short-term experiment in fertility control was apparently tried by the British peerage, which reduced its family size to 3.60 children by 1747, but then raised it to a high of 4.85 in 1824.[21] Especially between 1690 and 1720 the aristocracy, preoccupied by the problem of providing for younger sons and desiring to protect the health of mothers, limited its fertility. But after 1750 it returned, richer, more confident in the assistance midwifery could offer its pregnant wives and driven by a new zeal for domesticity to the large family pattern.[22]

A more consistent drop in fertility was detected on the continent. Louis Henry found that the Genevan bourgeoisie had 5.4 children per family for the period 1600–49, 3.6 for 1650–99, and 2.9 for 1700–49. By the eighteenth century, similar patterns were detected in the families of both the French court and country aristocracy. In Besançon, the number of children per Parlementarian family dropped from 6.8 in 1692 to 4.4 in 1771–90. In the small village of Loumarin, the number fell from 4.9 in 1726–55 to 4.2 in 1756–85, to 3.9 in 1786–1815.[23] In the later eighteenth century, fertility fell in the major French cities, in villages like Meulan and amongst the peasantry in the Paris region.[24]

The fullest account of fertility control in pre-modern Europe was revealed in Bardet's study of Rouen. The city's fertility fell consistently from 1642 to 1792, with a brief pause between 1730 and 1759. Births per family dropped from eight in 1670 to four in 1800; the age of the mother at last birth declined from forty to thirty-seven, and the proportion of childless wives rose from 5 to 10 per cent. The notables were the pioneers in Rouen's family limitation, but by the later eighteenth century were overtaken by members of the petite bourgeoisie. Births continued to be spaced about twenty months apart, but now were 'stopped' after ten years of marriage. 'Artificial' fertility control was thus employed by mature women, not young brides. Indeed, the fact that knowledge-able, remarrying widows had fewer children than women of the same age in first marriages seems to substantiate Bardet's claim that 'Contraception is both a question of knowledge and skill.'[25]

The fertility of eighteenth-century Europe accordingly revealed striking class and cultural cleavages. Proletarianization drove up the fertility of workers in both England and France, as did 'refeudalization' in eastern Europe; the peasantry and bourgeoisie of France swung round to embrace fertility control.

Up to this point we have been reviewing only the quantitative evidence. What meanings can we give to the findings of demographic historians? What social processes were involved that led to the growing employment of fertility controls? How did these birth-control practices – which most historians assume were 'new' – relate to the changing nature of the family? It has been the burden of the argument of a number of recent studies that in the early modern period the family went through an important transition. Put baldly, the thesis is that there was a movement from the instrumental, authoritarian families of the sixteenth century – marked by arranged marriages, subordination of women, brutal treatment of children – to the sentimental, egalitarian family of the late eighteenth – signalled by close relationships between husbands and wives and a new concern for the well-being of children. This evolution, which allowed individual families to free themselves from the constraints of community and kin, was, it is argued, sponsored by Bible-based literacy, new wage labour and social mobility. Protestantism, in nurturing a new respect for one's spouse, paved the way for companionate marriages. Capitalism legitimized individuals' giving priority to the interests of those inside their family rather than to those outside it. The modern state, in seeking to enlist impersonal and efficient bureaucrats, rewarded those who would be loyal to it rather than to clan or parochial interests. A key symptom of the family ethos was an increased concern for the welfare of children. Paradoxically, the argument runs, the very fact that children were beginning to be considered more important explained why in some instances attempts were made to limit their numbers.

Lawrence Stone has argued that birth control only became thinkable in the eighteenth century, with the emergence of 'possessive individualism'. The employment of contraception signalled primarily a moral change, as the pleasure principle was finally separated from the procreative function. As religion waned, sexuality was freed from the restraints of theology and a hedonistic eroticism flourished. Couples now felt they had the right and power to make choices about their childbearing. Medicine, in proving it was possible to overcome the scourges of disease, gave some reason to hope nature could be controlled. Birth control was accordingly possible in this new situation, when it was 'theologically and morally acceptable . . . to make planned choices rather than trust to the will of God'.[26]

Stone is clearly mistaken in believing that attempts at fertility control were not made prior to the Age of Enlightenment; his targeting of the decline of religion and the rise of medicine as key precursors to the wide-scale adoption of contraceptives is useful but simplistic. To begin with the 'restraints of theology' argument, it is true that the Catholic clergy sought to instill in Christian spouses the belief that they did not have the right to control procreation. Christianity propagated the idea that the child was sent by God and, unlike other religions, made few concessions to the social realities that justified the avoidance of pregnancy. If one had too many children it had to be viewed as a cross to bear. This doctrine did produce curious twists, condemning, for example, male masturbation as a sort of homicide, but defending female masturbation if employed for the purpose of completing intercourse by producing the necessary seed.[27]

The church was not unchanging. In the sixteenth century, Catholic marriage rites were revamped as part of the response to the Reformation. Procreation was maintained as the first purpose of marriage, but the Catholic church tended, as its adherence to Augustinianism declined, to be more discreet and understanding of marital lapses. Confessors were less vocal in condemning as a sin intercourse during menses or before communion. A slightly more optimistic view of marriage was taken, though sexual pleasure, even as a 'remedy' for fornication, was still viewed with suspicion. St Francis de Sales, for example, compared unfavourably the married man to the chaste and monogamous elephant which, he asserted, not only had the decency to mate only once every three years, but immediately thereafter retreated to some nearby river to wash.[28]

While the church maintained the argument that procreation was the main purpose of marriage, it declared itself aware of the burdens posed by parenthood. In 1550 de Soto defended the abstention of couples plagued by poverty, and in 1602 Thomas Sanchez accepted the legitimacy of coitus reservatus employed for reasons of poverty or of dangers posed to the mother's health.[29] Sanchez nevertheless declared that a nursing mother did not have the right to refuse her husband, even if she thereby risked the life of her infant; in the early eighteenth century Fromageau asserted that she did. Refusal was also permitted if a pregnancy threatened a woman with death.[30] The church even began to permit intercourse during the woman's period. St Alphonsus Liguori (1697–1787), the most influential of the church doctors, suggested that to avoid giving unnecessary offence discretion be used by confessors in dealing with all marriage matters.

But even the most lax confessors would not sanction the use of contraceptives. In the late sixteenth century, Benedicti condemned those who violated nature or employed unnatural acts so that their wives could not conceive. Pleading poverty was no excuse. 'Those who by potion, drink, or whatever other method prevent conception and generation', he asserted, 'out of a fear of having too many children, sin mortally.'[31] In the seventeenth century, Jean

Cordier lamented the fact that the 'best families' limited their numbers; Jacques Marchant referred to onanism and women employing 'herbs and other poisons'.[32] The old view that contraception by the married was a worse sin than if employed by the unmarried was sustained. Yet the church, in accepting the fact that large families could be a burden and in warning confessors not to be overzealous in questioning those who avoided them, played an unwitting role in legitimating such practices. Fears of such an accommodation were voiced at the time by the more conservative, inquisitorial faction within the church, represented by Père Féline who called for more, not less, clerical policing of bedrooms.

Celibate Catholic priests demanded that the 'conjugal debt' be paid, but highly esteemed virginity and were not really interested in large families. Ironically, the married Protestant clergy did not talk about sex as much as their Catholic counterparts. Luther did attack the misogyny of the Catholics and their celibate ideal. Protestants glorified marriage and the home. They declared women should be subject to their husbands, but honoured for their childbearing. Protestant women, if married and fecund, thus gained some status; they lost the option Catholic women had of entering a convent and leading a life of continence.

Protestantism, in removing the interceding priest and in diminishing the importance of the Virgin Mary, increased the powers of the patriarch. It has been asserted by a number of historians that Puritans, in stressing individual salvation, 'spiritualized' the household. Spouses were enjoined with the duty to delight their partners.[33] Calvin condemned onanism, but called for sexuality to be used joyously. Procreation was still one of the most important functions of marriage, but more important for Protestants was mutual help.[34] 'Love' was fostered by Puritanism and soon brandished by young people to justify marriages opposed by parents. But both Catholics and Protestants assumed that marriages should be freely consented to; they also insisted children obey their parents.[35]

The argument has been made that in Catholic France the Jansenists followed Protestants in seeking to avoid the discussion of intimate matters such as procreation. The result was that, as sexuality was 'secularized', recourse to fertility control depended increasingly on the nature of a couple's relationship rather than on the dictates of religion. In theory, however, Protestants were as opposed to contraception as Catholics. Luther in 1522 stated, much as had St Augustine, that procreation was, for women, 'the purpose for which they exist'. He later attacked those 'who seem to detest giving birth lest the bearing and rearing of children disturb their leisure'.[36] Turning to specific practices Luther declared, 'Onan must have been a malicious and incorrigible scoundrel. This is a most disgraceful sin. It is far more atrocious than incest and adultery. We call it unchastity, yes, a Sodomitic sin.'[37] Calvin agreed. In the early seventeenth century, Samuel Hieren condemned as 'a notable evidence of a miserable and faithless mind' the fact that some 'would prescribe the Lord how many [children] He should give them and set Him down a stint which He must not exceed'.[38]

Even if religious injunctions did lose much of their force in cowing those thinking of employing contraceptives, it is simplistic to attribute such changes directly to the rise of science. Scholasticism with its blind reliance on Aristotle and Galen only slowly declined. The great Renaissance anatomist Andreas Vesalius in 1555 described the follicles, and his pupil Gabriello Fallopio in the 1560s provided further proof of the complexity of the female genitalia. The discovery of the Fallopian tubes, Harvey's search for the ovum and the advances based on seventeenth- and eighteenth-century dissections and microscopic observation of the womb and testicles appeared to promise a new understanding of the process of reproduction. But changes occurred only in a piecemeal fashion. By 1600 there was less talk of the parallelism in anatomy of the two sexes, though still much debate over the role of heat. In Cosme Viardel's *Observations sur la pratique des accouchemens naturels* (1674), for example, there were familiar references, dating back to the Greeks, to the uterus as a field, both sexes producing seed, the womb as an oven and so on.[39]

More sophisticated observations did not end confusion. Harvey followed Aristotle in believing the egg to be the product rather than the cause of conception. It was not until 1667 that the Danish bishop Niels Stensen advanced the argument that before coitus the female testes contained eggs and so should be called ovaries. But it was the follicle rather than the egg itself which was observed by Regnier de Graaf and Jan Swammerdam. Their followers advanced the 'ovist' argument of preformation that held all beings were created at the beginning of time and encapsulated in eggs.[40] Their opponents, members of the 'animalculist' school, believed van Leeuwenhoek's discovery in 1678 of spermatozoa proved that such encapsulation in fact took place in the male, and that mothers were accordingly little more than incubators. What both schools dismissed was the old 'two-seed' theory. They thereby undermined the traditional view that men and women had similar sexual functions and needs. A 'natural' justification for women's subservience was produced.[41]

The new science had little practical information to offer the public. Indeed, it tended if anything to mystify the process of procreation by distancing it from the experiences of ordinary men and women. Whereas women were once viewed as lusty and passionate, indeed necessarily so if conception were to occur, now the basis for a new female passivity emerged. Whether women were viewed differently because of such scientific musings or new views of women *led* to such 'discoveries', the results were the same – amongst the intellectual elite, the old idea of the sexes fulfilling roughly complementary roles was discounted.

The embryologists basically declared that the female orgasm was not necessary. One should not exaggerate the impact of such views. Popular texts continued to portray women as being actively interested in sexual matters. The old humoral theories that attributed failure to conceive to wombs that were too hot or cold, or to seed that was too thin or thick, were still believed. Crude medical texts such as *Le bastiment des receptes* (1665) and *Petit trésor de santé* (1639) still contained traditional cures for barrenness, and well on into the eighteenth century the poorly endowed continued to consume aphrodisiacs, wear talismans and church keys, and make pilgrimages to Christian shrines, pagan menhirs and magic springs.[42] Children were highly valued and raised for more than simple economic reasons. Marriage as rite of passage was less important to a woman than to a man because it represented his establishment as the head of a new household; it was in becoming a mother that she confirmed her status. Demos has noted that in the New England witchcraft trials of the seventeenth century, a fear that was commonly expressed was that women who had few children would envy those more favoured.[43]

Those worried by the thought of barrenness turned to vulgarizations of traditional embryological lore carried in *Aristotle's Masterpiece*, the purported works of Albertus Magnus and the more up-market *Tableau de l'amour conjugal* (1686) by Nicolas Venette, each of which by the end of the eighteenth century had gone through dozens of editions.[44] In such texts the populace was provided with the familiar discussions of the male and female roles in reproduction, the origin of seed, the determination of sex and remedies for impotence and infertility. Embryological discoveries had, in short, next to no impact on popular attitudes towards procreation.

Nor had any revolution in medical practice occurred. The average late eighteenth-century physician had little more to say about childbirth beyond what was found in the Hippocratic texts. Life was still remarkably fragile; obstetrics primitive. Private letters reveal the bourgeoisie's constant concern for health.[45] Women, threatened by repeated births, faced a maternal mortality rate estimated at up to 25 per 1000 live births.[46]

Did the emergence of the eighteenth-century obstetrician signify an increased concern for the well-being of women and children? Upper-class women's child delivery was certainly taken over by men. The received view is that women welcomed such attentions, being 'increasingly eager to associate motherhood with dignity, more anxious to live lives free of artificial restraint, more likely to minimize the pains of birth and suffering in their lives'.[47] The difficulty is proving that such services were actually provided by medical men. And it must not be forgotten that the triumph of the skilled male practitioner took place at the expense of midwives. Those who had access to medical assistance might in fact have suffered more than those who did not. Though forcep deliveries had come into vogue, late eighteenth-century English obstetricians did at least recognize the danger of unnecessary intervention. But French doctors such as Baudelocque were so convinced of their surgical expertise that they campaigned vigorously in favour of the murderously unsuccessful Caesarian section.[48]

No new ideology appeared in the early modern period that justified fertility control; no new technology made it any easier to accomplish. Most no doubt simply fell back on the techniques already well established. Continence was, of course, the simplest way to prevent births. In Protestant as in Catholic Europe, intercourse continued to be avoided at certain times in the liturgical and agricultural calendars. No doubt some doctors provided upper-class women with excuses for avoiding their conjugal duties. Flandrin refers to an 'epidemic of migraines' used through the centuries by French women to avoid their husbands, and argues that in the civilizing eighteenth century women's right to refuse conjugal relations was increasingly recognized, even by Catholic confessors.

Recipes for herbal potions, anaphrodisiacs and lotions aimed at inhibiting intercourse (many dating back to the Greeks) were, thanks to the printing press, carried to a wide audience in a variety of popular herbals and chapbooks which went through countless editions. Benedicti condemned, in the late sixteenth century, druggists and pharmacists who gave women something to eat or drink that might prevent them from conceiving. This, he declared, was admittedly not homicide but still a grievous crime.[49] Edward Poeton described in 1630 a special oil, which he asserted 'forbidds Venus acts, if the genitals be therewith anointed'.[50] I have dealt at length in *Reproductive Rituals* with issues of traditional forms of contraception between the sixteenth and nineteenth centuries.[51] Suffice it to say that across western Europe there was much evidence to be found of a variety of herbal brews to prevent pregnancies. A clear decline in the belief in the efficacy of such potions, at least for contraceptive if not for abortive purposes, seems to have occurred in the west by the early 1700s.

In the eighteenth century, references to magical forms of fertility control were also made less frequently. Magical knots were, according to such eminent witnesses as the jurist Jean Bodin and the Swiss doctor Thomas Platter, in use on the continent in the sixteenth century.[52] Impotency and barrenness caused by diabolical means were condemned in seventeenth-century England by the medical commentators Nicolas Culpeper and John Pechey.[53] The powers of procreation were too mysterious ever to be disentangled completely from superstitious beliefs, but the literate at least discounted such ideas in the same century they overcame their fear of witchcraft.

Between the sixteenth and eighteenth centuries, as the discussions of magical and herbal contraceptives declined, references to onanism increased. There is little doubt that Europeans understood the effectiveness of coitus interruptus; the question was whether they would employ it in marriage. Many of the accounts of onanism appeared in reports of extra-marital affairs. Brantôme, for example, described sixteenth-century aristocratic adulteresses making their lovers swear they would not 'sprinkle a thing inside, not a single drop'.[54] Lower down the social scale, Martin Ingram found in the records of the English ecclesiastical courts references to what appear to be similar practices:

> Edward Harper, a married man of Hamilton, was said in 1617 to 'have to do with wenches when he list and would choose whether he would beget them with child or not'; while Jeremy Gibbons of Idmiston, accused in 1616 of begetting a bastard, was said to have remarked to a friend that 'what he had done was as much as nothing'.[55]

More explicit evidence was produced by a Venetian police investigation of 1457 that uncovered the employment of coitus interruptus by an incestuous father when assaulting his daughter: 'He . . . coming together with her when he came to the moment of emitting sperm, withdrew his member and ejected semen between the thighs of the said Antonia because he said that he did not wish to impregnate her.'[56] It is, of course, unlikely that onanism employed in marriage would ever be reported or investigated. Sodomy was also apparently turned to for contraceptive purposes in Venice. Complaints were made to the council by unhappy wives, but though it ruthlessly persecuted homosexuals for such perversions it avoided interfering with the married.

Recourse to onanism by the married was condemned by Puritans like Babington in 1596 and Gouge in 1626. J. F. Ostervald, the pastor of Neufchatel, alluded to it in attacking marriage abuses.[57] Catholics like St Francis de Sales, bishop of Geneva, seemed to suggest that some were openly defending coitus interruptus. He stated that Onan's actions had always been viewed as 'infamous and execrable' but noted that 'Certain heretics of our days . . . have been pleased to say it was only the perverse intention of that wicked man which displeased God. The scripture positively asserts the contrary and assures us that the act itself that he committed was detestable and abominable in the sight of God.'[58]

Onanism had become so common in early eighteenth-century England that quacks sought, by publishing a series of sensational tracts entitled *Onania*, to cash in on the concerns raised by the practice. At least nineteen editions appeared in the first half of the century. Their first purpose was to provide horrific accounts of the fate that awaited masturbators; a secondary theme was the castigation of males who sought to frustrate marriage by 'a criminal untimely Retreat'. But despite such censures, some editions of *Onania* carried a letter from a married man who protested that he and his poverty-stricken wife, already having three children, conscientiously employed withdrawal to prevent further pregnancies. 'My conscience seems to Clear me of ONAN'S crime for what he did was out of spite and ill-will, and contrary to the express Command of raising up Seed to his brother, in Contradiction to the Method of our Redemption: Whereas mine is pure necessity in respect both of Body and Soul.' This letter appears to be the first public defence made of the legitimacy of coitus interruptus.[59]

On the continent, attacks on onanism were launched in the 1760s in Lausanne by the pietist J. P. Dutoit-Mabrini and from Geneva by S.A.A.D. Tissot, author of what was to prove to be the classic study of masturbation. Both attributed the age's fixation on luxury as its cardinal sin. Tissot bemoaned the desire to protect one's patrimony, leading to the small family: 'As a result few marriages for those who are not rich; few children for those who marry.'[60]

Those who attributed recourse to onanism to economic calculation assumed that the decision was made by the man. They usually mentioned neither the fact that it required his sacrificing a certain degree of pleasure nor that his wife might be more interested in such practices than he. But some evidence suggests that men did not necessarily take the initiative in employing the withdrawal method. A seventeenth-century midwife like Jane Sharp was in a position to know that some women sought to avoid pregnancy; her reference to the ineffectiveness of 'Onan's Seed' suggests coitus interruptus was the method. She carefully noted that motherhood was 'the earnest desire if not of all yet of most women'. She opposed 'destructive means to produce barrenness' but acknowledged 'some persons have presumptuously ventured upon it'.[61] Venette similarly noted that women were more interested in forbidden positions than men, which may suggest that some men were cajoled by their wives into employing coitus interruptus. Père Féline certainly attributed the decline in family size to husbands caving in to their spouses' demands: 'The first reason being the excessive concern of husbands for their wives; the former make themselves too sensible to the latter's complaints of how much childbearing costs them.'[62] Whether or not one accepts the notion that women first persuaded men to employ coitus interruptus in extra-marital affairs and later introduced such practices to the marriage bed, it is clear that to describe the practice simply as a 'male method' can lead to unwarranted denial of women's active interest in controlling their fertility.[63]

Sponges and tampons were more obvious female contraceptives. Chaucer mentioned them,[64] and Mathurin Regnier in *Les Satyrs* (1609) described a prostitute's abode in which were found '*la petite seringue, une éponge, une sonde*'.[65] Sponges were perhaps what Henri Estienne was referring to in 1568 when he spoke of '*preservatifs*' that women employed to protect themselves from becoming pregnant.[66] There is a clearer reference to a sponge in 'The Duchesse of Portsmouth's Garland' (1690).[67] The Marquis de Sade referred to both condoms and sponges – '*des éponges*' and '*un petit sac de peau de Vénise*'.[68] Sponges and tampons were, as these reports made clear, usually associated with extra-marital affairs. Flandrin found no mention of them by confessors questioning married women in the seventeenth and eighteenth centuries. But the fact that Jeremy Bentham recommended, in 'Situation and Relief of the Poor' (1797), the use of sponges to keep down the poor rate suggests that by the end of the eighteenth century such devices were becoming domesticated.

To have been truly effective the use of a sponge would have to have been followed by douching. The use of astringent solutions can be traced back to Soranus and earlier. The French seemed to have employed douches more widely than other Europeans. This was Regnier's '*petit seringue*', and in Mme de Sévigné's letters there is a reference to '*les restringents*'. Such washings were abetted by the use of the *bidet* which is and was, as the English agricultural reformer Arthur Young noted in 1790, a particularly French institution.[69]

The condom, the only new and presumably the most effective contraceptive produced in the early modern period, ironically played little role in the decline of fertility. This was not because its utility was not appreciated. Lord Hervey informed Henry Fox in 1726 that he was sending him 'a dozen preservatives from Claps and impediments to procreation'.[70] But the condom was mainly used to avoid venereal disease. Gabriello Fallopio described in 1564 a small linen covering for the glans that could prevent infection. By the 1700s, condoms were being made of animal bladders or fine skins. In early eighteenth-century England, they were touted by the pornographer John Marten, sold by brothel owners like Mrs Philips, hailed by poets such as Joseph Gay and employed by roués like James Boswell and Giacomo Casanova. Moralists like Joseph Cam attacked them, some realistic doctors like Astruc considered them an unfortunate necessity. By the end of the century they were available at brothels in London, Paris, Berlin and St Petersburg, though their expense and association with venereal disease limited their use by the married. It was a token of the embarrassment with which they were viewed that the English called them French letters and the French named them 'la capote anglaise'.[71]

The invention of the condom expanded, however modestly, men's power over procreation. Women's control over their bodies was in the early modern period more closely policed than it had ever been before. Since one tends to associate the expansion of fertility control with an improvement in the status of women, it is curious that the early modern period witnessed an apparent erosion of women's rights. Both reformed Catholicism and Protestantism cultivated a domesticity that in many ways worked to women's disadvantage. A sharper line was drawn between the private and public worlds than had been the case in medieval times. A woman called before the Geneva Consistory for sleeping with her fiancé must have been thinking of earlier freedoms when she protested, 'Paris belongs to the king and my body belongs to me.'[72] One should not exaggerate the powers of women in the Middle Ages, but queens and noblewomen exerted an influence that would rarely be met with between the sixteenth and twentieth centuries. The women of the early modern period, in theory at least, were increasingly consigned to the private realm. In practice, of course, most still worked, but they were shut out of the new professions and guilds, and even the role of wife and mother was subjected to surveillance.

In seventeenth-century England, increased attempts were made to police marriage. Ante-nuptial sex was censured. Women were whipped for fornication and pre-nuptial conception was made a statutory offence. In the 1620s even the married were prosecuted for 'unnatural acts' by the church courts. Premarital pregnancies appear to have declined, but figures on bastardy have to be viewed with suspicion; the seventeenth-century decline was probably due more to failure to report than Puritan policing. In the seventeenth century, the fear of illegitimacy centred on morality; in the eighteenth century, on the cost of maintenance of the bastard. The unwed mother's right to welfare was traditionally defended, but placed under greater pressure by the end of the eighteenth century. Such pressures may have resulted in a rise in infanticide.[73]

The surge in witchcraft and infanticide denunciations suggests that in the rationalizing west the unruliness of women was viewed with increased concern. There is in fact no good evidence of increasing neglect or infanticide. What changed were the ways in which infanticide was prosecuted. In 1557, Henri II declared that any concealed pregnancy that ended with the death of the child would be presumed to be murder. A similar statute was passed in England in 1624.[74] Presumably this new rigour was associated with the religious reformist surge of the period.[75] In the medieval world the church punished both parents, but now investigations were narrowly focused on the woman. Indeed, these statutes were aimed only at the 'lewd' single woman. Such inequitable laws proved impossible to enforce with any consistency because juries were reluctant to convict women driven to such an extreme.[76] By the eighteenth century only the most flagrant cases were being brought before English courts.

It was argued at the time that the laws against infanticide simply drove women to abortion. The fact that in seventeenth-century Lancashire the miscarriage rate was 29–96 per 1000 live births, whereas in the twentieth century it would be closer to 10–20 per 1000, has been taken as evidence that many miscarriages were in fact induced abortions.[77] In seventeenth-century Essex, Jane Josselin's five miscarriages late in her childbearing career, her husband's diary suggests, might well have been induced.[78] In many of the popular medical tracts, such as Philibert Guybert's La médecine charitable (1630), recipes were provided for potions and pessaries 'to provoke the monthlies', and Paul Dubé, author of Le médecin des pauvres (1686), cautioned his readers not to inform pregnant women of the ways in which suppression of the menses could be cured.[79] Louise Bourgeois, midwife at the seventeenth-century French court, warned her daughter to be equally cautious:

> This I do not speak that thou shouldest refuse to give
> Remedies upon just occasions: but to take heed how you be
> cheated by subtle persons, who shall tell you fine stories of
> the diseases of their Wives, or Daughters, which they may say
> are very honest, hoping to get from you some Receipts to
> effect their wicked designs.[80]

By the end of the eighteenth century, medical students were given
the same warnings. 'We are frequently deceived', admitted James
Gregory of Edinburgh, 'by women with child who, wishing to get
rid of their burden, produce a miscarriage and attribute many
complaints to a cession of the menses, which they are cunning
enough to say happened many a month before'.[81]

Jonas Hanway, the eighteenth-century English philanthropist,
clearly assumed that abortion was a resort of the desperate when he
attacked the upper classes for preventing servants from marrying:
'We usually reject them when they are married, tempting them to
practice sinister arts and contrivances to conceal their situation.'
The outcome, he warned, was sometimes 'manslaughter'.[82] But the
upper classes were not immune. Guy Patin, a seventeenth-century
French surgeon, left an account of the abortion-related death of
Mademoiselle de Guerchi in June 1660 and the ensuing investigations,
in which priests asserted that in the previous year over 600 women
had confessed *'d'avoir tué et étouffé leur fruit'*. Pierre Bayle
countered that 'If the confessors gave us the list of those who took
early precautions, before ensoulment, they would not limit
themselves to six hundred a year in a city like Paris.'[83]

The public was always hostile to practices employed to remove
evidence of promiscuity, but married women clearly remained true
to the traditional notion that, until animation took place, they were
free to seek to restore their menses. In England these views were
legally sanctioned by the common law; only after the fetus had
'quickened' was induction of miscarriage a crime.[84] The continent
had less liberal laws. In Freiburg a 1494 ordinance penalized both
intentional and unintentional abortion and called for women
suspects to be examined by a midwife.[85] In France the apothecaries'
oath contained a promise not to sell abortifacients to any but well-
known doctors, and in 1556 Henri II sought to end abortions as
well as infanticides by demanding that single women publicly
declare their pregnancies.[86] Such laws had little impact because in

Catholic as in Protestant Europe the public was still obviously unclear as to the moral status of early abortion. In 1588 Pope Sixtus V, as part of a campaign against the prostitutes of Rome, declared in the bull *Effraenatam* that both contraception and abortion at any stage of fetal development were homicidal acts. The bull was regarded as excessive, and in 1591 Gregory XIV retroactively annulled all its stipulated penalties.[87] Thomas Sanchez and other church theorists continued to draw distinctions depending on whether abortion took place before or after animation, and whether it was a direct attack on the fetus or an indirect result of actions taken for the benefit of the mother.[88] Sanchez even implied that an abortion was not as morally evil as contraception, inasmuch as an argument of self-defence could be employed to legitimate inducement of miscarriage; it could not be mounted in defence of contraception.

A campaign for a more rigorous condemnation of abortion was launched in the eighteenth century by Abbé Cangiamilla of Palermo. He insisted on the notion of immediate ensoulment and asserted that the debate over animation simply provided women with a justification for seeking early abortions. He denied that even the woman's right to save herself from certain death justified such an operation. Since he assumed it was better that she should give up her corporal life for the fetus' spiritual life, he called on the authorities to bypass the opposition of family members and carry out forcible Caesarians on dying pregnant women.[89] Cangiamilla's views were too extreme for most members of the church; the 'lax' attitudes of theorists such as Sanchez were to hold sway on into the nineteenth century.

Cangiamilla's references to the Caesarian operation signalled, however, the increased role played by doctors in such discussions. M. de Jaucourt, who provided the *Encyclopédie* with the article on '*fausse-couche*', asserted that abortions were sought by married women to prevent the family's estate being divided between too many children and by the single to protect their reputation. Traditional herbal remedies were still employed, but Jaucourt also noted the increased use of instruments.[90] In the early 1700s, Jean Benedicti had condemned mothers who slept with their infants and so risked suffocating them and those who took medicines and drinks or engaged in excessive running, dancing and intercourse in order to abort.[91] By the mid-1700s, the church was concerned that English doctors were using sounds to puncture the amniotic sac and asserting the legitimacy of carrying out 'therapeutic' abortions.

At the very time doctors were voicing their right to provide abortions, women lost their traditional *de facto*, if not *de jure*, right to them. In France a 1791 statute stated that criminal abortionists would be prosecuted, and its amended form in 1810 also provided for the prosecution of their patients. In England abortion was made a statutory crime in 1803, though the concept of quickening was, like the notion that a woman could not be prosecuted for her own abortion, momentarily maintained.

Jaucourt noted that in France as in England the ferocious laws aimed at infanticide proved counter-productive and simply drove some women to commit abortion. He argued that such desperate acts could be best prevented by providing foundling homes for the deposit of unwanted children. The establishment of foundling homes, taken as a sign of a new solicitude for children, was marked by curious regional variations. These concerns were manifested earliest in Tuscany, where in the fourteenth century such homes were first established. England did not have a foundling home until Coram established the London Foundling Hospital in the 1740s; France by this time had something like fifty. Between 1670 and 1862, over 65,000 children were abandoned at Rouen, and at the end of the eighteenth century over 4000 a year were left in Paris. Most but not all foundlings were illegitimate; at Nimes up to a third had married parents.[92] It has been suggested that the French concern for the number of abandoned children was somehow linked to the early employment of birth control, the logic being that it was realized that rather than dispose of children it was better not to have them in the first place. But since it was the poor who abandoned their children and the better off who first employed contraceptives, the theory seems somewhat tenuous.[93]

A more compelling argument is that variations in attitudes towards nursing influenced the employment of contraceptives. Extended breastfeeding continued, from the time of the Renaissance, to be employed by women to space births and protect the health of their babies.[94] But despite its obvious benefits the custom waxed and waned in popularity. In the Florentine elite, the sending out of children to nurse, usually arranged by the father, was the dominant practice from the fifteenth century onward. The sending out of a child to a wet nurse signalled a degree of male disinterest; Klapische-Zuber notes that in Tuscany girls were left longer than boys.[95] Mothers who did not nurse had some free time when they were neither suckling nor pregnant, but were subjected to more pregnancies than those who nursed their babies themselves.

The Catholic church played an ambiguous role in all of this. On the one hand, the church stressed the duties of motherhood; in sixteenth-century France, Jean Benedicti declared that women who refused to nurse were worse than beasts.[96] But on the other hand, the church long argued that the man's demand for a resumption of intercourse was so pre-eminent that it had to be conceded even if it resulted in an interruption of maternal nursing and an endangering of the life of the newborn.

English aristocratic mothers often sent their first children to wet nurses, but with later births nursed the baby themselves in what appeared to be hopes of postponing subsequent pregnancies.[97] In the eighteenth century, doctors and philanthropists led a campaign in favour of women nursing all their children.[98] The new appreciation of the fact that the mother's first milk (colostrum) should not be eliminated but given to the infant led, according to Fildes, to a marked decline in English babies' deaths in the first twenty-eight days of life.[99]

The contrasting nursing practices of the French and English appear to have played an important role in explaining recourse to contraceptives. Indeed, the argument has been made that nursing was the primary cause of differentials in marital fertility.[100] The English breastfed their children more than their continental counterparts, with the result that their infant mortality rate was lower and births – spaced by about twenty months – more widely separated. Until the late seventeenth century the French notables sent out their children to wet nurses. This meant that mothers became pregnant soon after, and their families were accordingly far larger than those of artisans. It was also the case that urban dwellers were more prone to employ wet nurses and accordingly conceived more quickly than provincials. The children sent away were victims of high infant mortality rates. In Rouen, 18.7 per cent of infants nursed by their mothers died; the rate was at least twice as high for those sent to wet nurses.[101] There is good reason to believe that consequently the French notables turned in the eighteenth century to contraception, as a protection both for the mother against excess fertility and for children against the tragically high infant mortality rate.[102]

Philippe Ariès first posited the notion of this new concern, this 'discovery' of childhood which occurred in the early modern period. In the Middle Ages, he argued, children were viewed as simply small adults, but from the 1500s on a new appreciation of their being distinctly different and warranting special treatment emerged. The old indifference or emotional distancing of patriarchal families was eroded. New bourgeois concerns for privacy and domesticity emerged. Improved parenting led to more child survival and ultimately the need for birth control, since excess children could no longer be allowed simply to perish. This idea that children represented increased costs and investments in both psychological and material terms has been taken up by Stone, Shorter and Trumbach. They contrast earlier, brutal ages to the eighteenth century when, they assert, the decline of wet nursing and swaddling symbolized the growth of a new interest in mothering, an interest which the middle classes eventually passed on to the lower orders.

There is no doubt that many eighteenth-century middle-class educators and doctors pontificated on the need to reform childrearing. There is also evidence that the mortality rate of aristocratic children declined. What is not proven is that it resulted from a greater attachment of mothers to their children. Linda Pollack asserts that there was really no perceptible transformation in attitudes towards children; parents always loved their children.[103] Some things obviously did change, in particular the educational and leisure patterns of upper-class children. There clearly was a new belief expressed that children should be regarded differently. This did not mean, however, that the middle classes loved their children any more than their forebears or had any lessons in devotion to give to the labouring classes.[104]

The theory that a decline in the infant mortality rate, in posing the possibility of excessively large families, led to an adoption of contraception also has its weaknesses. The argument seems to work for France, where from the late seventeenth century onwards both fertility and infant mortality fell. But it is just as likely that the opposite was true; that the fall in fertility *preceded* and led to a fall in infant mortality. The fewer the children the better a mother could care for them.[105] A contemporary such as Sebastien Mercier certainly suggested this when he declared,

> There are others who would like to limit their fertility. Making a false calculation of the favors of Providence, which they distrust, they dare to fear to bring into the world a being which, according to them, they will not find room enough on the earth, nor this earth abundant enough to feed them.[106]

Priests chastised women for such cautions. Abbé Pierre Jaubert assumed that '*les mères coquettes*' would attack him for his opposition to small families.[107] Père Féline similarly recognized that women sought, by recourse to contraceptives, to protect not just their own health but also that of already existing children. He referred to the 'fear which the women have of finding themselves pregnant again too soon after their confinements' and their concern not 'to injure the children whom they are nursing'.[108] It should be recalled that the Catholic church held that, if the husband insisted, a nursing mother had to pay the conjugal debt even if in doing so she ran the risk of becoming pregnant, losing her milk and thereby placing her baby's life at risk. Certain rabbis had, as we noted, recognized as early as the first century that contraception offered a way out of such a dilemma. The Catholic church long condemned such stratagems.

There are thus good reasons to attribute the spread of contraception in France to the desire to protect children from the murderously high infant mortality rates they faced. In France, where the demands of the domestic economy placed great pressure on women's time, more children than in England were sent out to wet nurse and deposited in foundling homes, and accordingly a higher infant mortality rate was experienced.[109] Indeed, France probably had the highest rate of infant mortality in Europe. To counter this, birth control was employed. In England, since infant mortality rates were not so high, there was less incentive to employ contraceptives and, indeed, because of its earlier industrialization and the accompanying demands for labour there were actual incentives to marry early and have large families.

Contraception was employed to limit the number of children and to ensure their health. This explains why it was used more for spacing than stopping. Even with couples who adopted a 'stopping' strategy, births were not all concentrated in the first few years of marriage as would be the case in the twentieth century. And increasingly the concern was not just to avoid sending excess children to early deaths, but to take better care of the children people had. 'Depopulation' was accordingly attributed by French commentators to the desire of the lower orders to emulate the fashions of the bourgeoisie.[110]

Where did this concern for children come from? Most historians have pointed to the propagandizing role of doctors like Smellie and Cadogan and humanitarians like Rousseau and Condorcet. Some have pointed out that the Catholic church, with its cult of the Holy Family, played a key part in popularizing a new sense of responsibility for the children one brought into the world. The most glaring weaknesses of so much of family history is its slighting of women's active participation in decisions pertaining to reproduction. All the talk of family 'strategies' implies that the wife and husband did not differ in their attitudes towards childbearing. But clearly one often lost or benefited more than the other.[111] Giovanni Costeo observed in the 1560s that women's poor health was due not to humours, but to excessive childbearing: 'We observe daily that those of them who are more fecund grow older more quickly and die sooner.'[112] It is true that amongst the lower classes both men and women would have shared the simple concern of surviving. A number of studies have argued that the marriage and fertility rates of eighteenth-century English artisans responded directly to changes in economic opportunities. The problem with such studies is that they are so convinced that the demand for labour is the key to fertility-making decisions that no room is left in the equation for differing male and female views.

The evidence suggests that France was the first nation to experience widespread fertility control because of female solidarity. French women might not have had the legal rights of their English counterparts, but they clearly assumed they had a right to control their bodies. Witness the famous letters of Mme de Sévigné to her daughter in 1671 and 1672, warning her not to become pregnant again. 'I beg of you, my dear, do not rely on having two beds; it lends itself to temptation: have someone sleep in your bedroom. Seriously, have pity on yourself, on your health and mine.'[113]

French women actively sought to prevent conception with or without their husbands' aid. In south-west France, women tradition- ally married fairly young, but did not have large families.[114] Fromageau referred to the woman who 'after paying the conjugal due, expels all or part of the male seed', and Sanchez to 'the woman who, immediately after coition, urinates, stands up straight or does some other thing whereby she expels the seed.'[115] In the eighteenth century Moheau complained:

> You may consult those men whom Religion has appointed as depositaries of the secrets of the hearts and frailties of humanity, or those whom a taste for researches in natural philosophy important to the good of the State has made accurate observers of the customs of the country people and the poor; they will tell you that rich women, for whom pleasure is the greatest objective and the sole preoccupation, are not the only ones who regard the propagation of the species as a trickery of past times: already these deadly secrets, unknown to any animal other than man, these secrets have penetrated into the countryside: nature is cheated even in the villages.[116]

The Countess of Sutherland, after having had her third child in Paris in 1792, wrote to her mother-in-law, 'The French ladies are all astonished at how anybody can be *si bête* as to have *trois enfants*. They are perfectly right and I shall mind what they say another time.'[117]

The emergence in eighteenth-century France of this new morality that justified fertility control has been attributed to husbands' having a new concern for their wives. Marriages, it is suggested, were now refined and treated with the gallantry previously reserved for liaisons. Husbands sought to protect wives, who faced a 10 per cent chance of death in childbearing.[118] The same was not true in England because, as a result of a decline in infectious diseases and improvements in obstetrical care, maternal mortality was lower.[119] But women's own interests seem oddly absent in such an explanation. It is as likely that a decline in the threat of death in childbed, rather than raising women's confidence, would harden their resolve to avoid such dangers. Moreover, theories that stress male 'gallantry' skate around the evidence that the issue of fertility control could divide couples. A glimpse of such disputes was caught in a 1706 church declaration that a woman had to obey a husband who insisted on employing unnatural means to avoid having children, but that she did not have the right to suggest such means herself.[120]

The stress on the significance of the companionate couple as the key to employment of fertility controls appears unwarranted. Trumbach points out that in England a more 'egalitarian or domestic style of household relationships' in the later eighteenth century actually led to larger families. Curiously enough, the 'romantic marriages' of the English aristocracy seemed to limit the freedom of women. Such cloying unions meant that English women were less able to move in mixed company than their French counterparts.[121] What Trumbach inadvertently demonstrates is that domesticity, far from laying the basis for an egalitarian relationship, limited the woman's options.

The ideology of domesticity was clearly more successfully rooted in England than in France. But the growing privacy sought by the upper classes in their marriages, the decline of rituals of 'bedding' the couple and offering guests 'favours', did not mean that the needs of the new spouses were placed above those of the family. It meant rather that the upper classes had cut themselves off from the larger community. Presumably this laid the basis, not for a more 'egalitarian' relationship, but for one in which the woman was totally dependent on the man. English upper-class brides of the late eighteenth century, trained to hide any interest in sexuality, warned not to listen to the gossip of servants and cut off from the larger female community, were probably more ignorant of the workings of their bodies than their grandmothers had ever been.

French women enjoyed perhaps a less 'loving' relationship with their husbands, but carved out for themselves a less domestic, less fettered life. Père Féline recognized that French husbands did not impose contraception on their wives; rather they acceded to the latter's demands. 'They [the husbands] become too sensitive to the complaints that the wives make about all that it cost them to bring children into the world. [The husbands] treat kindly their excessive delicacy, they consent to spare them this trouble, without, however, renouncing the right that they believe they have of satisfying themselves.'[122]

Historians of the family always run the risk of mistaking doctrines and practices. A 'love' marriage at the start of the eighteenth century was construed as an unfortunate misalliance; by its end parents were insisting that their children marry for 'love'. The vocabulary had changed; not the concerns of the parents to make a good match. Similarly, the glorification of domesticity indicated that the enriched middle classes of the prosperous eighteenth century were, not more loving parents, but better able to afford such indulgences. The apparent neglect of and lack of interest taken in children in previous centuries were clearly a function of economic deprivation. Likewise the employment of contraception by French couples did not signify that husbands were suddenly overcome by some simple sense of gallantry; a more complicated development took place. Men wanted to maintain their conjugal rights and avoid the division of their property among numerous heirs; women wanted to protect their health and that of their children. Recourse was had to contraception in the light of these practical concerns, not in the rosy glow of romance.

Such private disputes were rarely documented. But the late eighteenth century did see the emergence of the first generation of women writers who criticized existing sex roles. Ironically, the early English feminists like Mary Wollstonecraft, who wanted motherhood to be esteemed and worried that its dignity might be undermined if undue stress was placed on women's pursuit of pleasure, defended their claims of sexual equality by advancing an ideology of 'passionlessness'.[123] Women had traditionally been portrayed as more lusty than men. Defenders of women accordingly took the moral high ground, stressed the importance of domesticity and played down the sexual issues. Wollstonecraft went so far as to argue against fertility control in insisting that procreation was not to be separated from pleasure. 'Surely nature never intended that women, by satisfying an appetite, should frustrate the very purpose for which it was implanted.'[124] Victorian arguments against birth control preceded Victoria by several decades.

Notes

1 Demographic historians concede that western European fertility has always been low, but insist on calling it a form of 'natural fertility',

inasmuch as they assume it was achieved by late marriage and extended nursing which resulted in a wide spacing of births. Skirting the notion that even this 'natural' fertility was a social construct, they assert that one can only speak of the 'artificial' restriction of fertility when family size was even further reduced.

2 Late marriage and high levels of never marrying were seen by contemporaries as creating a demand for prostitution. See Erica-Marie Benabou, *La prostitution et la police des moeurs au XVIIIe siècle* (Perrin, Paris, 1987), pp. 463–9.

3 Ralph A. Houlbrooke, *The English Family: 1450–1700* (Longman, New York, 1984), p. 67.

4 R. B. Outhwaite, 'Marriage as Business: Opinions on the Rise in Aristocratic Bridal Portions in Early Modern England', in *Business Life and Public Policy*, eds R.B. Outhwaite and Neil McKendrick (Cambridge University Press, Cambridge, 1986), p. 30; E. Le Roy Ladurie, *The French Peasantry, 1450–1660* (Scolar Press, London, 1987), pp. 280–4.

5 Peter Laslett, *Family Life and Illicit Love in Earlier Generations* (Cambridge University Press, Cambridge, 1977), pp. 21–45.

6 Cicely Howell, *Land, Family and Inheritance in Transition: Kibworth Harcourt, 1280–1700* (Cambridge University Press, Cambridge, 1983), p. 204; David Levine, *Reproducing Families: The Political Economy of English Population History* (Cambridge University Press, Cambridge, 1987), pp. 77–8.

7 John Demos, 'Demography and Psychology in the Historical Study of Family Life: A Personal Report', in *Household and Family in Past Times*, eds Peter Laslett and Richard Wall (Cambridge University Press, Cambridge, 1972), p. 552.

8 Jean-Louis Flandrin, *Families in Former Times: Kinship, Household and Sexuality* (Cambridge University Press, Cambridge, 1979), p. 56.

9 Ann Kussmaul, *Servants in Husbandry in Early Modern England* (Cambridge University Press, Cambridge, 1981).

10 Kussmaul, *Servants*, p. 26.

11 John R. Gillis, *For Better, For Worse: British Marriages, 1600 to the Present* (Oxford University Press, New York, 1985).

12 Richard Wall, ed., *Family Forms in Historic Europe* (Cambridge University Press, Cambridge, 1983).

13 Christiane Klapische-Zuber, *Women, Family and Ritual in Renaissance Italy* (University of Chicago Press, Chicago, 1985), p. 112.

14 Cicely Howell, 'Stability and Change, 1300–1700', *Journal of Peasant Studies*, 2 (1975), p. 476.

15 E. A. Wrigley and Roger Schofield, *The Population History of England, 1541–1871: A Reconstruction* (Cambridge University Press, Cambridge, 1981), p. 451.

16 David Levine, *Family Formation in an Age of Nascent Capitalism* (Academic Press, New York, 1977), p. 96.

17 Levine, *Family Formation*, p. 139.
18 For a similar situation elsewhere see Susan B. Hanley, 'The Influence of Economic and Social Variables on Marriage and Fertility in Eighteenth and Nineteenth Century Japanese Villages', in *Population Patterns in the Past*, ed. R. D. Lee (Academic Press, New York, 1977), pp. 165–200.
19 E. A. Wrigley, 'Family Limitation in Pre-Industrial England', *Economic History Review*, 19 (1966), pp. 82–109; and see also Richard B. Morrow, 'Family Limitation in Pre-Industrial England: A Reappraisal', *Economic History Review*, 31 (1978), pp. 419–28; E. A. Wrigley, 'Marital Fertility in Seventeenth Century Colyton: A Note', *Economic History Review*, 31 (1978), pp. 429–36.
20 Ronald Lee, 'Short Term Variation: Vital Rates, Prices, and Weather', in Wrigley and Schofield, *The Population History of England*, pp. 367–8, 400.
21 T. H. Hollingsworth, 'The Demography of the British Peerage', *Population Studies*, 18 supplement (1965), pp. 49–50.
22 Ralph Trumbach, *The Rise of the Egalitarian Family* (Academic Press, New York, 1978), p. 175.
23 Louis Henry, *Anciennes familles genèvoises* (PUF, Paris, 1956), pp. 71–110; Claude Levy and Louis Henry, 'Ducs et pairs sous l'Ancien Régime: caractéristiques démographiques d'une caste', *Population*, 15 (1960), pp. 807–30; R. Gresset, *Le monde judiciare à Besançon de la conquète à la révolution française* (PUL, Lille, 1975); Thomas F. Sheppard, *Loumarin in the Eighteenth Century* (Johns Hopkins Press, Baltimore, 1971), p. 38.
24 Marcel Lachiver, 'Fecondité légitime et contraception dans la région parisienne', in Lachiver (ed.), *Hommage à Marcel Reinhard* (PUF, Paris, 1973), pp. 383–401.
25 J. P. Bardet, *Rouen aux XVIIe et XVIIIe siècles: Les mutations d'un espace social* (Société d'enseignements superieurs, Paris, 1983), pp. 264–84.
26 Lawrence Stone, *The Family, Sex, and Marriage in England, 1500–1800* (Harper and Row, New York, 1977), p. 415.
27 Marcel Bernos, 'Le temps des mises en order', in *Le fruit défendu: les chrétiens et la sexualité de l'antiquité à nos jours*, ed. Marcel Bernos (Le Centurion, Paris, 1985), p. 150.
28 St Francis de Sales, *Introduction to the Devout Life*, tr. John K. Ryan (Harper and Row, New York, 1950), p. 170.
29 John T. Noonan, Jr., *Contraception: A History of its Treatment by Catholic Theologians and Canonists* (Harvard University Press, Cambridge, Mass., 1965), p. 333.
30 Adrien de Bussy de Lamet and Germain Fromageau, *Le dictionnaire de cas de conscience* (Coignard, Paris, 1733), vol. 2, col. 1225.
31 Jean Benedicti, *La somme des pechez, et les remèdes d'iceux* (Hierosme de Marnes, Paris, 1595), vol. 2, xi, p. 152.
32 Noonan, *Contraception: A History*, pp. 344, 364.

33 Edmund Leites, 'The Duty to Desire: Love, Friendship, and Sexuality in some Puritan Theories of Marriage', *Journal of Social History*, 15 (1982), pp. 383–408.

34 Rosemary Radford Ruether, *Religion and Sexism: Images of Women in the Jewish and Christian Traditions* (Simon and Schuster, New York, 1974), p. 300.

35 Thomas Max Safley, *Let No Man Put Asunder: The Control of Marriage in the German Southwest: A Comparative Study, 1550–1600* (Sixteenth Century Journal, Kirksville, 1984), p. 194.

36 Steven Ozment, *When Fathers Ruled: Family Life in Reformation Europe* (Harvard University Press, Cambridge, Mass., 1983), pp. 100, 216.

37 Jaroslav Pelikan, ed., *Luther's Works* (Concordia, St Louis, 1965), vol. 7, p. 20.

38 Susan Cahn, *Industry of Devotion: The Transformation of Women's Work in England, 1500–1660* (Columbia University Press, New York, 1987), p. 222, ft. 105.

39 On parallelism, see for example John Hall, *A Very Fruitful and Necessary Brief Worke of Anatomie* (Hall, London, 1565); Cosme Viardel, *Observations sur la pratique des accouchemens naturels* (L'Authour, Paris, 1674), pp. 1, 15.

40 R. V. Short, 'The Discovery of the Ovaries', in *The Ovary*, eds Lord Zuckerman and Barbara J. Weir (Academic Press, New York, 1977), pp. 1–25.

41 Ian Maclean, *The Renaissance Notion of Women: A Study of the Fortunes of Scholasticism and Medical Science in European Intellectual Life* (Cambridge University Press, Cambridge, 1980), pp. 36–46; Yvonne Knibiehler and Catherine Fouquet, *La femme et les médecins: analyse historique* (Hachette, Paris, 1983).

42 *Petit trésor de santé* (Hughes Seneuze, Chalons, 1639); *Le bastiment des receptes traduit d'italien en français* (Antoine de Raffle, Paris, 1665); Mireille Laget, *Naissances: l'accouchement avant l'âge de la clinique* (Seuil, Paris, 1982), pp. 46–51; Jacques Gélis, *L'arbre et le fruit: la naissance dans l'Occident moderne, XVIe–XIXe siècle* (Fayard, Paris, 1984), pp. 46, 52, 109.

43 John Putnam Demos, *Entertaining Satan: Witchcraft and Culture in Early New England* (Oxford University Press, New York, 1982), pp. 72–3, 170.

44 *Aristotle's Masterpiece: or Secrets of Generation* (How, London, 1690); *Les admirables secrets d'Albert le Grand* (Cologne, 1722); Nicolas Venette, *La génération de l'homme ou tableau de l'amour conjugal* (Ryckhof, Amsterdam, 1778); Roy Porter, 'Spreading Carnal Knowledge or Selling Dirt Cheap? Nicolas Venette's *Tableau de l'amour conjugal* in Eighteenth-Century England', *Journal of European Studies*, 14 (1984), pp. 233–55.

45 Steven Ozment, *Magdalena and Balthazar: An Intimate Portrait of Life in Sixteenth-Century Europe Revealed in the Letters of a*

Nuremberg Husband and Wife (Simon and Schuster, New York, 1986).

46 Edward Shorter, *A History of Women's Bodies* (Basic Books, New York, 1982), pp. 98–100; Audrey Eccles, 'Obstetrics in the 17th and 18th Centuries and its Implication for Maternal and Infant Mortality', *Society for the Social History of Medicine*, 20 (1977), pp. 8–11.

47 Judith Schneid Lewis, *In the Family Way: Childbearing in the British Aristocracy, 1760–1860* (Rutgers University Press, New Brunswick, NJ, 1986), p. 231. On France see Nicole Belmont, *Les signes de la naissance* (Plon, Paris, 1971).

48 Bernard This, *La requête des enfants à naitre* (Seuil, Paris, 1982), pp. 142–70.

49 Benedicti, *La somme*, vol. 2, iv, p. 110.

50 Edward Poeton, *The Chyrurgians Closet* (Miller, London, 1630), p. 183.

51 Angus McLaren, *Reproductive Rituals: The Perception of Fertility in England from the Sixteenth to the Nineteenth Century* (Methuen, London, 1984).

52 E. Le Roy Ladurie, *The Mind and Method of the Historian* (University of Chicago Press, Chicago, 1981), pp. 88–95. On the peasantry see also J. L. Flandrin, *Les amours paysannes: amour et sexualité dans les campagnes de l'ancienne France* (Gallimard, Paris, 1975).

53 John Pechey, *The Compleat Midwife's Practice Enlarged* (Rhodes, London, 1698), p. 243. The belief that a woman could prevent conception by urinating immediately after intercourse continued to be held; see John Garfield, *The Wandering Whore*, numbers 1–5, 1660–1 (University of Exeter, Exeter, 1977), pp. 12–13.

54 Brantôme, *Les dames gallantes* (Hilsum, Paris, 1933), p. 51. Eighteenth-century French erotic poetry referred to lovers being asked to '*décharge à la porte*'. Georges Pillemet, *La poésie érotique* (Desforges, Paris, 1970), p. 123.

55 Martin Ingram, *Church Courts: Sex and Marriage in England, 1570–1640* (Cambridge University Press, Cambridge, 1988), p. 159.

56 Guido Ruggiero, *The Boundaries of Eros: Sex Crime and Sexuality in Renaissance Venice* (Oxford University Press, New York, 1985), p. 42; and see also p. 118.

57 Gervais Babington, *Certaine Plaine, Briefe, and Comfortable Notes, Upon every Chapter of Genesis* (Charde, London, 1596), p. 278; William Gouge, *Of Domestical Duties* (John Beale, London, 1626), p. 12; J. F. Ostervald, *Traité contre l'impureté* (Lombrail, Amsterdam, 1707), pp. 271–5.

58 St Francis de Sales, *Introduction*, p. 170.

59 *Onania; or the Heinous Sin of Self-Pollution and All its Frightful Consequences, in Both Sexes Considered* (Crouch, London, 1723), p. 101.

60 J. P. Dutoit-Mabrini, *L'Onanisme ou discourse philosophique et*

moral sur la luxure artificielle sur tous les crimes relatifs (Grasset, Lausanne, 1760); pp. 59–60; S. A. A. D. Tissot, *Avis au peuple sur la santé* (Grasset, Lausanne, 1761), p. 9.

61 Jane Sharp, *The Midwives Book or the Whole Art of Midwifery Discovered* (Simon Miller, London, 1671), pp. 93, 99, 165.

62 Père Féline, *Catéchisme des gens mariés* (Gay, Paris, 1880 [original Caen 1782]), p. 7.

63 Venette, *La génération de l'homme*, vol. 1, pp. 305–8; Flandrin, *Families*, pp. 223–5. The vicomte de Valmont boasted of having taught his seduced victim everything about love but '*les précautions*'; Choderlos de Laclos, *Les liaisons dangereuses* (Rocher, Monaco, 1948), vol. I, p. 272.

64 *Parson's Tale*, lines 575–6.

65 Mathurin Regnier, *Les Satyrs* (1609) in *Oeuvres complètes* (Les belles lettres, Paris, 1958), pp. 160–1.

66 Henri Estienne, *Apologie d'Hérodote* (Vandellin, Antwerp, 1568), p. 226, cited in Pierre Bayle, *Dictionnaire historique et critique* (Desoer, Paris, 1820), vol. 2, p. 458.

67 Clive Wood and Beryl Suitters, *The Fight for Acceptance: A History of Contraception* (MTP, Aylesbury, 1970).

68 Marquis de Sade, *La philosophe dans le boudoir*, in *Oeuvres complètes* (Du livre precieux, Paris, 1966), vol. 3, p. 414; Etienne van de Walle, 'Motivations and Technology in the Decline of French Fertility', in *Family and Sexuality in French History*, eds Robert Wheaton and Tamara Hareven (University of Pennsylvania Press, Philadelphia, 1980), pp. 135–78.

69 Arthur Young, *Travels in France and Italy During the Years 1787, 1788, and 1789* (Dutton, London, 1934), p. 324. The bidet was associated with prostitution, hence a pimp was called a '*chevalier de bidet*'. The employment of bidets and syringes for contraceptive purposes is missed in Georges Vigarello, *Concepts of Cleanliness: Changing Attitudes in France Since the Middle Ages* (Cambridge University Press, Cambridge, 1988), pp. 162–3.

70 Robert Halsbad, *Lord Hervey: Eighteenth Century Courtier* (Clarendon, Oxford, 1973), p. 63.

71 Norman E. Himes, *A Medical History of Contraception* (Williams and Wilkins, Baltimore, 1936), pp. 188–200. Himes's assertion that Mme de Sévigné described the condom is incorrect. See McLaren, *Reproductive Rituals*, pp. 82–6.

72 Natalie Z. Davis, 'Boundaries and Sense of Self in Sixteenth Century France', in *Reconstructing Individualism: Autonomy, Individuality, and the Self in Western Thought*, eds Thomas C. Heller, Morton Sosna and David E. Welbery (Stanford University Press, Stanford, 1986), p. 63.

73 Stone, *The Family*, pp. 400–2; that Catholics were also attempting to instill a new rigour and austerity was evident in counter-reformation France, where from the 1690s increasing numbers of men were cited

for forcing abortions on their mistresses. See Kathryn Norberg, *Rich and Poor in Grenoble, 1600–1814* (University of California Press, Berkeley, Cal., 1985), pp. 38–9, 56, 99.

74 Peter C. Hoffer and N. E. H. Hull, *Murdering Mothers: Infanticide in England and New England, 1558–1803* (New York University Press, New York, 1981), pp. 19–20.

75 Natalie Zemon Davis, *Fiction in the Archives: Pardon Tales and their Tellers* (Stanford University Press, Stanford, 1987), pp. 85–7.

76 Susan Dwyer Amussen, *An Ordered Society: Gender and Class in Early Modern England* (Blackwell, Oxford, 1988), pp. 111–15; John Beattie, *Crime and the Courts in England, 1660–1800* (Princeton University Press, Princeton, NJ, 1986), pp. 113–24.

77 *Local Population Studies* (1970), 11–16, cited in Houlbrooke, *The English Family*, p. 128.

78 Alan Macfarlane, *The Family Life of Ralph Josselin: A Seventeenth Century Clergyman* (Cambridge University Press, Cambridge, 1970), p. 83.

79 Philibert Guybert, *La médecine charitable* (David Ferrand, Rouen, 1630), p. 24; Paul Dubé, *Le médecin des pauvres* (Edme Coterot, Paris, 1686), pp. 231–2.

80 Pechey, *Compleat Midwife*, p. 346. Another midwife in 1709 attributed the birth of a deformed child to the fact that the mother 'had sworn to herself that she should not get with child, that she knew better'. Hilary Marland, ed., *'Mother and Child were Saved': The Memoirs (1693–1740) of the Frisian Midwife Catharina Schrader* (Rodopi, Amsterdam, 1987), pp. 61–2.

81 G. B. Risse, 'Hysteria at the Edinburgh Infirmary: The Construction and Treatment of a Disease, 1770–1800', *Medical History*, 32 (1988), p. 18.

82 Trumbach, *Rise of the Egalitarian Family*, p. 147; and see also Claude Grimmer, *La femme et le bâtard: amours illégitimes et secrètes dans l'ancienne France* (Renaissance, Paris, 1983), pp. 215–23.

83 Bayle, *Dictionnaire historique et critique*, vol. 2, pp. 449–52.

84 McLaren, *Reproductive Rituals*, pp. 121–2.

85 Merry E. Weiner, *Working Women in Renaissance Germany* (Rutgers University Press, New Brunswick, NJ, 1986), pp. 60–1, 71.

86 L. Lewin, *Die Fruchtabtreibung durch Gifte und andere Mittel* (Springer, Berlin, 1922), pp. 154–5.

87 Noonan, *Contraception: A History*, p. 362.

88 'Avortement', *Dictionnaire de droit canonique* (Letouzey, Paris, 1935), vol. I, 1536–40.

89 F. E. Cangiamilla, *Abrégé de l'embryologie sacrée*, ed. J. A. T. Dinouart (Nyon, Paris, 1762), pp. 8, 12, 63, 110.

90 *Encyclopédie ou dictionnaire raisonné des sciences, des artes et des métiers* (Amsterdam, 1777), vol. 6, pp. 450–3.

91 Benedicti, *La somme*, vol. 2, iv, pp. 109–10.

92 Nicole and Yves Castan, *Vivre ensemble: ordre et désordre en Languedoc (XVIIe–XVIIIe siècles)* (Gallimard, Paris, 1981), p. 171.

93 Peter Laslett, *The World We Have Lost Further Explored* (Methuen, London, 1983), p. 118; Bardet, *Rouen*, p. 331.

94 Klapische-Zuber, *Women*, p. 158; Patricia Crawford, 'The Suckling Child: Adult Attitudes to Child Care in the First Year of Life in Seventeenth-Century England', *Continuity and Change*, 1 (1986), pp. 23–53.

95 Klapische-Zuber, *Women*, p. 104.

96 Benedicti, *La somme*, vol. 2, ii, pp. 95–6.

97 Lewis, *In the Family Way*, p. 212.

98 See, for example, Ambroise Ganne, *L'homme physique et moral* (Treuttel, Strasbourg, 1791), p. 9.

99 Valerie Fildes, 'Neonatal Feeding Practices and Infant Mortality During the Eighteenth Century', *Journal of the Biosocial Sciences*, 12 (1980), pp. 313–24. See M. L. Saucerotte, *Examen de plusieurs préjugés et usages abusifs concernante les femmes enceintes* (Gay, Strasbourg, 1777), p. 49.

100 V. A. Fildes, *Breasts, Bottles, and Babies: A History of Infant Feeding* (Edinburgh University Press, Edinburgh, 1985), pp. 107–9; Chris Wilson, 'The Determinants of Marital Fertility', in *The World We Have Gained: Histories of Population and Social Structure*, eds Lloyd Bonfield, Richard M. Smith and Keith Wrightson (Blackwell, Oxford, 1986), pp. 224–8.

101 Flandrin, *Families*, pp. 203–5.

102 Bardet, *Rouen*, p. 303.

103 Philippe Ariès, *Centuries of Childhood*, tr. Robert Baldick (Cape, London, 1962); Edward Shorter, *The Making of the Modern Family* (Basic Books, New York, 1975); Linda Pollack, *Forgotten Children: Parent-Child Relations, 1500 to 1900* (Cambridge University Press, Cambridge, 1983).

104 Gillis, *For Better, For Worse*; Alan Macfarlane, *Marriage and Love in England: Modes of Reproduction, 1300–1840* (Blackwell, Oxford, 1986).

105 Flandrin, *Families*, pp. 198–203.

106 Louis-Sebastien Mercier, *Mon bonnet de nuit* (Imprimerie de la société typographique, Neuchâtel, 1784), pp. 142–3.

107 Abbé Pierre Jaubert, *Des causes de la dépopulation et des moyens d'y remédier* (Dessain, London, 1767), p. vi.

108 Féline, *Catéchisme des gens mariés*, p. 7

109 In seventeenth-century England, the fertility of peers fell when infant mortality rose, and then after 1750 reversed itself and climbed back to a height at which it remained for the next century, despite falling infant mortality rates. High infant mortality rates acted as a check in some places, but not everywhere. S. Ryan Johannson, 'Centuries of Childhood/Centuries of Parenting', *Journal of Family History*, 12 (1987), pp. 343–66.

110 Bernard Christophe Faust, *À l'Assemblée nationale sur un vêtement libre, uniforme et national, à l'usage des enfants* (L'Auteur, Paris, 1792), p. 5.

111 Miranda Chaytor, 'Household and Kinship: Ryton in the Late Sixteenth and Early Seventeenth Century', *History Workshop Journal*, 10 (1980), p. 28; Margaret George, *Women in the First Capitalist Society: Experiences in Seventeenth-Century England* (University of Illinois Press, Urbana, 1988), pp. 207–15.

112 Nancy G. Siraisi, *Avicenna in Renaissance Italy* (Princeton University Press, Princeton, NJ, 1988), p. 303.

113 M. Gerard-Gailly, ed., *Mme de Sévigné: lettres* (Gallimard, Paris, 1953), vol. 1, p. 437; see also *Les caquets de l'accouchée* [1622] (Marpen, Paris, 1890), pp. 120–1.

114 An abrupt drop in the birth rate occurred after 1789; E. Le Roy Ladurie, 'Démographie et funeste secrètes en Languedoc', *Annales historiques de la Révolution Française*, 37 (1965), p. 385.

115 Flandrin, *Families*, p. 213; Noonan, *Contraception: A History*, p. 368.

116 Moheau (attributed to A.J.B.R. Auget de Montyon), *Recherches et considérations sur la population de la France* (Moutard, Paris, 1778), vol. 2, pp. 101–2.

117 Lewis, *In the Family Way*, pp. 228–9.

118 Flandrin, *Families*, p. 223–4.

119 Roger Schofield, 'Did Mothers Really Die? Three Centuries of Maternal Mortality in the World We Have Lost', in Bonfield, *The World*, pp. 231–60.

120 J. M. Gouesse, 'Le refus de l'enfant au tribunal de la penitence', *Annales de démographie historique*, (1973), p. 238.

121 Trumbach, *Rise of the Egalitarian Family*, p. 98.

122 Féline, *Catéchisme des gens mariés*, pp. 7–8.

123 Katherine M. Rodgers, *Feminism in Eighteenth Century England* (University of Illinois Press, Urbana, 1983).

124 Mary Wollstonecraft, *A Vindication of the Rights of Women* (Dent, London, 1929), p. 152.

6

Neo-Malthusianism and the Fertility Transition

'Let us sin without conceiving'
Alexandre Boutique (1894), *Les Malthusiennes*

In the nineteenth century, America and western Europe entered a new demographic age. These societies had never produced the maximum number of children biologically possible, but fertility rates were from the sixteenth to the nineteenth century relatively stable; suddenly in the mid-1800s a sustained decline in fertility began. By World War I, family size was cut in half. The extensive use of contraception was signalled not so much by the drop in number of large families – which might have been explained by lengthy periods of continence and extended nursing – as by the increasingly early age at which women stopped giving birth.

Western women traditionally began their birthing careers rather late and widely spaced their pregnancies, but in eighteenth-century France the widespread employment of birth control was aimed at reducing family size. By 1830 the country's birth rate dropped below thirty per thousand, and the term 'French family' was henceforth discreetly employed by the English when referring to the two-child household.[1] The United States, which in the eighteenth century had experienced a fertility higher than that of Europe, also saw its rate begin to decline steadily from the first decades of the nineteenth century, dropping by 50 per cent between 1800 and 1900. The lead was taken in the north-east; in Utica, New York, for example, native-born middle-class women who had begun their childbearing in the 1820s had on average 5.8 children; those who began ten years later had only 3.6 children.[2]

Until the 1870s, most European nations maintained much higher levels of fertility. What demographers call the 'demographic transition' was the dramatic drop in such rates that occurred between 1870 and 1920. In Germany, marital fertility fell by about 65 per cent in the space of two generations. In England, couples who married in 1861–9 had an average of 6.16 children, those of 1890–9 had 4.13 children, and those of 1920–4, had 2.31 children.[3] Marriage, delayed in bad times and entered early in good times, was the primary means of controlling fertility in pre-industrial Europe. In the late nineteenth century, nuptiality rates remain fairly stable. What changed was the extent to which fertility was now clearly being reduced by the married. Fertility was, thanks to the widespread adoption of birth-control practices, brought to very low levels. The question is, why?

Demographers, approaching the question from the macro level, provide a rather mechanistic portrayal of the process. In traditional societies, they argue, population was relatively stable due to the balancing of high levels of mortality and fertility. In the eighteenth century, mortality rates began to fall, but fertility rates did not. The result was the great population boom of 1750–1850. Eventually a new stability was achieved, due not to the deaths and diseases which traditionally followed surges of over-population, but to the use of artificial fertility controls. Such controls, the demographers argue, were somehow spontaneously produced by a secularized, urbanized society. What is advanced is in effect an 'adjustment' theory; the modern, conception-limiting family was created by new environmental realities, chief of which was declining mortality.[4] Unfortunately the theory does not really explain why the French fertility decline preceded by a century that of other nations. Even in nineteenth-century industrializing Belgium and England, marital fertility fell before infant mortality. But the greatest failing of the demographic account is its indifference to the specific problems posed by reproduction to past generations.

Innovation theorists, in contrast to proponents of the adjustment theory, have shown far more interest in what nineteenth-century men and women thought and said as opposed to what the census tables tell us they did. A literate, modern individual who believed in the possibility of controlling nature would, the advocates of innovation suggest, be the sort to limit family size. They have argued that in tracing the adoption of birth control one can accordingly anticipate who would be the 'leaders' and who would be the 'laggards'. First came the enlightened upper classes at mid-century; the working classes followed suit a generation or two later as middle-class mores were diffused. The Bradlaugh–Besant trial of 1877, in giving unprecedented publicity to the birth-control propagandists and finally dispelling the workers' ignorance of effective contraceptive methods, is thought to have played a crucial part in making such progress possible. The notion that the ability to make freer, more rational choices meant fewer children was certainly voiced at the time. By the 1880s the swarms of ragged children produced by the poor were regarded by the bourgeoisie, so Zola's novels inform us, as evidence of the lower orders' ignorance and brutality.

In France, limitation of family size was attributed from the eighteenth century on to the peasantry's intent to avoid dividing land between heirs and the bourgeoisie's efforts to maintain a civilized life style. By the mid-nineteenth century, the birth rates of English and German civil servants and professionals began to decline; the middle and lower-middle classes clearly having good reasons to curb their fertility before workers and farmers. German bureaucrats, for example, had to think twice about marrying and procreating when regulations required their maintenance of a life style appropriate to their rank.[5] The English middle classes, argued J. A. Banks in *Prosperity and Parenthood*, managed to maintain large families until faced with the 'Great Depression' of the 1870s. When forced to choose between either protecting unprecedented levels of gentility or having more children, they opted for the small family.[6] The lower classes followed their lead a generation or two later.

The fact that the well-to-do led in the abandonment of large families has been advanced as proof by Banks and others that the adoption of birth control was a cultural innovation. The nineteenth century, it is argued, witnessed increased well-being and an expansion in the range of satisfactions. Those who first restricted births did so not to escape poverty, but to protect new-found prosperity; they were in effect carrying out a revolution of rising expectations. Their lead, according to such innovation or 'trickle-down' theories, would be followed by the lower classes as they became more rational. Modernization and urbanization meant greater mobility and secularization. In the city, occupational structures evolved, individuals – not families – were paid for their labour, and migrants escaped the 'dead hand of the past'. City fertility was generally lower than that of the countryside, just as upper-class fertility was lower than that of the lower classes.

The diffusionist argument highlights the power of ideas, but clearly slights the importance of material conditions. It implies that all classes and ethnic groups ultimately saw the wisdom of adopting the small-family model propagated by the middle class. But did such a consensus emerge? Fertility declined across classes and across regions, but was it always for the same reasons? Would not men and women view fertility control differently, as would the church, the medical profession and the state? An examination of the nature of the developing population discussion, the appearance of new contraceptive technologies, and the ways in which changing economic and ideological forces shaped the responses men and women of different classes made to them, allows one to test the assumptions of both the adjustment and innovation theorists.

The proponents of the innovation theory, assuming as they do that many births in the past were unwanted, have presented the advocates of birth control as playing a crucial role. Given the masses' lack of motivation and instruction, it is argued that a 'movement' was necessary to make fertility control 'thinkable'. Once it was seen as a legitimate choice it could spread like wildfire. Such information was always available to some, but as one English doctor noted in 1837, whereas once most felt they had no alternative but to accept stoically each pregnancy, now 'a spurious modern philosophy of our day inculcates the contrary, and has even suggested unnatural means for the limitation of offspring'.[7]

The history of the birth-control movement is customarily traced back to late eighteenth-century France, when fertility-limiting practices were first publicized and defended. Condorcet, one of the few *philosophes* who could be considered a feminist, suggested that to avoid misery artificial means be employed to constrain population. In the nineteenth century the argument was followed by Senancour, who spoke of the necessity of *'une précaution, une réserve'*.[8] Such suggestions, though condemned by the respectable, were taken up and pursued by English and American propagandists.[9] These birth-control advocates were ultimately to be known as neo-Malthusians. Although Thomas Malthus was opposed to contraception, his *Essay on Population* (1798) was enormously influential in focusing attention on the social impact of fertility.[10] Western states traditionally welcomed population increases in the belief that greater numbers led to greater prosperity. Malthus advanced the radically new argument that this was no longer true. Since population always placed pressure on resources, he argued, social improvements could only be attained by the lower classes demonstrating 'moral restraint' in prudently postponing early and reckless marriages. The brunt of Malthus's pessimistic message, which was welcomed by the propertied, was that poverty could not be legislated away by the charitable; it was a problem caused by the poor which they would have to solve themselves.

Malthus made reproductive decision making a respectable topic of conversation. In the turbulent first half of the nineteenth century, when Owenites and Chartists were asking how the English working class might best survive the misery spawned by the industrial revolution, they were answered by the first advocates of birth control. Most – Jeremy Bentham, Francis Place, Richard Carlile, Robert Dale Owen and George and Charles Drysdale – accepted Malthus's view that the pressure of numbers contributed to social misery, but they drew on the French example to argue that the employment of contraceptives offered a way out. Their audience was mainly limited to readers of handbills and radical journals.[11] To spread the message, the Drysdales created in 1877 the first neo-Malthusian organization, the Malthusian League. The same year the trial of George Bradlaugh and Annie Besant for having republished an early birth-control tract by the American Charles Knowlton gave the movement enormous publicity. Extraordinary numbers of birth-control publications were in circulation by the end of the century. Annie Besant's *Law of Population* sold 175,000 copies between 1877 and 1890; Knowlton's once obscure pamphlet was reprinted in the hundreds of thousands. There was now clearly a demand for such literature.[12]

From Britain, neo-Malthusian propaganda spread to the continent. Aletta Jacobs, who in 1878 became the first woman physician in the Netherlands, learning of neo-Malthusianism while on a stay in London, established a birth-control clinic in Amsterdam in 1882.[13] Paul Robin, a French libertarian who had been in contact with the English neo-Malthusians in the 1870s while in exile in England, established in 1896 the French *Ligue de la régéneration humaine*. In Spain at the turn of the century the message was spread by Bullfi; in Barcelona in 1904 a league for *Regeneracion humana* was created. In Italy George Drysdale's work circulated in translations and neo-Malthusian ideas were espoused by the popular writer Paulo Mantegazza.[14]

Though few in number, the birth-control advocates were extremely active. Determining their actual influence is difficult. Most were Malthusians and saw contraception as a way of responding to the problems of poverty posed by over-population, a stance that alienated labour. Others such as Richard Carlile embraced birth control because they were freethinkers or libertarians, which had the effect of driving away the respectable. Quacks' exploitation of interest in birth control frightened off doctors. Free-love advocates interested themselves in the issue and so respectable feminists necessarily kept their distance. The fact that family limitation was associated in the public mind with the mores of revolutionary France did not endear it to the socially conservative, who believed 1789 was itself a result of libertinism and criminal indulgences.[15] In the nineteenth century, birth control was never presented simply as a means of limiting family size; it was portrayed as having as much if not more to do with poverty, politics and promiscuity. The advocates of birth control were as responsible as their opponents for clouding the issue.

But even if the defenders of birth control presented a confused message, the argument could still be made that they at least instructed the masses on new, effective means of contraception. If technological innovations were important in bringing down the birth rate, then such information would clearly have been vital. Upon investigation, however, it appears that there is little evidence to suggest that new contraceptives played a major role in reducing fertility.

Bentham declared in 1797 that population could be controlled not by a 'prohibitory act' or a 'dead letter' but by 'a sponge', indicating that a range of contraceptives was already known to the late eighteenth-century, middle-class readers of the *Annals of Agriculture*. Carlile, in the first book published in England on birth control – *Every Woman's Book: or What is Love?* (1826) – described the woman's use of a sponge, the man's employment of a *baudruche* or 'glove' and partial or complete withdrawal.[16]

Dunglinson described condoms in 1816 made of sheep gut with a ribbon used to close the open end. In Europe they were still being made of animal skins and silk into the twentieth century; French propagandists provided information on how housewives could make condoms or *baudruches* from intestines purchased at butcher shops. In 1844 Goodyear and Hancock publicized their vulcanization of rubber process, and by the 1850s relatively cheap rubber condoms were available in the United States, A. M. Mauriceau offering to sell them at $5.00 a dozen.

But even if washed, dried and re-used, condoms were too expensive for the lower classes and had limited use. Knowlton mentioned but did not recommend them; Drysdale thought them unaesthetic and an impediment to enjoyment. A birth-control advocate described them in the 1870s as 'somewhat unsafe and . . . in every way inconvenient'.[17] The danger referred to was that of bursting; the prudent first tested them by inflating them with air or water. Napheys, an American doctor, suggested they only be used if the husband had a venereal complaint. Their association with disease and prostitution necessarily limited their acceptability in nineteenth-century households.

Francis Place recommended the woman's use of a sponge to absorb semen in his famous 1823 'diabolical handbills' that were explicitly directed at a working-class audience. Carlile asserted that sponges were widely employed by upper-class women on the continent. Robert Dale Owen, son of the English socialist Robert Owen and author of *Moral Physiology; or, A Brief and Plain Treatise on the Population Question*, published in New York in 1831, agreed with Carlile that the sponge was important because it provided the woman with some control, but warned that it was not always effective. Nevertheless, the insertion of a small, damp sponge tied to a ribbon continued to be recommended by English birth controllers and declared by the French, if accompanied by a douche or bidet, to be the woman's best protection. In the United States it was noted in an 1839 manual attributed to Jean Du Bois.[18]

The invention of the diaphragm did represent a significant innovation in fertility control. Nineteenth-century doctors popularized the use of pessaries to correct prolapsed uteruses; it was a short step to employ them as a barrier method of birth control. Such a device was presumably what Dr Edward B. Foote meant when referring to an India-rubber 'womb veil'.[19] The German physician W. P. J. Mensinga provided a clearer account of his diaphragm in 1882; a soft rubber shield which the woman inserted into the vagina to block entry to the uterus. Mensinga's explicit intent was to protect unhealthy women from undesired pregnancies.

The diaphragm was, when accompanied by douching, an effective female contraceptive; unfortunately its expense and the fact that it had to be fitted by a physician long restricted its use to a middle-class clientele.

Commercial houses began at the turn of the century to develop acidic powders and jellies to block and kill sperm. Easier to use was the soluble quinine pessary or suppository developed by the Rendell company in England in the 1880s and popularized by Dr Henry Arthur Allbutt. Similar home-made products which countered conception with both a barrier and a spermicide were soon being made from cocoa butter or glycerine by innovative housewives across Europe and North America.[20]

Diaphragms and pessaries to be fully effective had to be followed by douching. Douching after intercourse with a vaginal syringe to destroy 'the fecundating property of the sperm by chemical agents' was recommended by the Massachusetts doctor Charles Knowlton in his *Fruits of Philosophy*, published in 1832. Knowlton was prosecuted for obscenity, but his douching advice was repeated by others, such as Frederick Hollick in 1850 in his *Marriage Guide*.[21] Simple cold water was suggested by some; Knowlton stressed the need to add a restringent or acidic agent such as alum, various sulphates or vinegar. Douches, like diaphragms, were regarded as providing a woman with contraceptive independence. By mid-century they were readily available in pharmacies and drug stores and sold via respectable mail-order catalogues, purportedly for purposes of hygiene. They were, for this reason, promoted by the German Health Insurance Programme and provided free to members of local Funds.[22] Douching did entail expenses and required both a privacy and a water supply that was not available to many working-class couples. Perhaps this was just as well, since simply douching after intercourse was in fact less effective than coitus interruptus.[23]

In the latter decades of the nineteenth century, contraceptives and abortifacients were advertised in newspapers and magazines, sold in barber shops, rubber good stores and pharmacies, and brought to villages by itinerant pedlars and to working-class neighbourhoods by door-to-door hucksters. Irish doctors were astonished at the display by London chemists of 'antigestatory appliances' and 'orchitological literature'.[24] A quack like Horace Goss advertised a 'Preventive Mucilage' – presumably a soluble pessary – and abortifacient pills, and if all else failed promised that he and Mrs Goss could restore regularity 'from whatever causes it has been interrupted'.[25] Given the amount of such advertising, it is tempting to believe, as one historian has claimed, that the 'mass production and mass advertising' of the condom, diaphragm, pessary and syringe led to the sudden drop of the birth rate in the 1870s.[26] But there is little evidence that the new methods were extensively employed. It was estimated that only 16 per cent of English couples who married before 1910 used mechanical contraceptives.[27] Moreover, the birth rate dropped in parts of Europe where such devices were not available. The sudden decline in fertility was no doubt aided by, but clearly not dependent on, any technological breakthrough in contraception. The costs of the new contraceptives were appreciable, their supply limited and hostility to their employment – even by those seeking to limit family size – widespread. The claims doctors, quacks, and charlatans made for new, reliable contraceptives were chiefly of significance in demonstrating that enormous number of couples were – without the benefit of any modern technology – already controlling their fertility.

Since the fall in nineteenth-century fertility was so dramatic, it was natural that scholars should have assumed that a new method of contraception was primarily responsible. But nineteenth-century Europeans' first means of limiting births was, as it had been for their forebears, simply abstaining from intercourse. Marital continence was preached as ever by the churches, but given added impetus in the 1800s as feminists campaigned in favour of male self-control. The same ideology employed to counter masturbation and prostitution was turned to limiting marital intercourse, and may well have lessened coital frequency. Western Europeans always had high levels of celibacy; males postponed marriage until their late twenties. In England at the end of the nineteenth century, such unions were even further delayed, and the percentage of celibate women rose from 12 per cent in 1851 to 16 per cent in 1911.[28] It is likely that the idea of relying on long periods of continence after marriage would not have appeared impossible to couples already accustomed to the postponement of sexual gratification.[29] One should accordingly not brush aside as completely irrelevant the feminist and evangelical pleas for sexual moderation. To facilitate such abstinence, separate beds, if not separate bedrooms, were employed by the French upper classes. Such tokens of civilized behaviour could, of course, be afforded by only a few. Perhaps some shared the belief of a birth-control advocate like William Thompson, who recommended couples sleep separately, not so much to ensure continence as in the expectation that the act of walking back to bed immediately after intercourse might prevent the wife from conceiving.[30]

Some doctors, true to older theories, warned that prolonged abstinence was not healthy. But others defended periodic continence and provided scientific support for the belief that the woman's period, resembling as it did oestrus in animals, was followed closely by her most fertile period. Accordingly an avoidance of intercourse at such times, or intermittent continence, would, it was argued, provide a natural method of fertility control. Bischoff's, Pouchet's and Raciborski's purported discovery that ovulation occurred at or within a week or so of menses was hailed by feminists such as Dr Elizabeth Blackwell as confirming woman's rightful role as 'regulator of sexual intercourse'. Dr John Cowan agreed that 'if there is one direction more than another in which "Women's Rights" should assert itself, it is in this one of choice of time for sexual congress.'[31]

Doctors in the main opposed 'artificial' birth control. The fact that many publicly interested themselves in the 'natural' rhythm method implies that they were under pressure from their patients to come up with some alternative. In America, Gardner suggested conceptions could be avoided if intercourse were delayed until twelve days after the menses; R. T. Trall recommended ten to twelve days. In England, Henry Arthur Allbutt suggested eight days.[32] Unfortunately, the cycle was completely miscalculated. It is now known that ovulation typically occurs about ten days after menses, just when doctors asserted women entered their 'safe period'. Some physicians by chance suggested a calendar that was correct; some couples possibly struck on a system that worked for them. At the very least a restriction of intercourse, whatever the underlying theory, could have had some effect in limiting births.

Extended nursing, along with late marriage, remained a key means of limiting births.[33] In France the relationship seems clear. In the south-west, a region of prolonged nursing, there occurred wide spacing of births and low infant mortality. In the north there was shorter nursing, higher infant mortality rates and the threat of an increased rate of pregnancies, which presumably was only obviated by recourse to contraception. Many doctors ridiculed the old belief in its efficacy, but Charles Loudon explicitly called for extension of nursing to space the pregnancies of the working class.[34] Lactation was obviously affected by women's work patterns; factory labour, in interrupting the ability to breastfeed, pushed up the fertility rates of the urban poor. Even among the better off, who could afford the purchase of cow's milk and the newly produced feeding bottles and nipples, there occurred in the 1890s a decline in nursing and an increasing recourse to artificial feedings. Some birth controllers such as Annie Besant and Henry Arthur Allbutt attacked extended nursing as dangerous and weakening to mothers.[35] Their stance can perhaps be understood inasmuch as some opponents of birth control argued that the protection offered by nursing made birth control unnecessary. It is possible, however, that the critique of the birth controllers, complementing as it did that of doctors opposed to lengthy breastfeeding, actually undermined working-class confidence in a measure that offered an important margin of protection to both mother and child.

The most important form of contraception remained coitus interruptus. William Thompson, in a veiled 1824 reference to withdrawal, argued that, 'A mental effort on the side of refinement, not of grossness, is all the price to be paid, and by only one party, for early marriages and mutual endearments, where the circumstances of society permit no increase of population.'[36] Richard Carlile was foolish enough to recommend partial withdrawal, a tactic whose dangers Robert Dale Owen pointed out when recommending coitus interruptus in *Moral Physiology*. Some seemed to need to be instructed on this simplest of birth-control techniques. In France, written directions on employment of '*la retrait*' were provided.[37] In America in 1849, one woman complimented her husband – 'I do think you are a very *careful* man' – and suggested he teach his skill to a neighbour whose wife was burdened with repeated pregnancies.[38] A variant of coitus interruptus popularized in John Noyes's New York state Oneida colony was coitus reservatus, in which the male refrained completely from ejaculating.[39] Both methods were obviously extremely risky and placed great demands on the couple's cooperation.

An indication of the popularity of the withdrawal method was the number of attacks made on it. Doctors opposed it as a depraved form of masturbation leading to physical and mental illnesses. At the end of the century Freud expressed his concerns about the problems it might pose the psyche.[40] But such warnings probably did not impress that many. A forty year old German farmer when told of the purported dangers coolly replied, 'I don't believe that. Otherwise everybody would be sick.'[41]

Contraceptive failure might well lead to recourse to abortion, and indeed the two strategies were traditionally confused. In the nineteenth century, both doctors and neo-Malthusians sought to promulgate the idea that the two actions were clearly different. In 1827 the existence of the human egg was established as a scientific fact, and the idea of 'conception', in the sense of an instantaneous event when sperm and egg meet, was finally crystallized. Previously conception had been viewed as a process that was only completed after several days, if not weeks; in the Middle Ages it had sometimes been equated with ensoulment. Now doctors used the new discovery to condemn abortion at any stage and drew a sharp line between contraception and inducement of miscarriage. But for the general public the dividing line was still hazy, and herbal teas, purgatives and suppositories continued to be employed to keep women 'regular'. Many insisted on viewing abortion as simply one more step on a continuum of fertility-controlling practices. Doctors reported with alarm that there were poor women who actually preferred abortion to contraception. And there were Catholics who believed it less immoral than contracepting, since only one party was involved.[42] Abortion remained for most a 'back-up' method of fertility control, obviously necessary when all methods of contraception were unreliable. It was clearly a female form of fertility regulation and provided the most dramatic evidence of the lengths women would go to, even against the wishes of their spouses, in controlling their fertility.

The reported upsurge in abortion that took place across the western world from the mid-nineteenth century onwards was taken as a sign of the increased desire to limit family size. A swell was reported from the 1840s on in America by Dr Hugh L. Hodge and Dr Horatio Storer. In France by the end of the century, claims were being made that 100,000 to 500,000 abortions a year were being carried out.[43] Most western countries passed new legislation against such practices. Doctors led the campaign against abortion as much to destroy professional paramedical competitors as to protect the unborn.[44] The Catholic church followed the physicians in taking a harder line on abortion. Whether or not animation had taken place, abortion was, declared Pope Pius IX in 1869, worthy of excommunication. Previously the church threatened with such sanctions only those *'procurantes abortum foetus animati'* ('attending to the abortion of unensouled progeny'); now it hit out more generally at those *'procurantes abortum effectu secuto'* ('attending to an abortion, with the effect having followed').[45]

Doctors continuously expressed their shock that respectable, church-going women resorted to abortion. The author of *Satan in Society* indignantly cited the letter of a clergyman who had the temerity to defend his wife's right to abort. 'If Mrs —— is in such a condition, it would be entirely proper now, before life or animation has commenced, that something be done to bring on the regular periods. We are both very anxious it *should* be done, and in her present condition there would be nothing wrong.'[46] Women in particular clearly refused to accept the new medical message that life was present from the moment of conception, and remained true to the traditional view that until quickening they had the right to take whatever measures necessary. ' "But", says our client, "quickening is not till the four-and-a-half month, and so, abortion before that time is no sin." '[47] The law in fact only slowly embodied the new theory. Quickening was retained in the first English statute on abortion in 1803, and not until 1867 was it made clear that a woman could be tried for precipitating her own miscarriage. Likewise in America anti-abortion state legislation only emerged at mid-century; some states did not criminalize abortion until the twentieth century.

Most advocates of birth control were also opposed, if only for safety reasons, to abortion. An innocent preventive was better, in Robert Dale Owen's words, than the 'noxious drugs' to which both the married and single had recourse.[48] In France, where abortion was in the 1890s apparently more prevalent than elsewhere, it did win public defenders such as Georges Hardy and Madeleine Pelletier.[49] A. M. Mauriceau, who few knew was the husband of the notorious New York abortionist Madame Restell, was one of the rare American writers to assert that the operation could be carried out safely.[50]

In the early nineteenth century, doctors attributed abortions to the unmarried; in the late nineteenth century to the married. What was not clear was the extent to which women were acting independently. Did they have recourse to abortion because the control of fertility was viewed as their responsibility, or because the contraceptive use agreed on by a couple in a companionate marriage had failed? The former situation was described in a California divorce suit. Susan Gilbert declared that she had aborted four times because her husband 'could not, or would not restrain himself so as to prevent her becoming with child'.[51] It is certainly important not to romanticize abortion, which always posed great dangers. Corsican seducers forced abortifacients on their mistresses, and English ruffians, warned a moralizing tract of the 1870s, would similarly advise their victims 'to take the means to get rid of the child, either before or as soon as it is born. Such things happen every day; the papers are full of them.'[52]

Whatever the cause for recourse to abortion, quacks and abortionists used new advertising mediums to peddle wares purportedly designed to respond to the demand. An idea of the profits to be made was revealed in the 1897 trial in Exeter of Louisa Fenn, who sold abortifacients under the name of 'Madame Douglas'; in six months she spent £600 (roughly twelve times a working man's yearly wage) on advertising.[53] Most women before purchasing such pills probably first tried hot baths, gin and strenuous walks. Lead in the form of diachylon pills was consumed in large amounts in England, while in Sweden and Germany phosphorus taken from match heads was turned to the same purposes. Rural women continued to concoct their own brews or turn to herbalists and *officiers de santé* for aid. In the cities, patent medicines which were guaranteed to cure irregularity of the monthly period began to edge out traditional remedies.[54] But even the new concoctions were based on traditional emmenagogues – aloes, iron, savin, ergot of rye, rue, tansy, quinine, cotton root oil (in the United States) and pennyroyal. Instrumentation spread with increased availability of cheap catheters, sounds and probes; douchings and injections were also employed.[55]

There was no hard statistical evidence available on the number of abortions, but doctors asserted that up to a quarter of all conceptions were terminated.[56] Such a surge of abortions was to be expected in countries going through a fertility transition, in which the desire to limit births could not be completely met by contraception. This was to be the case in twentieth-century Chile and Japan. Such 'abortion epidemics' tend to be attenuated once effective contraception is made widely available, yet twentieth-century experience indicates that even in societies in which there is no shortage of reliable contraceptives demands for abortion remain high.

If all else failed the poor might have been forced to abandon their children. French foundling homes introduced in 1811 *tours* in which children could be discreetly left. The numbers increased from 63,000 to 127,000 by 1833. The argument that the *tours* actually induced parents to leave their children led to the government's closing them in the late 1830s.[57] Because such refuges were lost, claimed the concerned, abortion and infanticide rates were pushed up. Even in the prosperous England of the 1860s, infanticide fears were raised by sensational accounts of mercenary wet nurses and 'baby-farming'.[58]

There was no important technological breakthrough which explained the widespread decline of fertility in the late nineteenth century. The available methods required a sacrifice of pleasure (condoms, coitus interruptus, extended lactation and continence) or posed real danger (abortion). The fact that such means could be exploited successfully indicates the determination with which couples employed them. But the causes of such determination varied according to class and sex.

As industrialization and urbanization appeared to pose new threats to existing family forms, middle-class men and women increasingly turned to professional counsellors for advice on the appropriate roles to be played by husbands, wives and children. The birth-control pamphlets are best understood when located in the context of the flood of marriage advice literature produced in the nineteenth century. The prosperous bourgeois was told that respectability was based on a man's ability to separate his public and private lives.[59] Middle-class wives were in fact increasingly less able to act as their husbands' business partners, as production ceased to be a domestic activity and was concentrated in the factory or office. The 'home' now emerged as primarily a centre of consumption, and as often as not was relocated in the suburbs, far from the masculine world of work. It was to be a 'walled garden' offering protection from the savagely competitive world of commerce.

Its middle-class chatelaine was purposely cut off from the real world, her apparently inconsequential duties only ennobled by the devotion with which they were carried out.[60] But though society's intent was to make femininity more dependent than ever, complete submissiveness was only an ideal. Though rarely acknowledged, many middle-class men's business successes continued to depend on their wives' crucial contribution of capital and unpaid labour.

Respectable nineteenth-century women were, according to most marriage manuals, to be as ignorant of sexuality as they were of economics. 'Woman, as is well known, in a natural state – unperverted, unseduced, and healthy – seldom, if ever makes any of those advances, which clearly indicate sexual desire; and for this very plain reason that she does not feel them.'[61] Traditionally women were regarded as sexually active, if indeed not more demanding than men. Now sexual passivity was taken to denote civility and sexual aggressiveness as evidence of lower-class mores. Workers' poverty was attributed not just to their excessive numbers, but to their purported licentiousness, promiscuity and illegitimacy. But the bourgeois sexual ideology was racked by inherent tensions. It exalted the passionless female, yet assumed that the companionate marriage was based on love; it lauded male continence while tacitly accepting a sexual double standard that fueled fears of venereal disease and prostitution.

The doctrine of the separate spheres that exalted the ideal of the active man and the 'idle' woman left the middle-class lady in a curious limbo. She was emancipated from the drudgery of domestic chores passed on to domestics, but cut off from the world of business, politics and education. Cossetted and constricted, she was steered back to her 'natural' role of mothering. The nineteenth-century 'cult of motherhood' made reproduction so important that the diligent matron was expected to turn to doctors and teachers for advice. The rise of education clearly changed the ways in which children were viewed. They were supposed to be pampered rather than productive members of the bourgeois household. Childrearing was accordingly taken to be as important as childbearing.

The concept of passionless females was inculcated, while women, increasingly cut off from the public world, had their attention narcissistically focused on their health, their body, their childbearing.[62] The intent of moralists was to make reproduction chaste by distancing it from sexuality. The irony was that those who purportedly sought to protect middle-class women from sexuality in fact exalted procreation as their most important function. Girls' education was designed to instill just this ethos of middle-class domesticity.[63]

Both middle-class men and women were informed by the writers of advice literature that the specialization of gender roles would result in domestic bliss. Both parties were clearly prepared to make sacrifices to ensure happy, companionate marriages. But was such domestic harmony possible with large numbers of children under foot? 'The ostensible motives' advanced by American couples to justify restriction of births, a contemporary noted, 'are a regard to each other's feelings and convenience.'[64] From the 1850s on, middle-class men worried about their ability to make the necessary increased economic investments in their children's education; middle-class women became ever more emotionally involved in their offsprings' well-being. The role of wife and mother became 'professionalized' as the purportedly 'idle' woman was forced to meet ever higher standards of childcare. The greater concern taken in each additional pregnancy led logically to a pondering of the question of the wisdom of restricting their number. Could not fertility control be employed, many wondered, not as a protest against motherhood, but as a means of improving it? Such a cool weighing up of options clearly was undertaken in 1881 by Mabel Todd, wife of a New England academic. 'I will *never* have another', she confided to her diary, 'unless David has a salary of at least three or four thousand.'[65]

The traditional counsellors of married couples were churchmen. In both Catholic and Protestant countries, religion was 'feminized' in the 1800s as men turned to other centres of sociability. Priests, playing to their predominantly female parishioners, provided an increasingly sentimentalized, domesticated form of religion.[66] The Catholic church was especially concerned by the fertility issue, given the fact that France was the first country to restrict births on a massive scale. In Germany the Catholic birth rate was higher than the Protestant, but by the last decades of the century also declining.

Some suggested that the birth controllers were spreading what was in effect a new religion. So Alexandre Boutique began his novel *Les Malthusiennes* (1894) with the ditty:

> Holy Mother we believe
> Without sin thou didst conceive:
> Holy Mother, so believing,
> Let us sin without conceiving.[67]

The nineteenth-century Christian churches had little original to say in response. Attempts by the church to inculcate ignorance and fear of sexuality, as for example in France where convent girls had to embroider *'Dieu le veut'* over the openings of the *'chemises à trou'* they prepared for their trousseaux, were as likely to incite as curb curiosity.[68] The Protestant denominations, wary of pastoral interference in family matters, largely avoided discussion of sexual issues. Women in the social purity camp did oppose contraception as simply offering another means by which women could be subordinated to men. 'Voluntary motherhood' was defended by Protestant women, who at the same time feared that male forms of contraception, associated as they were with prostitution, would increase immorality. The Catholic church for its part long managed to postpone coming to grips with the problem of family planning by arguing that a woman who simply consented to her husband's insistence on employing coitus interruptus was not herself sinning. From the 1870s on, the increased vehemence of the church's opposition to contraception was primarily due to the fact that it came to be regarded as a symptom rather than as a cause of such evil forms of modernism as materialism, socialism and feminism. But the fact that the church tacitly accepted the legitimacy of the rhythm method as a means of avoiding coitus interruptus was its way of acknowledging that some curbs on fertility had to be tolerated.[69]

It was a sign of the times that churchmen increasingly employed medical rather than moral arguments when arguing against contraception. Doctors became in the nineteenth century the acknowledged authorities on procreation. They had linked ovulation to menstruation and publicized the rhythm method that the church grudgingly accepted. But doctors were unwilling to go much further in responding to their patients' requests for information. The self-help aspect of the birth-control movement and a clear suspicion of doctors' self-serving concerns were obvious in works of birth controllers like William Thompson and Robert Dale Owen. In response, most doctors publicly attacked birth control as the brainchild of quacks and midwives. American doctors such as Augustus Gardner declared in the 1870s that all forms of fertility control were physically dangerous. Others retreated to the moral heights and asserted that sexual excesses would result if pregnancy could be avoided.[70]

Doctors did warn unhealthy women to avoid pregnancies, but rarely would say how. More common was the argument that giving birth actually improved health in that it released 'energy'.[71] Deliveries were made safer by the training of midwives and the popularization of Lister's antisepsis theories in the 1880s. Nevertheless, unnecessary medical intervention still posed a great danger: home deliveries were actually safer than those done in hospital and upper-class women more likely to fall victim to sepsis than their lower-class counterparts.[72]

Doctors clearly limited the size of their own families, but did not wish to be linked with birth control, a subject too unseemly for reputable professionals to discuss, associated as it was by males with the arcane knowledge of prostitutes and midwives. In England, only a few physicians like Henry Arthur Allbutt came out in favour of family limitation.[73] In America, where the line between regular and irregular practitioners was not so clearly drawn, there was more open medical support. Dr Edward Bliss Foote saw birth control as protection against exhausted mothers and defective children; Dr J. Soule claimed it would end the fear women had of the illnesses and pain associated with pregnancy.[74] By the 1880s, birth-control methods were beginning to be described in American medical journals. But the medical profession in general remained hostile to what it called 'sexual fraudulency, conjugal onanism' and 'indirect infanticide' that was not only immoral but, in leading to excessive indulgences, caused cancer, leucorrhoea, ovaritis, mania and neurasthenia. As late as 1904 John W. Taylor, president of the British Gynaecological Society, declared that 'mechanical shields' caused 'purulent vaginitis' and 'sexual onanism' resulted in 'brain fag'.[75]

Many of the leading feminists with similar concerns for public propriety avoided, as the Bankses pointed out in *Feminism and Family Planning*, any discussion of contraception. Of course, the first women's movement was preoccupied by the plight of the single – the unmarried, widowed, divorced and deserted. Moreover, Linda Gordon has made the argument that suspicion of male neo-

Malthusians' defence of fertility control was understandable given the fact that motherhood still provided most nineteenth-century women with a good deal of status.[76] The fear was that contraception might make women sexual playthings, more rather than less dependent on men. Feminists did defend 'voluntary motherhood'. Although they did not at first directly defend the artificial limitation of fertility, they asserted that no woman should be forced to have children against her wishes. This defence of 'her own person' laid the ground for the eventual embracing of birth control. The ends were agreed on; the means were to be decided.[77] John Stuart Mill's prediction that women would defend their right to free themselves of their physical function as their political rights increased was to be borne out in the early twentieth century. 'To be relieved from it [excessive childbearing] would be hailed as a blessing by multitudes of women who now never venture to urge such a claim, but who would urge it, if supported by the moral feeling of the community.'[78]

Some nineteenth-century women did openly defend birth control, England's Annie Besant being the most notorious. In the United States Alice B. Stockham, though opposed to coitus interruptus and the condom, defended coitus reservatus, or what she called 'karezza'.[79] The most isolated feminists were the ones most likely to go the furthest. Thus in Germany Helene Stocker and Marie Stritt, and in France Madeleine Pelletier, called for the use of contraceptives and the legalization of abortion.[80] And even when most leaders of the women's movement publicly condemned contraception, its male opponents insisted on attributing a feminist stance to women who limited births. In the French Assembly it was noted that birth controllers advanced 'cette thèse que la femme est maitresse de son corps'. René Berenger reported that the working women he talked to declared,

'We are mistresses of ourselves!'
   And then I asked: 'Have you read this little [neo-Malthusian] tract?'
   She tells me: 'I read it, I didn't understand a thing in it. In the books that we are sold, nothing is understandable, but it's for the illustrations and the addresses that are at the back that we buy them.'[81]

Such was the association of birth control with 'advanced women' that the first generation of women doctors found that both their colleagues and patients assumed they would provide advice on abortion and contraception.[82]

The middle classes paid lip service to the official pro-natalist teachings of the church and medicine. In practice they came to accept, in the latter half of the century, the explicit argument of the birth controllers and the implicit argument of the feminists that only limitation of births would ensure the sort of economically secure, companionate family life that was now idealized. The new white collar or lower middle class, rapidly expanding in the last decades of the century, and having the pretensions but enjoying neither the prosperity nor the property of the middle classes, found even greater reasons to curtail its fertility.[83]

Did the working class follow suit in also aping middle-class manners? It first has to be recalled that nineteenth-century workers were already controlling their fertility; the real difference was that from the mid-century on, the bourgeoisie was employing such controls more intensively. Was this new model, small family copied? No doubt domestics observed and sought to emulate some of the customs of their masters, but of more far-reaching importance was the impact of economic change on the family structure of the labouring classes. In England the mechanization of industry began in the eighteenth century, but for another hundred years most production was still done in familial units, the factory only triumphing in the late 1800s. The growth of waged industrial labour initially provided inducements for early marriages and the bearing of children who could contribute to the family economy. Lack of economic certainty also encouraged workers to live in more complex households by taking in kin and lodgers.[84] Proletarianization and population growth thus went together.[85]

England was infamous for its extensive use of child and female labour in mines and mills, but the 'family wage' was common across Europe. In the first half of the nineteenth century, German fertility rose along with mechanization, and in eastern and southern Europe the process continued into the early twentieth century. In central and southern Italy, for example, fertility continued in the inter-war period to be pushed up by demands for unskilled workers.[86] Middle-class observers went so far as to claim that the lower orders had children for no other reason than to add to their supply of cheap labour. Absent in such analyses was the fact that workers, while recognizing the essential contribution every able-bodied family member made to the household economy, were themselves ambivalent about the morality of child labour.[87]

Why did working-class fertility finally fall? It was traditionally low in textile areas where women found employment outside the home; where such options were not available, as in mining and heavy industry regions, it remained high well into the twentieth century. The occupational status and attitude of husbands, not just their wage level, were particularly important. Skilled workers, aware by the end of the century that the middle class had smaller families, often felt they were being kept in ignorance of the methods employed. Such concerns were played up by the editors of the French left-wing journal *Le Père Peinard*.

> The more proletarians there are, the less does it cost to feed them. Hence whenever a poor girl has a child which is not viable, you hear these camels braying that they have been cheated. They fling the mother to the bears, and they cry out they have been robbed. If you read, however, the journals of the *grand ton*, you will easily see that their wives despise conjugal fidelity, and that they are often nothing but sluts, whose children may have thirty-six fathers . . . generally they have two little ones, the rest are avoided.[88]

The various socialist parties were opposed to neo-Malthusian economic theories, but divided over the wisdom of defending the workers' right to birth-control information.[89] Nevertheless, workers ultimately restricted family size, not in order to ape the behavior of the upper classes, but largely because the wages of children and women, which in the early industrial society often added up to more than half of the family's income, were radically diminished as the economy matured. In England and Germany after 1870, the demand for skilled male labour increased and that for unskilled female and child labour declined. Moreover, workmen, organizing to protect themselves from the competition of cheap workers, increasingly opposed child and female labour and demanded for men a 'breadwinner's wage'. The state responded by 'protective legislation' which narrowed the occupational opportunities of women and young people.[90]

A new working-class household slowly emerged – with the woman in the subordinated position of full-time housewife – as a result of a complex struggle by labour against economic exploitation and in pursuit of a secure domestic life. Given their preoccupations with the insecurity of their employment and the fragility of their households, it was understandable that workmen idealized a new sexual division of labour, in which the man would be the sole wage-earner and the woman free to devote all her energies to the duties of wife and mother. The status of the former supposedly increased outside the home, that of the latter within.[91] The wife, according to this new code of working-class, female respectability, was no longer to be an economic partner, but keeper of the home and children. She was to set higher standards of domestic competence; a real 'home', so the popular and socialist press declared, was not a productive centre, but a haven of reproduction and consumption in which the wife cared for the family.[92]

The reality was that it would be the rare nineteenth-century, working-class woman who could hope to make this transition to full-time motherhood. In England it was pointed out in the late 1880s that, 'It must be remembered that, as a matter of fact, *the majority of men do not support their wives and their families*. The wife, already exhausted with her special duties, has, in addition, to labour to bring in a contribution to the household purse, and the children also contribute.'[93] And even though the number of women working outside the home declined at the end of the century, many still did piecework and played a key role as manager of the family's budget, frequently being handed over the pay packet of both husband and children. Such women necessarily knew more about the family's financial situation than the middle-class matron. And given the lack of privacy available in workers' dwellings, it is unlikely their daughters could have been as ignorant of the working of their bodies as were their middle-class counterparts.

With the fall in the demand for agricultural and unskilled labour, the large family lost its economic rationale. Children, no longer needed by the economy, were free to be educated; schooling could not impose itself as long as there were financial incentives for truancy. Offspring ceased making economic contributions to the family; indeed, they became consumers of resources. They were kept longer at their studies and prevented by factory acts from working. In the French mining town of Anzin, 50 per cent of the boys aged 10 to 14 were working in 1872; only 16 per cent in 1906. Compulsory education accentuated age differences and 'infantilized' children, making them less autonomous and more dependent.[94] Workers, though they doubted schooling would provide much social mobility, did accept the new notion that parents should work for their children, not the other way round. Even the idea of having them to provide possible economic support in one's old age was unintentionally undercut by the emergence of modern pension and welfare programmes.

As the cost of rearing children rose, their numbers in working-class households began to decline.[95] In their reappraisal of family strategies, working-class parents sought not only to space births, but to limit them. It is probable that the rise of regular employment and the creation of stable working-class neighbourhoods increased the ability of workers to plan their future. Once they could predict their life chances, they were likely to have been better prepared psychologically to envisage the limiting of births. But many workers appear to have regarded limitation of family size as essentially a defensive stratagem turned to for protection in a threatening world; they did not perceive themselves as having made any great gains. Presumably varying mixes of such motives underlay most decisions to curb fertility.

Workers had their own reasons for restricting births. They were not ignorant of the new family form adopted by the upper class, but they had to think first of their own concerns. There was a percolation downward of ideas, but they were met with both accommodation and resistance. Workers' adoption of fertility control, which could be taken as a symptom of the lower classes' search for 'respectability' and an aspect of their 'embourgeoisement', represented in reality their desire not so much to enter the middle class as to maintain their position in the working class.

Having dwelt on the material concerns of labour, it is necessary to acknowledge that there is the danger, when discussing the decline of both middle- and working-class fertility, of attributing everything to economic calculation. The concept of couples' pursuing fertility 'strategies' is a seductive notion, but can give the unwarranted impression that every birth was determined. Clearly, every pregnancy faced by a working-class woman was not planned. Many family changes must have been the result of environmental shifts which had an unintended impact on fertility. Migration to cities led to unforeseen increases in infant mortality rates; waged labour permitted earlier marriage, which was desired, as well as a larger number of conceptions, which often was not. But the greatest trap in focusing on the economic causes of fertility decline is that, in positing the idea of 'family strategies', one can forget that a household might very well have been split by the differing views of the husband and wife.[96]

If the fertility rate had been simply dictated by economic forces it could have been expected to oscillate, going up in good times and down in bad. But once the birth rate started to come down it never returned to its old level; it is difficult not to believe that women played an important role in such decision making. Once women knew they did not have to become pregnant, they viewed childbirth in a radically new way. The stoicism they often assumed when facing pregnancy was replaced with fears and concerns, despite the fact that the actual number of births they faced was declining. Giving birth did not, of course, suddenly cease to be so dangerous; that would not be true until the 1940s, when sulpha drugs became available to counter post-delivery infections. But the increased ability to avoid pregnancies and their resulting complications made women more, not less, determined to avoid them.

Carl Degler has attributed the rise of birth control to nineteenth-century women's growing sense of individualism.[97] No doubt it did play a role. Individualism was fostered by literacy; those who could read had a greater expectation of controlling their own destiny. And the literacy of women made the great difference; studies of nineteenth-century America revealed that literate wives had a lower fertility than illiterate wives married to men of the same class.[98] Officially the neo-Malthusian line stressed individual decision making. But working-class women put great stress on reciprocity, community, neighbourhood assistance and mutuality. They took a pragmatic, unromantic view of marriage, taking domestic disputes in their stride and accepting the fact that the primary source of personal fulfilment would not be necessarily found in their spouse. Other women – mothers, sisters, friends – provided emotional support. Contraceptive information accordingly spread via such networks. Population density was often correlated to fertility control, no doubt because a concentration of women allowed a passing on of advice. And the rapid diffusion of the low fertility ideal was, moreover, possibly due to the fact that female culture was less divided than male. In the dissemination of birth-control information, old sociability networks were turned to fresh purposes and new ones created.

Such discussions were not always explicit. Bonnie Smith has suggested that French women's discussions of rituals and everyday household chores had embedded in them implicit references to suitable family size and ways to achieve it. But women were not always so guarded. Most wives were told of fertility control methods by their mothers, sisters, or female friends. In the winter of 1877 Mary Hallock Foote, after being enlightened by her sister-in-law, wrote from California to her friend Helena Gilder in New York to pass on such information.

> Of course, I know nothing about it practically and it sounds dreadful; but every way is dreadful except the one which it seems cannot be relied on. Mrs. H. said Arthur must go to a physician and get shields of some kind. They are to be had also at some druggists. It sounds perfectly revolting, but one must face anything rather than the inevitable result of Nature's method.[99]

And women's networks crossed class boundaries. Domestics exchanged information with their employers. In England in the mid-1860s Susan Harris, a servant, found herself in the position of informing her mistress of how best to attempt to abort.[100]

What was the husband's role? The two sexes often took different views of birth control inasmuch as procreation imposed a heavier burden on the woman. All the evidence suggests that women were more anxious than men to limit family size. Conflicts were thus to be expected, although some sort of resolution was no doubt usually found. The first question was which sex would regulate births. The older view was that this was the woman's responsibility. George Drysdale stated that women had to be in charge of contraception (via the douche and sponge) since the man was too impulsive to be trusted and both condom and coitus interruptus were unsatis-factory.[101] Annie Besant, the first woman defender of contraception, who referred to the condom as 'used by men of loose character as a guard against syphilitic diseases, and occasionally recommended as a preventive check', clearly preferred the woman's retaining control by using the sponge.[102] The assumption amongst the working class at least was that family planning should remain the woman's responsibility. A unique survey of middle-class women's contraceptive habits in the United States, compiled by Dr Celia Mosher between 1892 and 1920, revealed that thirty-nine of the forty-three women in the sample used some sort of contraception. Twice as many favoured the female method of douching over the male methods of withdrawal or condom.[103]

The argument that men should assume the responsibility of regulating breeding was voiced by William Thompson in the 1820s, and gained support as the century wore on. Inconsiderate drunkards and louts who thoughtlessly impregnated their wives were the arch villains of the birth controllers' tracts. Many women did say they had thoughtful spouses. 'My husband takes whatever trouble is necessary', wrote a Sussex woman in 1910, 'and I think a husband cares more when he has to take trouble for you.'[104] But the fact that working women praised those who were 'careful' suggested that such male foresight was not always the rule. Studies done of German workers just prior to World War I casts a revealing light on the mix of motives, the absence of contraceptives and the separate male and female sexual cultures. A Berlin working woman, asked how she avoided pregnancies, answered, ' "My husband always takes care of himself." How? "I don't know. We never talk about that. He only says that now nothing more can happen." '[105]

Birth control was presumably more likely to be successfully achieved in cooperative households. It is possible that an un-intended consequence of mass education was that it broke down some of the barriers that once divided male and female cultures, and made it easier for men and women to communicate. But that such harmony was not always expected is suggested in the striking number of advertisements for female contraceptives that stated that they could be used without the knowledge of the husband. Family historians have commonly assumed that the spread of birth control was a symptom of the growth of more equitable, egalitarian family forms. There is no doubt some truth in the argument, but one should not go too far in heralding the arrival in the early twentieth century of new symmetrical relationships. If it is likely that to be successful in limiting family size with unreliable methods couples had to have shared concerns, the question still remains – was it a result of increased female assertiveness, greater female dependence on the male or a more egalitarian relationship? Any one of these paths could have led to the same result.

At the turn of the century it was commonly assumed that the decline of family size represented women's attempt to free themselves of their traditional duties. The reality was more complex. Existing gender roles were in many ways strengthened rather than weakened. Indeed, a new patriarchy emerged as working-class husbands became sole breadwinners and working-class wives were increasingly relegated to the home. The social price paid by the unwed mother was greater than it had been in the pre-industrial world, and the single necessarily reassessed the pleasures and dangers of sex. Married women found themselves in a society in which their status was increasingly based on the quality of childcare given rather than the number of children produced. Contraception was accordingly employed to improve, not undermine motherhood. Men could not fully appreciate women's fears of the dangers additional pregnancies posed their health and that of their children; they did come to share with their wives a new concern with the impact additional births could have on the economic well-being of the family. The neighbourhood esteem a respectable working man enjoyed increasingly came to be based on his ability to be a 'good provider', not siring more children than he could support.

In 1910, the German socialist Karl Kautsky noted that the working class was adopting the 'clever practices' of the middle class in restricting its fertility. Birth control had once been brutal, repulsive and harmful; now, thanks to advances in science and technology which produced manufactured preventives, he claimed, it was easy. This was wishful thinking.[106] Economic development, technological innovation and growing rationality all played some role in preparing an environment in which birth control would be employed on a mass scale, but it did not result from a simple combination of such forces. The fertility decline is better understood if seen, not as a product of a growing social consensus, but as the consequence of the competing interests of men and women, individuals and the community.

The social elites, having been the first to restrict family size, castigated such actions when carried out by the masses. Fears of 'depopulation' were voiced earliest in France in the 1860s.[107]

Everything conservatives disliked – hedonism, taxation, feminism, equal inheritance, socialism, secularism, education – was blamed for the fertility decline. Women who avoided childbearing were labelled debtors to society. 'The woman who flinches from childbirth', declared Theodore Roosevelt, 'stands on a par with the soldier who drops his rifle and runs in battle.' In the United States Anthony Comstock, agent of the US Post Office and the New York state-supported Society for the Prevention of Vice, succeeded in having a law passed in 1873 forbidding the use of the mails to communicate any information regarding contraception or abortion, and in the following year seized over 60,000 'rubber articles' and 3,000 boxes of pills.[108] In Germany, the satiric journal *Simplicissimus* spoofed the fears of the pro-natalists:

> The modern woman – haughty bag –
> Thinks yearly childbirth is a drag.
> And German men have lost their starch
> They don't say 'Into bed! Now march!'

The 1900 revision of the German Criminal Code included provisions against obscene advertising much like the 1857 British statute that limited explicit advertising of contraceptives.[109]

In France, Jacques Bertillon created the '*Alliance nationale contre la depopulation*', which fought the 'criminal propaganda' of the birth controllers, sought tax reforms to raise fertility and campaigned for the laws against contraception and abortion which were ultimately passed in 1920.[110] These laws, although they must have made life more difficult for poor families looking for more efficient forms of fertility control, had no obvious effect on the birth rate. Such statutes, passed by members of the middle and upper classes who were already successfully limiting family size, simply served the reassuring ideological function of attributing national 'degeneration' to the isolated activities of neo-Malthusian propagandists.

The wide-scale adoption of birth control and the sudden decline in family size that occurred within a few generations at the turn of the century necessarily appear, when viewed in hindsight, as utterly revolutionary. There is the temptation to seek a simple explanation for such a phenomenon, linking it directly, for example, to economic or social development. An equally convincing argument can be made that ideas and aspirations were the first to change and economic developments merely buttressed fertility shifts already made. There was not one fertility transition; each class and region had its own. At the neighbourhood level, family planning was no doubt regarded by most couples as simply a short-term strategy adopted in order to ensure household survival. They rarely regarded themselves as enjoying some new liberation or freedom. The new norms of the small family were quickly internalized. This should not blind us to the fact that the fertility decline was indeed remarkable and took place in the absence of major improvements in contraception and in the face of the avowed public hostility of the medical profession, the churches, and the state. Clearly, enormous restraint and determination were exercised by millions of ordinary women and men. What counted was their desire and motivation; it overcame any inadequacy of means.

Notes

1 Etienne van de Walle, *The Female Population of France in the Nineteenth Century, A Reconstruction of Eighty-Two Departments* (Princeton University Press, Princeton, NJ, 1974). Remaining regions of high fertility within France such as Brittany saw their birth rates drop, as in the rest of Europe, in the last third of the nineteenth century.

2 Mary P. Ryan, *Cradle of the Middle-Class: The Family in Oneida County, New York 1790–1865* (Cambridge University Press, New York, 1981), p. 155; Mark J. Stern, *Society and Family Strategy in Erie County, New York, 1850–1920* (SUNY Press, Albany, 1987).

3 John Knodel, *The Decline of Fertility in Germany, 1871–1939* (Princeton University Press, Princeton, NJ, 1974), pp. 246–7; E. A. Wrigley, *Population and History* (McGraw Hill, New York, 1969), p. 197.

4 Ansley J. Cole and S. C. Watkins, eds, *The Decline of Fertility in Europe* (Princeton University Press, Princeton, NJ, 1986).

5 Reinhard Spree, *Health and Social Class in Imperial Germany: A Social History of Mortality, Morbidity, and Inequality* (Berg, New York, 1988), p. 84.

6 J. A. Banks, *Prosperity and Parenthood: A Study of Family Planning among the Victorian Middle Classes* (Routledge and Kegan Paul, London, 1954); on the United States see Richard Sennett, *Families*

Against the City: Middle Class Homes of Industrial Chicago, 1872–1890 (Harvard University Press, Cambridge, Mass., 1970), pp. 110–19.

7 Michael Ryan, *The Philosophy of Marriage* (Baillière, London, 1837), p. 119.

8 A. N. de Condorcet, *Esquisse d'un tableau historique des progrès de l'esprit humain*, ed. O.H. Prior (J. Vrin, Paris, 1933), pp. 222–3; E. Pivert de Senancour, *De l'amour* (Ledoux, Paris, 1834), vol. I, p. 245; see also 1808 edition, pp. 41, 145–9.

9 D. E. C. Eversley, *Social Theories of Fertility and the Malthusian Debate* (Oxford University Press, Oxford, 1959).

10 Thomas Malthus made his hostility to optimistic doctrines clear in entitling his work *An Essay on the Principle of Population as it Affects the Future Improvement of Society with Remarks on the Speculations of Mr. Godwin, M. Condorcet and Other Writers* (Johnson, London, 1798).

11 Norman E. Himes, 'The Birth Control Handbills of 1823', *Lancet*, 2 (1927), pp. 313–64.

12 Angus McLaren, *Birth Control in Nineteenth Century England* (Croom Helm, London, 1978).

13 Samuel van Houten, *Darwinisme en Nieuw-Malthusianisme* (Nieuw Malthusiaansche Bund, Amsterdam, 1883).

14 Angus McLaren, *Sexuality and Social Order: The Debate Over the Fertility of Women and Workers in France, 1770–1920* (Holmes and Meier, New York, 1983); Francis Ronsin, *La grève des ventres: propagande néo-malthusienne et baisse de la natalité en France, 19e–20e siècles* (Aubier Montaigne, Paris, 1980); Paulo Mantegazza, *Igiene dell'amore* (Bemporad, Firenze, 1903 [first ed. 1889]), ch. xxi. Benito Mussolini, though once in power a rabid opponent of birth control, in his pre-war syndicalist stage undertook with Angelica Balabanoff the translation into Italian of a Swiss neo-Malthusian tract, and as late as 1913 supported the birth-control activities of Dr Luigi Berta. Laura Fermi, *Mussolini* (University of Chicago Press, Chicago, 1961), p. 65.

15 Alexander Walker, *Woman Physiologically Considered* (Churchill, London, 1840), p. 99.

16 Norman Himes, 'Jeremy Bentham and the Genesis of English Neo-Malthusianism', *Economic Journal*, 3 (1936), pp. 267–76; Richard Carlile, *Every Woman's Book; or What is Love? Containing Most Important Instructions for the Prudent Regulation of the Principle of Love and Number of the Family* (Carlile, London, 1826).

17 Jno. Hy. Palmer, *Individual, Family and National Poverty* (Truelove, London, 1875), p. 15; George H. Napheys, *The Transmission of Life* (Fergus, Philadelphia, 1872), p. 108.

18 Robert Dale Owen, *Moral Physiology; or, A Brief and Plain Treatise on the Population Question* (Wright and Owen, New York, 1831), pp. 66–7; Carl Degler, *At Odds: Women and the Family in America*

from the Revolution to the Present (Oxford University Press, New York, 1980), p. 217.

19 James Reed, *From Private Vice to Public Virtue: The Birth Control Movement and American Society Since 1830* (Basic Books, New York, 1978), 16. The smaller cervical cap also required medical fitting; see Norman E. Himes, *A Medical History of Contraception* (Williams and Wilkins, Baltimore, 1936), pp. 318–20.

20 McLaren, *Sexuality and Social Order*, p. 166.

21 Charles Knowlton, *Fruits of Philosophy or, the Private Companion of Young Married People* (Watson, London, 1841), p. 34; Frederick Hollick, *The Marriage Guide or Natural History of Generation* (Excelsior, New York, 1883), p. 264.

22 James Woycke, *Birth Control in Germany, 1871–1933* (Routledge, London, 1988), p. 14.

23 Reed, *From Private Vice to Public Virtue*, p. 11.

24 *The Chemist and Druggist*, 10 July 1897, p. 64.

25 Horace Goss, *Man and Woman: Their Physiology, Functions, and Sexual Disorders* (Author, London, 1857), pp. 37, 52, 70.

26 Patricia Branca, *Silent Sisterhood: Middle Class Women in the Victorian Home* (Croom Helm, London, 1975), pp. 130, 138. Branca claims birth control advertisements appeared in middle-class women's magazines in the 1880s, but gives no examples; p. 135.

27 Royal Commission on Population, *Papers*, 1949, I, and *Report on an Enquiry into Family Limitation*, pp. 7–8, tables 2, 5, 7.

28 E. A. Wrigley and Roger Schofield, *The Population History of England, 1541–1871: A Reconstruction* (Cambridge University Press, Cambridge, 1981), pp. 437–8.

29 For the argument that middle-class Victorian prudery was 'instrumental' inasmuch as it supported restraint, see Paul A. David and Warren C. Sanderson, 'Rudimentary Contraceptive Methods and the American Transition to Marital Fertility Control', in *Long Term Factors in American Economic Growth*, eds Stanley L. Engerman and Robert E. Gallman (University of Chicago Press, Chicago, 1986), pp. 307–90; Paul Thompson, *The Edwardians: The Remaking of British Society* (Weidenfeld and Nicolson, London, 1975), pp. 71–2.

30 William Thompson, *Practical Directions for the Speedy and Economical Establishment of Communities* (Strange, London, 1830), p. 239.

31 McLaren, *Sexuality and Social Order*, pp. 60–3; Elizabeth Blackwell, *Essays in Medical Sociology* (Bell, London, 1902), vol. I, p. 77; John Cowan, *The Science of a New Life* (Cowan, New York, 1869), p. 109.

32 Augustus K. Gardner, *Conjugal Sins Against the Laws of Life and Health and Their Effects upon the Father, Mother, and Child* (Redfield, New York, 1870), pp. 90–7; R.T. Trall, *Sexual Physiology: A Scientific and Popular Exposition of the Fundamental Problems in Sociology* (Holbrook, New York, 1881); H. Arthur Allbutt, *The Wife's Handbook* (W. J. Ramsey, n.d.), p. 36; Anon., *Valuable Hints*

to Fathers Having Increasing Families But Limited Incomes (London, 1866).

33 M. S. Pember Reeves, *Round About a Pound a Week* (Bell, London, 1913), p. 102; Agnès Fine-Souriac, 'La limitation des naissances dans le sud-ouest de la France: fecondité, allaitement et contraception au Pays de Sault du milieu du XVIIIe siècle à 1914', *Annales du Midi*, 90 (1978), pp. 166–88.

34 Charles Loudon, *Solution de la problème de la population* (Galignani, Paris, 1842).

35 Henry Arthur Allbutt, *Evils Produced by Over-Childbearing and Excessive Lactation* (Malthusian League, London, 1878); George Sussman, *Selling Mothers' Milk: The Wet Nursing Business In France, 1715–1914* (University of Illinois Press, Urbana, 1982), pp. 11–12.

36 William Thompson, *An Inquiry Into the Principles of the Distribution of Wealth* (Longman, London, 1824), p. 549.

37 Jean Marestan, *L'education sexuelle* (Silvette, Paris, 1916), pp. 165–6.

38 Degler, *At Odds*, p. 211.

39 Alice Stockham, *Karezza: The Ethics of Marriage* (Fenno, New York, 1896); Lawrence Foster, *Religion and Sexuality; Three American Communal Experiments of the Nineteenth Century* (Oxford University Press, New York, 1981); Louis Kern, *An Ordered Love: Sex Roles and Sexuality in Victorian Utopias* (University of North Carolina Press, Chapel Hill, 1981).

40 Angus McLaren, 'Contraception and Its Discontents: Freud on Birth Control', *Journal of Social History*, 12 (1979), pp. 513–29.

41 R. P. Neuman, 'Working-Class Birth Control in Wilhelmine Germany', *Comparative Studies in Society and History*, 20 (1978), p. 419.

42 *Malthusian*, (December 1879), p. 84.

43 Jacques Dupaquier, 'Combiens d'avortements en France avant 1914?', *Communications*, 44 (1986), pp. 87–105.

44 James C. Mohr, *Abortion in America: The Origins and Evolution of a National Policy 1800–1900* (Oxford University Press, New York, 1978); John Keown, *Abortion, Doctors and the Law: Some Aspects of the Legal Regulation of Abortion in England from 1803 to 1982* (Cambridge University Press, Cambridge, 1988).

45 G. J. Witkowski, *Histoire des accouchements chez tous les peuples* (Steinheil, Paris, 1887), p. 135.

46 'A Physician', *Satan in Society* (Vent, New York, 1872), p. 119.

47 Mrs R.B. Gleason, *Talks to My Patients; Hints on Getting Well and Keeping Well* (Wood, New York, 1870), p. 159.

48 Robert Dale Owen, *Moral Physiology* (Brooks, London, 1832), pp. 36–7.

49 G. Hardy [Gabriel Giroud], *Moyens d'éviter la grossesse* (L'auteur, Paris, 1908), p. 5.

50 A. M. Mauriceau [Charles Lohman], *The Married Woman's Private Medical Companion* (The Author, New York, 1847), p. 169, cited in Degler, *At Odds*, p. 243.

51 Robert T. Griswold, *Family and Divorce in California, 1850–1890* (SUNY Press, Albany, 1982), p. 137.

52 Stephen Wilson, 'Infanticide, Child Abandonment and Female Honor in Nineteenth Century Corsica', *Comparative Studies in Society and History*, 30 (1988), p. 772; Henry Butter, *Marriage for the Millions: For the Lads and Lasses of the Working Classes* (Guest, London, 1875), p. 11.

53 *The Chemist and Druggist*, 26 June 1897, p. 1004.

54 Agnès Fine, 'Savoirs sur le corps et procédés abortifs au XIXe siècle', *Communications*, 44 (1986), pp. 107–33; Hilary Marland, *Medicine and Society in Wakefield and Huddersfield, 1780–1870* (Cambridge University Press, Cambridge, 1987), pp. 216, 240–1

55 Edward Shorter, *A History of Women's Bodies* (Basic, New York, 1982), pp. 177–224.

56 Norman Barnesby, *Medical Chaos and Crime* (Kennerley, London, 1910), pp. 222–3; Mohr, *Abortion in America*, pp. 78–85.

57 Albert Dupoux, *Sur les pas de Monsieur Vincent: trois cents ans d'histoire parisienne de l'enfance abandonnée* (Revue de l'assistance publique, Paris, 1958), pp. 187–201; Rachel Fuchs, *Abandoned Children: Foundlings and Child Welfare in Nineteenth Century France* (SUNY, Albany, 1984). On Russia, where abandonment was practised on a wide scale into the twentieth century, see David L. Ransel, *Mothers of Misery: Child Abandonment in Russia* (Princeton University Press, Princeton, NJ, 1988).

58 See the *British Medical Journal*, 1 (1868), pp. 127–8, 175–6, 197, 276–7, 301–2; Lionel Rose, *The Massacre of the Innocents: Infanticide in Britain, 1800–1939* (Routledge, London, 1986).

59 The argument has been made that such was the idealization of family life that the number of households in America and Britain containing extended kin increased from 10 per cent in 1750 to about 20 per cent in 1900. Steven Ruggles, *Prolonged Connections: The Rise of the Extended Family in Nineteenth Century England and America* (University of Wisconsin Press, Madison, 1987).

60 Bonnie G. Smith, *Ladies of the Leisure Class: The Bourgeoises of Northern France in the Nineteenth Century* (Princeton University Press, Princeton, NJ, 1981); Leonore Davidoff and Catherine Hall, *Family Fortunes: Men and Women of the English Middle Class, 1780–1850* (University of Chicago Press, Chicago, 1987); Leonore Davidoff, *The Best Circles: Society Etiquette and the Season* (Croom Helm, London, 1973); Nancy F. Cott, *The Bonds of Womanhood: 'Women's Sphere' in New England, 1780–1815* (Yale University Press, New Haven, 1977).

61 William Allcott, *The Physiology of Marriage* (Jewett, Boston, 1856), p. 167.

62 Nancy F. Cott, 'Passionlessness: An Interpretation of Victorian Sexual Ideology, 1790–1850', *Signs*, 4 (1978), pp. 219–36.

63 Luc Boltanski, *Prime éducation et morale de classe* (Mouton, Paris, 1969).

64 Allcott, *The Physiology of Marriage*, p. 181; Peter Stearns, *Be a Man* (Holmes and Meier, New York, 1979), pp. 88–9.

65 Peter Gay, *The Bourgeois Experience: Victoria to Freud* (Oxford University Press, New York, 1984), vol. I, p. 258.

66 Ann Douglas, *The Feminization of American Culture* (Knopf, New York, 1977).

67 Alexandre Boutique, *Les Malthusiennes* (Dentu, Paris, 1894), i.

68 Françoise Loux, *Le corps dans la société traditionelle* (Berger-Levrault, Paris, 1979), p. 87.

69 John T. Noonan Jr., *Contraception: A History of Its Treatment by Catholic Theologians and Canonists* (Harvard University Press, Cambridge, Mass., 1965), pp. 439–46; J. L. Flandrin, *L'église et le controle des naissances* (Flammarion, Paris, 1970).

70 Gardner, *Conjugal Sins*; George M. Beard, *Sexual Neurasthenia* (Putnam, New York, 1884).

71 Pat Jalland, *Women, Marriage and Politics, 1860–1914* (Clarendon, Oxford, 1986), pp. 175–7; William Woods Smith, *A Baneful Popular Delusion on the Subject of Motherhood* (Simpkin, London, 1895), p. 13.

72 Shorter, *A History of Women's Bodies*, p. 129.

73 Dr Henry Arthur Allbutt, *Artificial Checks to Population*, 14th edition (Standring, London, 1909).

74 J. Soule, *Science of Reproduction and Reproductive Control* (Author, Cincinnati, 1856).

75 John W. Taylor, *On the Diminishing Birth Rate* (Baillière, London, 1904), p. 13; C. D. Routh, *The Moral and Physical Evils Likely to Follow if Practices Intended to Act as Checks to Population be not Strongly Discouraged and Condemned* (Baillière, London, 1879), pp. 8–21.

76 J. A. and O. Banks, *Feminism and Family Planning in Victorian England* (Liverpool University Press, Liverpool, 1964); Linda Gordon, *Woman's Body, Woman's Right: A Social History of Birth Control in America* (Grossman, New York, 1976), pp. 95–115.

77 Ethel Snowden, *The Feminist Movement* (Collins, London, 1911), p. 24; Cicely Hamilton, *Marriage as a Trade* (Chapman and Hall, London, 1912), pp. 156–9.

78 John Stuart Mill, *Principles of Political Economy* (University of Toronto Press, Toronto, 1965), p. 372.

79 Alice B. Stockham, *Tokology: A Book for Every Woman* (Sanitary Publishing, Chicago, 1887).

80 Richard J. Evans, *The Feminists: Women's Emancipation Movements in Europe, America, and Australia, 1840–1920* (Croom Helm, London, 1977), pp. 107–8.

81 René Berenger, 'La propagande néo-malthusienne', *La Réforme sociale*, 1 August 1908, p. 170; René Berenger, *Journal Officiel*, 25 November 1909, p. 2931.
82 Gloria Moldow, *Women Doctors in Gilded-Age Washington* (University of Illinois Press, Urbana, 1987), p. 104.
83 J. A. Banks, *Victorian Values: Secularism and the Size of Families* (Routledge, London, 1981).
84 Michael Anderson, *Family Structure in Nineteenth Century Lancashire* (Cambridge University Press, Cambridge, 1971).
85 David Levine, 'Production, Reproduction, and the Proletarian Family in England, 1500–1851', in *Proletarianization and Family History*, ed. David Levine (Academic Press, New York, 1984), p. 103; David Levine, 'Industrialization and the Proletarian Family in England', *Past and Present*, 107 (1985), pp. 168–203.
86 David I. Kertzer, *Family Life in Central Italy, 1880–1910* (Rutgers University Press, New Brunswick, NJ, 1984), pp. 58–60.
87 George Alter, *Family and Female Life Course: The Women of Verviers, Belgium, 1849–1880* (University of Wisconsin Press, Madison, 1988), pp. 179–88.
88 Cited in *Malthusian*, (October 1893), p. 73.
89 R. P. Neuman, 'The Sexual Question and Social Democracy in Imperial Germany', *Journal of Social History*, 7 (1974), pp. 280–6.
90 Mary Lynn Stewart, *Women, Work, and the French State: Labour Protection and Social Patriarchy, 1879–1919* (McGill–Queen's University Press, Montreal, 1989).
91 On the 'domestication' of women, see John Gillis, *For Better, For Worse: British Marriages, 1600 to the Present* (Oxford University Press, New York, 1985), pp. 242ff.; John Gillis, 'Peasant, Plebian, and Proletarian Marriages in Britain, 1600–1900', in Levine, *Proletarianization and Family History*, p. 155–6.
92 Barbara Taylor, *Eve and the New Jerusalem* (Virago, London, 1983), pp. 263, 272.
93 E. Fairfax Byrrne, 'Women and Their Sphere', *Our Corner*, February 1888, p. 71.
94 Joan Scott and Louise Tilly, *Women, Work and the Family* (Holt, Rinehart and Winston, New York, 1978), p. 171; Mary-Jo Maynes, *Schooling in Western Europe: A Social History* (SUNY, Albany, 1985), p. 136.
95 Gay L. Gullickson, *The Spinners and Weavers of Auffay: Rural Industry and Sexual Division of Labour in a French Village, 1750–1850* (Cambridge University Press, Cambridge, 1986), pp. 154–60.
96 Diana Gittens, *Fair Sex: Family Size and Structure, 1900–1939* (Hutchinson, London, 1982).
97 Degler, *At Odds*, pp. 189–92.
98 Degler, *At Odds*, p. 207.
99 Degler, *At Odds*, p. 224; John Mack Faragher, *Women and Men on the Overland Trail* (Yale University Press, New Haven, 1979),

p. 123. See also Elizabeth Hampsten, *'Read This Only to Yourself'*: *The Private Writings of Midwestern Women, 1880–1910* (Indiana University Press, New York, 1982), pp. 102–11.

100 W. Talley, *He, or Man Midwifery* (Caudwell, London, 1865), p. 12.

101 George Drysdale, *The Elements of Social Science* (Truelove, London, 1867), pp. 349–50.

102 Annie Besant, *The Law of Population* (Freethought Publishing, London, 1877), p. 34.

103 Carl Degler, 'What Ought to Be and What Was: Women's Sexuality in the Nineteenth Century', *American Historical Review*, 79 (1974), pp. 1467–90; James Mahood and K. Wenbury, *The Mosher Survey* (Arno Press, New York, 1980).

104 *Malthusian*, (May 1911), p. 42.

105 Neuman, 'Birth Control in Wilhelmine Germany', p. 421.

106 Karl Kautsky, *Vermehrung und Entwicklung in Natur und Gesellschaft* (Dietz, Stuttgart, 1910), pp. 178, 193, 252.

107 Yves Charbit, *Du Malthusianisme au populationisme: les économistes français et la population, 1840–1870* (PUF, Paris, 1981), pp. 34–41.

108 Clifford Browder, *The Wickedest Woman in New York: Madame Restell the Abortionist* (Archon, New York, 1988), p. 149.

109 Ann Taylor Allen, 'Sex and Satire in Wilhelmine Germany: "Simplicissimus" Looks at Family Life', *Journal of European Studies*, 7 (1977), p. 34; Woycke, *Birth Control in Germany*, pp. 49–50.

110 Roger H. Guerrand, *La libre maternité, 1869–1969* (Casterman, Paris, 1971), p. 83; Robert Talmy, *Histoire du mouvement familial en France, 1896–1939* (UNAF, Paris, 1962), pp. 41–123.

7

The Triumph of Family Planning

'*Birth control is essentially an education for women*'
Margaret Sanger (1922), *The Pivot of Civilization*

In the 1920s a popular Sicilian joke concerned a man who, informed by his priests that it was a sin to spill his seed on the ground, put it in his purse. Italians doubted they had the self-discipline of the French, necessary to employ coitus interruptus successfully. ' "These people," they marvelled, "can pick up a glass of water, drink half of it, and put it down again, in contrast to Sicilians, who cannot but finish the whole thing." '[1] In point of fact, the French birth rate was the lowest in the world in the inter-war period. This despite the fact that there was no organized birth-control movement and every political party presented itself as pro-natalist. Maurice Chevalier left it unclear whether he was spoofing or supporting the populationists when he crooned:

> *Ah! Faites des enfants,*
> *Faites des enfants*
> *Et ne cessez jamais d'en faire,*
> *Oui, mais sans tricher,*
> *Car ce serait un gros péché.*[2]

The restriction of family size that was achieved in western Europe and North America at the end of the nineteenth century was still being pursued in southern and eastern Europe in the first decades of the twentieth century. But curiously, both the birth-control advocates and the medical professionals to whom the dramatic advances in fertility control have been usually attributed opposed many of the traditional means employed – including those envied by the Italians – as ineffective and dangerous. For much of the twentieth century, ordinary men and women continued to control their fertility in spite rather than because of the advice of experts.

In the United States, the anarchist Emma Goldman began about 1910 to defend publicly, on libertarian rather than on Malthusian economic grounds, the necessity of birth control. Goldman, in part because of her radical politics, did not create a mass movement, but she helped to win to her views a woman who would – Margaret Sanger.[3] Sanger (1879–1966) was a New York housewife with a vague desire to do something with her life. She had been raised in a progressive atmosphere. Her father – a friend of Henry George – was a socialist and feminist; her husband, an architect, was active in the Socialist Party. In 1911 Sanger moved to New York city, and in her capacity as a nurse began to discover the plight of poor women burdened by series of unwanted pregnancies. At the same time she shifted her support from the Socialist Party to the more radical Industrial Workers of the World, in which some members advanced birth control as a revolutionary creed.

Sanger later dated her conversion to birth control not to the time of her contact with Goldman, whom she came to see as a rival, but to a 1913 trip to France, where she was amazed at the sexual sophistication of ordinary mothers. Back in America she coined the term 'birth control', as a positive description of family limitation to replace the old, gloomy economic label, 'neo-Malthusianism'. She thus began to separate the issue of fertility restriction from some of its nineteenth-century political and economic associations. Her first efforts to win mass support had limited success. Sanger's tract, *Family Limitation*, which described for the benefit of working-class couples the use of douches, condoms and pessaries, was prosecuted by the federal government. She left America and met in England another woman also preoccupied by sexual issues – Marie Stopes. These two brilliant but egocentric people would never each recognize the talents of the other, but were in many ways similar. They both, for example, learned to exploit legal forums to spread their doctrines.

The charges against Sanger created unexpected positive publicity, and on her return to the United States in 1916 the government dropped them. Her name had become known across the country, however, and in the future Sanger sought court confrontations.[4] She started out on her first lecture tour in 1916, turning the defence of birth control into a free speech issue. She also established a birth-control clinic in Brooklyn, for which she was arrested and jailed. In response, she founded the American Birth Control League and began a campaign for legislative reform to permit the opening of medically supervised clinics for the poor. She herself was not to open another until 1923. Meanwhile, Marie Stopes set up her clinic in London in 1921.

Marie Stopes (1880–1958) was raised in an enlightened upper-middle-class family. She was the first Englishwoman to receive a doctorate in palaeobotany, but was not unhappy that many assumed 'Dr Stopes' was a physician. In truth, she came to her understanding of the physiology of reproduction rather late in life, following her own particular voyage of self-discovery. In 1912, after a year of marriage to a Canadian botanist, it slowly dawned on her that all was not well. It says something about the sexual ignorance of even some university-educated women, pre-World War I women that she did not realize at first that her husband was impotent and that the marriage had not been consummated. Only in 1914 did she start proceedings for an annulment. More importantly, shocked by her own blindness, she began the serious study of sexuality. The product of this research was her book *Married Love*. It appeared in 1918 and was an overnight sensation, going through seven printings and eventually selling more than a million copies.

Stopes's main argument in *Married Love* was that the married woman had as much right to sexual pleasure as her spouse. Stopes only noted the issue of birth control in passing, but in the huge number of letters she received from her readers learned that the inability to limit fertility was the source of much marital misery.[5] In response, she brought out another book at the end of 1918, *Wise Parenthood*. In this second text she directly broached the issue of birth control by providing diagrams of the reproductive organs and descriptions of a variety of contraceptives. She realized after a year or so that it was not sufficient to describe to poor mothers various forms of fertility control. They had to be made accessible. Doctors, dispensaries, chemists and local health officials made it clear that they did not see it as their duty to provide cheap devices for the working class; as a result, in March 1921 Stopes opened her Mothers' Clinic in Holloway Road, London. The purpose of the clinic was to show to public officials how such services could be carried out. The clinic was to serve primarily as a model and the chief aim of Stopes's Society for Constructive Birth Control and Racial Progress, also established in 1921, was to pressure government officials into taking over the responsibility for such work.[6]

Stopes and Sanger shared many of the same concerns. They both were alarmed by the high maternal and infant mortality rates associated with large families, and exploited the eugenic concerns for the need to improve the 'quality' of the race. Knowing that the middle class already restricted births, they sought to make accessible to lower-class women the contraceptives limited as yet to the better off. They both stressed the need for clinics supported by the government and directed by trained personnel to educate the public in contraceptive use. But most important of all, they sought on the one hand to play down the old, pessimistic, economic arguments usually trotted out by the neo-Malthusians in favour of birth control, and on the other to purge the movement of any associations with sexual or political radicalism. Stopes and Sanger believed that the challenge was to make limitation of family size appear not simply economically necessary but morally acceptable. To do this, they developed the positive argument that contraception was not only compatible with pleasure but essential if the woman's passions were to be allowed full expression.

But Stopes's and Sanger's message was not simply a hymn to marital bliss; they wedded it to a warning of the dire social consequences that could result from uncontrolled fertility. Their propagandizing activities were so successful that it is often forgotten that by the time they appeared on the scene, average family size in both America and Britain was only half of what it had been in the nineteenth century. Most working-class couples were already employing some means to attempt to limit pregnancies; Stopes and Sanger reflected the eugenic preoccupations of the age in their conviction that working-class fertility had to be much more rapidly diminished.

Although there was considerable confusion as to the cause of the fertility decline, there was by 1914 general agreement amongst serious researchers that it was volitional, and not as some pessimists had declared a result of racial decay. If the quantity of the population could not be increased, government officials concluded, attempts at least had to be made to improve its quality. Accordingly the concern for both high infant and maternal mortality rates led to increased state intervention in childbearing, with the establishment of health visitors' schemes, nurseries and welfare centres.[7] The eugenicists, who raised the alarm that the struggle for survival was being reversed inasmuch as contraception was employed primarily by the better off, who thereby increased the fertility differential, were at first opposed to birth control. But in the 1920s neo-Malthusians and eugenicists began to close ranks. Progressive English eugenicists like Dr C. P. Blacker swung round in defence of birth control; since the 'fit' already limited family size, dysgenic consequences could only be avoided if the 'drunken unemployables' were cajoled into following their lead. In a special 1923 issue of the medical journal *The Practitioner*, which for the first time dealt openly with contraception, Lady Florence E. Barrett agreed. 'To attempt to lower the number of the efficient while the inefficient multiply', she wrote, 'spells disaster in the future.'[8] In America, where the fertility of black people and immigrants raised an even greater 'race suicide' clamour, the eugenic lobby succeeded in having state laws passed for the sterilization of the feeble-minded and federal restrictions placed on immigration. It was in the context of the alarmed discussions of the inverse relationship of class and fertility rates and its potentially dysgenic results that Sanger began her work.[9]

Stopes's social preoccupations were made clear in the *Birth Control News*, which was filled with columns on the racial and national necessity of birth control. Stopes, like the neo-Malthusians, was as concerned to raise the fertility of the upper classes as to lower that of the working classes. She accepted, as did Sanger, who soon dropped her ties with the American Left, the eugenic argument that the struggle for survival was being reversed, with the 'unfit' now outbreeding the 'fit' and the country threatened by 'race suicide' and degeneration.[10] Birth control offered a way of improving the unskilled and the ignorant and of limiting their numbers. The working woman had to be taught birth control, Stopes asserted, because 'such knowledge is not only essential to her private well-being, but essential to her in the fulfillment of her duties as a citizen.'[11] 'Birth control', agreed Sanger, 'is essentially an education for women.'[12]

Although the purchasers of the birth-control books were no doubt mainly members of the middle class, Stopes and Sanger were primarily concerned with the working class. Stopes criss-crossed England during the 1920s, lecturing to labouring audiences. Her goal was to make available to them the rational methods of fertility control employed by the wealthy and well-educated. It would, she believed, not only improve their lives; it would also ease the load of the middle class, weighed down as it was, in her words, by 'crushing' taxes. 'Contraception is obviously indicated', she wrote, 'rather than the saddling of the community with children of a very doubtful racial value.'[13] Surprisingly enough, the grassroots defenders of birth control tended to be American radicals or British Labour party supporters, who seemed able simply to ignore Stopes's and Sanger's ludicrously elitist outbursts.

'Soon', Stopes prophesied, 'the only class callously and carelessly allowing themselves to hand on bodily defect will be the morons of various grades, sometimes called the "social problem group".'[14] For the careless, the haphazard and the mentally deficient who refused to employ birth control devices made available to them, she envisaged the more stringent measure of sterilization. Her repeated references to 'the thriftless, unmanageable, and the appallingly prolific' and to 'the hopelessly rotten and racially diseased' made it more than apparent that she had little sympathy for the life of the lower classes.[15] Such prejudices determined the methods of contraception she sought to popularize.

Stopes's first concern was for the family, which she presented as the foundation stone of a stable society. Few would have denied that the economic well-being of families was important, but what preoccupied Stopes was their emotional well-being. 'The only secure basis for the present-day State', she wrote, 'is the wedding of its units in marriage; but there is rottenness and danger at the foundation of the State if many of the marriages are unhappy.'[16] Stopes's goal was the creation of the sexually happy couple, in which the husband would be sensitive and caring. She elaborated the idea of a woman's sensuality being dominated by a 'fundamental pulse' that the man would have to learn to interpret. The sex act, in her romantic view, had to be a *mutual* affair, not the mere indulgence of a man'. She set her readers the goal of achieving mutual orgasm, or what she referred to as the 'coordinated function'. In unlocking the passions, she promised, one would shift marriage from being 'brutalized and hopeless and sodden' to something 'rapturous, spiritual and vital'. Her model man and wife were 'young, happy, and physically well-conditioned'.[17]

Stopes was one of the first of the modern marriage counsellors who made it obligatory for the twentieth-century husband and wife to 'adore' each other, to be 'married lovers' constantly 'wooing' each other, when not reading up on how it was to be done. In passing she condemned lesbianism and masturbation, not on moral grounds, but because they reduced the woman's ability to have a 'real union'. Stopes thus became one of the main architects and defenders of modern heterosexuality.

The letters written in their thousands to Stopes and Sanger provide striking first-hand accounts of the motives of those seeking birth-control information. Women confessed to living in dread from month to month, of having their sex lives blighted by fear of pregnancy, of actually avoiding orgasm in the hopes that they could thereby avoid conceiving. These apparently candid confessions have to be used with care, however, because the writers unconsciously knew what they had to say. A 'script' for the correspondent seeking help had in effect been created by Stopes and Sanger and others who popularized new notions of modern sexuality. The writer usually was a married woman with children. She would state that others clearly had access to contraceptive information that she did not. Some methods had already been employed but had proved unreliable. If a doctor had been approached for help he had not responded to her pleas. Turning to specifics, she asked if the pessary was reliable or the condom dangerous; did contraceptives lower sexual sensitivity; could premature ejaculation be cured? Her central concern was to limit family size to avoid jeopardizing the health and well-being of both herself and her existing children. But what was especially striking was the writers' insistence that they sought contraceptive information not out of simple economic self-interest, but so they could become better wives and mothers.

These women were concerned with the 'romance' in their marriages. They accepted the idea that the 'safeguarding of passion [was] of critical import for marital adjustment'.[18] Clearly a new, twentieth-century role of sensuous wife and conscientious mother had been created that could only be fulfilled if family size were limited. Of course, with a decline in family size the role of wife became more significant and that of mother less. But a 'sentimental-ization' if not 'sacralization' of childhood also occurred in western societies just as the number of births declined.

The middle-class family had, by the twentieth century, given up to outside agencies most of the provision of health and educational services. Its household was smaller, having fewer children and having shed the many relatives, servants and occasionally lodgers it once had sheltered. 'Home' was where one now expected only to find domestic happiness. In the past such high expectations of connubial bliss were uncommon. Now a new image of the sensual, married woman was advanced throughout the media, which portrayed her marrying young, being passionately attached to her spouse and raising no more than two or three children. Implied, but rarely mentioned, was the fact that only contraception would permit the resolution of the inherently contradictory implications of the cult of domesticity. That the small, privatized family had already arrived was implicit in the very fact that advice on intimate sexual matters was now sought by some middle-class women, not from neighbourhood friends or female relatives, but from marriage manuals, magazine columns, doctors or strangers like Stopes and Sanger, living perhaps thousands of miles away. Many of the letter writers openly confessed their sexual ignorance and lamented their not having a mother or female confidante to turn to.

Stopes and Sanger sold so many books and received so many letters because they appeared to have the answer to the question of how the twentieth-century woman could reconcile the conflicting pressures in her life. The war had highlighted women's contribution to every country's national effort, and was followed in many states with the reward of the franchise. There seemed, to the fearful, to be some basis for talking of a blurring of sex distinctions. The war certainly did break down much of the resistance to the public discussion of such sexual issues as venereal disease and birth control. But if the reading public was more enlightened in the 1920s, one should not exaggerate the impact of feminism, psychoanalysis or sexology on the mass of the population. Nor should it be assumed, as it often has been in references to women bobbing their hair and taking up smoking, that in the post-war world gender roles were radically changed.[19] Indeed, as if in response to the modest extension of political and economic rights made to women (to which were attributed rising divorce and falling fertility rates), social commentators took up the new cultural emphasis on the inescapable sex differences promulgated by psychoanalysts, sociologists and sexologists.

At the turn of the century, new concepts of female desire and pleasure were constructed and the notion of 'normal' sexual behaviour was elaborated. 'Biological needs' were defined by sexologists like Havelock Ellis, who provided ammunition for the acknowledgement of woman's right to pleasure that had been demanded by feminists like Emma Goldman and Ellen Key.[20] Birth control played a key part in such scenarios in that it provided a release from the fear of pregnancy and therefore undermined old arguments in defence of abstinence. But women were not to be 'freed' of their traditional responsibilities. Such contraceptives were not meant for the unmarried; they were to be used rather to shore up a stable, heterosexual relationship. Indeed, most of the sex and marriage manuals sought to define the male and female roles more narrowly so that more efficient parenting would result. In a popular marriage text like Theodore van de Velde's *Ideal Marriage*, in which the limitation of family was assumed, the doctor was presented as the guide, the husband the initiator, the wife the pupil. In an unexpected swing away from Victorian mores, sex manuals implied that it was now not simply a woman's right, it was her duty, to enjoy sex. Her failure to achieve orgasm was presented as a threat to family stability and therefore to society.[21] Any lack of heterosexual ardour could be taken as a sign of either frigidity or latent homosexuality.[22]

It is unlikely that these appeals to 'romance' made much headway in labouring districts. Working-class women could not fully escape, however, the new stress on woman as efficient wife, mother and homemaker. As part of the effort to compensate for the losses of World War I, a barrage of propaganda was spread by 'child-savers' in favour of 'mothercraft' and 'well-babies clinics'.[23] Middle-class mothers led the way in seeking to meet the high standards of mothercraft set by such reforming child experts as Dr Frederick Truby King, with his complicated schedule of mandatory nursings. Working-class parents were said by investigators to 'spoil' their children, that is irrationally care for them, and therefore to be in need of instruction in mothering. The inhabitants of tenements were forced to suffer the intrusive inspections of social workers and health visitors; a typical report of one American investigator announced that Italian immigrant mothers did not love their children 'in the right way'.[24]

Given their higher fertility, it was also assumed that working-class women did not love their husbands in the right way either.

Many working-class men continued to see unfettered sex as their 'right'. Working-class wives tended to value 'careful', decent, sober husbands more than passionate spouses. Margaret Eyles reported hearing women say they liked everything about marriage except 'the going to the bed side of it'.[25] To her astonishment, Stopes found working-class women wanted to know how to make their husbands less rather than more passionate.

> The demand for a simple pill or drug to solve such troubles [she wrote] is astonishingly widespread. After lecturing to working-class audiences, in the question time, and even more when talking individually to members of the audience afterwards, I am surprised by the prevalence of the rumour that there are drugs which can safely be taken to reduce the man's virility, and that such drugs act directly and only on the sex organs. I think it may not be out of place, even in a book specifically addressed to educated people, to explode this popular fallacy, and warn everyone that *no reliable drug of this nature exists*.[26]

Working-class life did change in the inter-war period. Many traditional forms of women's work – particularly in agriculture – declined. But in the cities, a surge in white collar employment required an army of 'respectable' working-class women who, though ceasing to work after marriage, snatched a brief taste of independence. A concern to retain some margin of freedom was reflected in the 'feminist' line advanced in some of the letters to Stopes by women stating that they had the right to control their own bodies. 'Birth-control use', notes Linda Gordon, 'almost always represented, in fact, a raised self-evaluation of women's own work as child-raisers, a change that increased women's self-identification as workers, even without being wage laborers.'[27] But letters were also written to Sanger and Stopes by concerned working-class men, and in the women's correspondence husbands were increasingly praised for being 'careful' or 'considerate'.[28] The older, male, work-centred culture revolving around mine or factory, pub and football club was slowly being eroded. As men's work became more regimented and sedentary, they looked increasing to their families for emotional fulfilment. Married men were 'domesticated' as working hours were reduced, holidays provided and housing improved, and they spent more leisure time with their wives. They took greater interest in their children as the children's numbers declined. Working families, in acknowledging the importance of educational degrees and credentials, accordingly became more child centred. Poverty became associated with the large family in a way in which it never had been before.

Diana Gittens has argued that in England the working-class couples that were most successful in limiting family size tended to be the ones with a more home-oriented, communicative, negotiated relationship.[29] Their first desire was to protect the health of the mother; their second to assure the family budget. Working-class women until at least the Second World War relied on neighbours for advice and the chemist for contraceptives. They did not feel at ease in discussing their fertility either with a doctor or with the staff at a birth-control clinic.[30]

Middle-class couples were more likely than working-class couples to employ appliance methods and to adopt them early in marriage to postpone or space births. Working-class women tended to have the number of children they desired and then turn to some method to stop. It was not so much that they had a predetermined idea of a perfect number; they just decided when they had had enough. A socialist like Edward Bernstein recognized early on that their limitation of family size was not due simply to adherence to the Malthusian wage fund theory. The decline in labouring families' size was due to a whole range of changes in life styles and living conditions, including new types of housing, furnishing, leisure activity, entertainment and education.[31]

The Malthusian League had supported fertility control on economic grounds. Birth control for Stopes and Sanger was essentially an instrument that, by sparing the woman unwanted pregnancies, would permit the emergence of the happy, sensual family unit in which she could have the leisure for delighting in motherhood.[32] It followed that the contraceptives Stopes and Sanger favoured could not be any that violated this image of the rational, caring couple. The myth of domesticity they conjured up must have drawn the interest of working-class women; their lives would necessarily have improved if their husbands became more responsible spouses. But Stopes and Sanger then proceeded to condemn most of the fertility-control measures already employed by working men and women. They condemned continence in describing the single bed as the enemy of marriage. Extended nursing, widely employed to space births, was damned as weakening for the mother.[33] Coitus interruptus Stopes declared to be extremely unreliable and physically and psychologically dangerous. According to Sanger it prevented 'the satisfactory fulfillment of the act of physical communion, and produces a nervous reaction fatal to the well-being of both participants'.[34] It not only left the woman psychologically tense; Stopes also held the curious belief that it had deleterious physiological side-effects. 'The woman, too, loses the advantage (and I am convinced that it is difficult to overstate the physiological advantage) of the partial absorption of the man's secretions, which must take place through the large tract of internal epithelium with which they come in contact.'[35] Moreover, men, she asserted, could be lured into dangerous over-indulgence by the simplicity of withdrawal. The douche Stopes opposed as possibly harmful; she described the sheath as unromantic and unaesthetic.[36]

Were there, wrote one woman to Margaret Sanger, 'any real sure-enough things women can do to keep from having children?'[37] In their beseeching letters written to the birth-control advocates, women of all classes made it clear that they wanted more effective contraceptive protection; the question was could they use what was on offer? Stopes's favoured method of contraception (which allowed the purported absorption of 'male secretions') was the cervical cap. Sanger backed the use of the diaphragm. There was a clear feminist argument underlying their preference for such contraceptives. The condom and coitus interruptus were, asserted Sanger, 'of no certain avail to the wife because they placed the burden of responsibility solely upon the husband – a burden which he seldom assumed. What she was seeking was self-protection she could herself use, and there was none.'[38]

But female contraceptives had to be fitted by a physician. In opting for such techniques, Sanger and Stopes necessarily also had to argue in favour of the establishment of clinics in which such fittings could be provided for working-class women. The hope was that the clinics would, on the one hand, serve to distance birth control from the shady world of rubber goods shops and, on the other, attract the support and interest of doctors.[39] The flaw in such a strategy was that most doctors refused to have anything to do with birth control, and the few clinics that were established had difficulty in attracting working-class women, who were intimidated if not repelled by their male, middle-class, medical aura. Stopes and Sanger condemned the very contraceptive measures the working class found easiest to use and exalted those that, though the most 'effective', were the least likely to be employed.[40] And ironically, while they called for greater male responsibility they opposed coitus interruptus, the contraceptive practice which required the greatest degree of male cooperation.[41]

Stopes and Sanger particularly opposed abortion. 'I have worked in a factory eleven years', wrote a working woman to Margaret Sanger, 'and the majority of women of my acquaintance procure abortion as their means of family limitation, regardless of the suffering and ill-health which it produces.'[42] Women continued to try to abort themselves by taking all kinds of drugs. Alice Jenkins recalled in the 1950s that even as a child she knew what it meant when one woman said of another, 'She takes things.'[43]

In Germany, it was claimed that the number of abortions climbed from 300,000 prior to the war to a million in the 1920s, and resulted in between 5000 and 8000 abortion-related deaths a year. Three-quarters of the women involved were married.[44] In a 1922 investigation of 281 women delivering at the Toronto General Hospital in Toronto, Canada, it was discovered that 527 of 1207 pregnancies had been terminated by abortion.[45] In England, Dr Janet Campbell shocked the public with reports that not only were abortion deaths numerous but that they were driving up the maternal mortality rate, from 3.91 per thousand births in 1921 to 4.41 per thousand in 1934. Abortion-related deaths in England increased from 10.5 per cent to 20.0 per cent of all maternal deaths between 1930 and 1934.[46] Marie Stopes informed *The Times* in 1931 that in a three-month period she received 20,000 requests for abortion.[47] Kinsey's subsequent investigations revealed that one out of every five married American women had had an abortion.[48]

By the 1930s it was clear that in the first trimester medical abortion was as safe (indeed, safer once sulphonamides were available) than delivery at term. Dilation and curettage was the most common method utilized. The old argument in defence of the law based on risk to the mother was thereby undermined. Now it was the criminalization of abortion itself which, by driving women into the arms of abortionists employing vaginal salves, instruments and uterine syringes, was putting women in danger. The Depression forced the abortion rate up to new heights. Dr W. D. Cornwall wrote that in Canada,

> I think most general practitioners can testify to the increasing frequency with which they are approached to terminate undesired pregnancies. Pregnancy is looked upon as an economic and social disaster. I note that England has recorded the lowest birth rate in 1932 for many decades. If it were possible to compile statistics it would be shown that abortion among the intelligent has increased tremendously.[49]

In the United States, Frederick J. Taussig reported that something like a fifth of all pregnancies ended in abortion.[50]

The idea that the woman less than three months pregnant who sought to 'put herself right' was committing a crime was clearly not accepted by a large section of the female public. Havelock Ellis stated that women felt no regret and could not understand the legal and medical opposition to abortion. The Birkett Committee on abortion reported in 1937 that 'Many mothers seemed not to understand that self-induced abortion was illegal. They assumed it was legal before the third month, and only outside the law when procured by another person.'[51] Working-class women clung to the traditional view that life was not present until the fetus 'quickened'. They took pills, not to abort, but 'to bring on a period'. That they did not intend to harm a new life was indicated by their abandonment of such tactics once quickening was perceived. The abortionists who aided them were sometimes exploitative charlatans, but often neighbourhood women who provided services as much out of kindness as for any monetary gain. Of the forty-four interviewed in Holloway Prison in the 1950s by Moya Woodside, all had been married, all but three had children, thirteen were grandmothers and twenty-two were over sixty. There were few crimes in which one would expect to find involved so many elderly women. Woodside noted that they viewed their activities not as 'criminal' but as gestures elicited by 'compassion and feminine solidarity'.[52]

For some women, abortion was a primary, rather than a back-up, method of birth control. An investigator of a Liverpool slum reported that the Catholic resident of Ship Street 'regards birth control as a sin but abortion before the age of three months a perfectly legitimate measure . . . though so few of the Mums use contraceptives the majority have at some time or another tried to bring on an abortion. Pills, jumping down stairs, etc., are perfectly legitimate up to the end of the third month, after which the woman stops in case she hurts the baby.'[53]

The legalization of abortion in Russia following the 1917 revolution proved the safety of the procedure, but confirmed in the minds of its opponents its association with the forces subverting existing class and sex relations.[54] In the west, the abortion laws were clearly class biased, because a well-off woman could usually find a doctor who would justify her need for a therapeutic abortion. In fact there were, as improvements in obstetrics increased the chances of safe deliveries, fewer and fewer medical justifications for such intervention. The abortion issue emerged increasingly as an issue of women's rights, and the campaign for decriminalization began to find advocates. Dorothy Dunbar Bromley argued America could avoid 8000 maternal deaths a year by legalizing abortion, at least until adequate contraceptives were made available.[55] In England, F. W. Stella Browne declared, 'The right to prevent the conception of life must logically and justly include the right to remove the life-seed which has been fertilized against the mother's will, either through accident or intention.'[56] To fight for liberalization Browne, along with Alice Jenkins and Janet Chance, formed the Abortion Law Reform Society in 1936.[57]

By the 1920s, there were also some lawyers and doctors willing to express their own unhappiness with the 1861 law on abortion. The statute was an obvious embarrassment to the police, who recognized that abortion was largely condoned and prosecutions unpopular. Eugenically minded judges in the 1930s wondered aloud why impoverished mothers should be punished for seeking to avoid the birth of congenitally unhealthy children. And physicians in both Britain and the United States – who for the most part believed that abortion was 'wrong' but sometimes 'necessary' – worried that their freedom to provide or withhold therapeutic abortions would be jeopardized if they were subjected to the dictates of either their patients or the courts.[58] Doctors on the one hand loathed being pressured by their patients; on the other hand they knew that if they did not provide such services others would. Professional control in both England and America was maintained by progressive physicians' continual broadening of the definition of 'health' – in particular by adding psychiatric indications – so that abortion would always be justified on medical rather than on social grounds.

A woman three days overdue wrote to Stopes in August of 1923, complaining that *Wise Parenthood* only dealt with 'pre-conception', and went on to threaten, 'If I do not get anyone with *knowledge* to help me, I shall try other means, as I feel I shall go mad if I have to go through it all again.'[59] In her clinic established off the Holloway Road, Stopes made her staff take an oath against providing any information on inducement of miscarriage. In *A Letter to Working Mothers* (1923), Stopes set out her arguments against such tactics. She envisaged the woman 'caught', and went on, 'So you do, or try to do, a desperate thing; you try to get rid of the baby before it has "gone too far".' This, she informed her readers, was 'what is called an abortion' and was opposed to both law and nature. Some might feel the law to be wrong, conceded Stopes: 'I know that many thousands of you feel all this is cruel and unjust, but I want to tell you that the law is not cruel, and that it is not unjust.'[60]

Margaret Sanger received so many enquiries about abortion that she had a form letter made up stating she could not respond to such requests. It has been argued that she presented herself as a campaigner against abortion as a way of claiming a moral impulse for her work; certainly both she and Stopes sought for tactical purposes to draw a sharp line between contraception and abortion.[61] But working-class women made it clear in their letters that, though they feared the risks posed by abortion, they did not accept the idea that the employment of one method of birth control required the sacrifice of the other; rather they saw both as having a place on a continuum of fertility-control measures.

The fact that working-class women wanted to provide themselves with the greatest possible degree of flexibility in dealing with reproductive decisions was reflected in their use of language. They did not usually employ the term 'abortion' because it clearly conjured up the image of a doctor carrying out an operation, something qualitatively different from the traditional means of limiting family size. The woman described herself as attempting to 'restore her menses' or 'make herself regular'. Likewise, women did not say they had 'conceived', which had an irremedial ring to it; they said they were 'caught' or had 'fallen', 'am that way again', 'my monthly courses are ten days late', 'am a month over my time', 'am four months on the way', 'am two months on the road', all of which implied a process which might or might not be terminated.[62]

Stopes and Sanger made slow headway in their attempts to turn working women towards complicated methods of contraception.[63] Birth controllers often chose to interpret such intransigency as evidence of 'ignorance'. What they ignored was that the ideological baggage with which middle-class contraceptive methods were lumbered often deterred their acceptance by the working class. Labouring families clearly wanted more effective contraceptives, but they would have had to become almost middle class in mentality to use many that the birth controllers offered. Stopes and Sanger envisaged a model family, in which the far-sighted and prudent husband would employ or assist his wife in employing mechanical means of contraception for the purposes of ensuring the family's upward economic mobility. The rational mother would not work outside the home but devote herself to her appropriate, maternal, childrearing duties. For advice on the suitable method of fertility control the couple would turn to their friendly, progressive physician. He would explain to them not only the efficacy of the medically fitted cap or diaphragm but the dangers of other methods of contraception and the immorality of abortion.

The dangers the birth controllers saw in abortion and withdrawal were as much social as physiological. Such tactics represented not the harmonious couple but two separate sexual cultures, in which the man demanded his 'rights' and the woman relied on her female friendship network for support; they epitomized not the consumption-oriented, far-sighted, rational middle class, but the short-sighted, risk-taking working class. Abortion conjured up the image of relying, not on the doctor, but on the neighbourhood wise woman. The ambition of Stopes and Sanger was to remake not only the fertility-control decision but the family that made it. The modern marriage could only be saved, declared the birth controllers (and like-minded progressives in favour of sex education and liberalization of divorce) if it evolved towards the companionate model.[64]

Stopes and Sanger 'medicalized' contraception in part to attract the legitimating support of doctors. In 1922, Stopes established a Medical Research Committee with the intent of enlisting such backing. But if the clinic appealed to some doctors, it did not appeal to many patients. By 1930, the sixteen clinics and two private consultants in Great Britain had seen a mere 21,000 clients, and despite Stopes's claims of success their failure rates were high.[65] The caps and diaphragms proved too demanding to be consistently employed. The vast majority of the population continued to rely on traditional methods.

Arguably the greatest good served by the birth-control clinics was in tabulating and publicizing both the threats posed to women's health by their frequent attempts at abortion and the physical disabilities associated with childbirth. Of her first 10,000 clients, Stopes reported that 1321 had slit cervices, 335 serious prolapses and 1508 internal deformations.[66] Doctors seriously concerned by maternal health could hardly ignore such shocking statistics. But one way of sidestepping the issue of contraception was for doctors to assert that maternal mortality and morbidity rates could be brought down by the medicalization of birthing. Such a campaign was remarkably successful. In England, hospital deliveries climbed from 15 per cent in 1927 to 54 per cent in 1954; in America, the rate was even higher. Women, told that such institutions offered superior care, naturally sought access to them. Doctors believed they could minimize the risks of childbearing in such a setting; in fact, given the greater chance of instrumental intervention, it is doubtful if hospital births were safer than home deliveries.[67]

The birth controllers constantly warned women to spurn the contraceptive advice of ill-informed local gossips and instead turn to trained professionals. But English doctors, though the 1911 census revealed that they had the smallest families of all occupational categories, long opposed discussion of contraception. In the 1920s, eminent British physicians still described the subject as a 'highly nauseous' one that could only attract the 'prurient-minded'. Women who employed contraceptives were condemned as selfish and self-centred. Mechanical contraceptives were attacked by purportedly well-trained gynaecologists as 'sordid and unnatural' and posing 'physiological dangers'.[68] 'The professional and well-to-do practice it [contraception]', a Saskatchewan correspondent of Sanger's American Birth Control League wrote in 1923, 'as in any other city in the U.S. An increasing number of people are applying to the doctor for birth control information.'[69] The problem was that doctors would not respond. They might advise the spacing of births, but few would say how.

Some doctors were simply opposed to birth control on moral grounds, but in England and North America the profession as a whole was obviously afraid of the loss of respectability that an association with Stopes and Sanger might entail, worried by confusions over abortion and contraception and simply ignorant of contraceptive techniques. The graduates of the London School of Medicine for Women were as ill-informed as their male counterparts. 'A young woman doctor, being interviewed for her first assistantship, was asked for her views on birth control. She replied tentatively that she had always thought large families rather jolly, and was relieved when this appeared to be the right answer.'[70] Even after British welfare centres began in the 1930s to provide birth-control information, doctors had little to contribute and did not take the initiative in broaching the subject with patients. In England, the first medical training lectures on the subject were started in 1936 but neglected by the majority of schools on into the 1950s.[71]

In America, the profession was even slower to support birth control. The very fact that clinics had been established by Sanger and others allowed doctors to send their patients to them for diaphragm fittings rather than engage themselves in such unglamorous activities. Doctors presented themselves as defenders of public morality, and were concerned that if they appeared to be critics of society their medical schools would lose the support of wealthy philanthropists. Nevertheless, Sanger continued to woo the medical profession by demonstrating that her Clinical Research Bureau could provide valuable data on the health histories of its clients. Dr Robert Latou Dickinson finally succeeded in getting the American Medical Association to pass a 1937 resolution acknowledging the importance of contraception and calling for its teaching in medical schools. This did not mean that doctors had become enthusiastic defenders of contraception. The Depression had simply forced them to provide grudging acknowledgement of the importance of the issue. Most continued into the 1960s to argue that the healthy woman was the childbearing woman.[72]

Nevertheless, in the 1930s a breakthrough of sorts was made in the public acceptance of birth control. This change has usually been attributed to the remarkable propaganda work of Marie Stopes and Margaret Sanger. They did succeed in presenting birth control as a positive force that would serve both the interests of individual couples in improving their health and happiness and the interest of the state in scientifically improving the quality of the race. For these reasons the birth controllers disarmed much of the opposition of the Protestant churches and the medical profession.

In truth, the churches had by the 1930s little to say in opposition. The Anglican bishops at the Lambeth Conference of 1908 referred to contraception as 'preventive abortion', but the eugenically minded clergy were slowly won over by the birth controllers' utilitarian argument that contraception would spare society high social costs.[73] Stopes and Sanger received a good number of requests for information from Protestant ministers and their wives who both employed it and helped disseminate it in isolated communities.[74] Pius XI's encyclical, *Casti connubi*, which was in part a response to the Anglicans' tepid acceptance of contraception announced at the 1930 Lambeth Conference, crystallized Catholic opposition to 'artificial' fertility regulation. But at the same time the new rhythm method, elaborated by Knaus and Ogino in 1929, was publicized by the church and sanctioned by the Vatican. 'A knowledge of a woman's rhythm', wrote Leo J. Latz in a church-approved text, 'enables married people to know *when*, by performing the married act, they are cooperating with God in the procreation of a new human being.'[75] Use of the rhythm method allowed the regulation of family size to take place 'naturally' and would, Latz hoped, be a way of winning back Catholics, who were over-represented among the birth-control clinics' clients.

In England, maternal and child welfare centres were, after the Labour victory of 1929 and as a result of the vigorous lobbying of feminist and birth-control societies, allowed to give out birth-control information if warranted for medical reasons. By 1937, only 95 of 423 centres did provide such information, but an important breakthrough had been made. Moreover, the Anglican Church and the British Medical Association conceded that birth control could be sanctioned if a further pregnancy was deemed detrimental to a mother's health. In Canada, a 1937 court case sanctioned the distribution of birth-control information when made for the 'public good'.[76] In the United States, the seizure by the customs of a shipment of diaphragms led federal appeals court justice Augustus Hand to strike down the provisions of the 1873 Comstock Law, which prevented the use of the mails by physicians to provide contraceptives or contraceptive advice.[77]

Stopes and Sanger provided new, sentimental justifications for family limitation and elaborated an often emotional vocabulary with which to describe the reasons it would be sought. They successfully used books, public lectures and courtroom forums to spread their message. But all the birth-control clinics combined provided only a tiny fraction of the population with new means of regulating fertility, and the main motive for employing them remained the old one of economic survival. Pro-natalists continued to castigate the immorality of birth control; they could not bring themselves, however, to attack the class and income inequities that impoverished large working-class families.[78] Fear of poverty drove the fertility rate down to a new historical low in the depths of the Depression; the simple acknowledgement of such social realities underlay the public acceptance of birth control. Social conservatives and eugenicists were finally forced to support birth control, if only in the hopes of reducing welfare expenditures.

In the United Kingdom, the crude birth rate (number of births per 1000 of the population) dropped continuously, from 34.1 per 1000 in 1870–2 to 24.5 per 1000 in 1910–12 to 15.8 per 1000 in 1930–2.[79] In America, the cohort of women marrying in the 1920s produced fewer children than any other between the 1880s and the 1950s.[80] The fertility of the working class fell faster than that of the middle class, but differentials in family size and contraceptive method remained. The evidence collected at the birth-control clinics revealed that coitus interruptus was the main form of contraception employed by the mass of the population. In England, the percentage of middle-class couples utilizing appliance methods of birth control grew from 9 to 40 per cent between 1910 and 1930, while amongst the working class the rise was only from 1 to 28 per cent.[81] Indeed, there appears to have been a peaking in the use of non-appliance methods in the 1920s, and only then a shift to new techniques. In the 1930s, the most popular methods used in Britain, were, in order, withdrawal, sheath, safe period and pessaries. Condoms in the 1930s were made of more comfortable latex rather than rubber. World War I had clearly popularized their use, though primarily for protection from venereal disease. Their association with prostitution, as opposed to marriage, was thus confirmed.

Male methods of contraception were slowly supplanted by female methods; the process took place earliest in the United States, where by the 1930s employment of the cap, douche and rhythm method was already high.[82] The cervical cap, invented in the late 1830s, was popularized by Stopes in the 1920s. It could be left in for up to a month, but required medical fitting. The diaphragm and cream were especially popular amongst the middle class. It was estimated that in the 1950s one in three American wives employed this method. The problem was that since the spring-rim vaginal diaphragm required medical fitting, few working-class women found it satisfactory and a low success rate resulted.[83]

In Belgium, Fernand Mascaux argued that for the proletariat simplicity and cheapness were essential; cotton wool dipped in vinegar or lemon juice could provide a vital margin of protection.[84] An appreciation of the social forces that inhibited the use of contraceptives was best represented by A. R. Kaufman. He began his Canadian birth-control work in the 1930s by funding clinics that fitted diaphragms. He soon became impatient with the low success rate, which he realized was due to the medicalization of the process. He withdrew his support from the clinics and instead began to send out, from his Parents' Information Bureau, kits of condoms and contraceptive creams. A less effective form of contraceptive, if used, clearly was more successful than its rivals that were not used.[85] In the United States, Clarence James Gamble (of the soap dynasty) followed a similar path in experimenting with the mass delivery of simple contraceptives like lactic-acid jelly.[86] Social conservatives like Kaufman and Gamble were sensitive to the argument that welfare costs could be kept down by limiting the size of working-class families. It was for them not a question of women's rights, but of class concerns.

Some new methods of birth control were produced in the early twentieth century; none proved satisfactory. Surgical sterilization of men and women was made possible in the 1890s, but usually only carried out for eugenic reasons on the mentally ill. The accurate plotting in the 1920s of ovulation by Ogino and Knaus resulted in the publicizing of a new rhythm method; although superior to its nineteenth-century counterpart, its high failure rate led to its being dubbed 'Vatican roulette'. Similar frustrations met

German researchers who, before the First World War, began work on intra-uterine devices that prevented the implantation of the fertilized egg. The first were made of silk, but in the 1920s Grafenberg announced his invention of a ring made of gold and silver. Stopes provided some patients with a similar device she called the 'gold pin'. The dangerous internal irritations caused by such methods created a host of medical problems that limited their employment.[87]

Where scientists failed, businessmen stepped in. Taking advantage of the demand for contraceptive protection, commercial houses produced a wide range of spermicidal creams and jellies. Rendells, Norforms, Sanitabs, Zonite and Zonitors were all advertised as offering contraceptive security. But because of the nature of the merchandise, there were no brand names or government regulations; customers had no guarantees of the products' efficacy. Some douches, whose makers claimed they could protect 'married happiness', might have contained spermicidal agents but often were no more than vaginal deodorants. Disinfectants such as Lysol and Dettol that could, according to their discreet marketers, be turned to the same purposes proved to be dangerously irritating. Despite such shortcomings, the 'feminine hygiene' industry, which included contraceptives, became a multimillion-dollar business, with an estimated $250 million a year spent in the United States on such products in the 1930s.[88]

In the 1950s, the situation was not that much improved. The medical profession continued to see itself playing the role of moral guardian. In England, as late as the 1970s, 'the Medical Defence Union advised practitioners not to fit an intra-uterine device for a woman without the consent of her husband.'[89] In America, the Depression had spurred on the establishment of birth-control clinics, but they still provided limited services and no new contraceptives were available. Most people depended on friends or acquaintances for information on birth control, not on doctors, who claimed there was little demand.

The war had, of course, put an end to the birth-control movement on the continent. In the Soviet Union, Stalin had in the 1930s restricted access to abortion. The fascist regimes were ferociously hostile to attempts by the 'fit' either to practise contraception or to abort. Mussolini, though a defender of neo-Malthusianism in 1913, passed repressive laws against birth control in 1926.[90] The Nazis followed suit. While deriding women's rights and presenting themselves as defenders of the family, they pushed eugenic theories to their logical conclusions by carrying out 56,000 sterilizations of the 'unfit' in their first year in power, and a quarter of a million by 1940. Abortionists were executed; contraceptive information suppressed. The Nazis succeeded in limiting access to therapeutic abortions; they were as helpless as previous regimes in trying to prevent criminal operations.[91] Birth rates rose after 1933, but not because of Nazi pro-natalist policies; fertility increased in every country (except for France) once the worst years of the Depression had passed.[92]

The post-war democracies, although preoccupied by the need for a population policy and essentially pro-natalist, did not want to be seen as sharing the fascist regimes' hostility to contraception. Indeed, in Britain family planning was supported as part of the National Health Service. Curiously, a blossoming of clinics occurred just as fertility rates rose. This post-war 'baby boom' was a surprise. Though it was more of a 'boomlet' on the continent and in Britain, in North America and Australia birth rates remained high on through the 1950s and into the 1960s. In England, the birth rate rose from 15.8 per 1000 in 1931 to a peak of 20.5 in 1947, and then declined in the 1950s; in the United States it was up to 24.5 in 1951. The three-child family once again displaced the two-child family as the norm. Old class fertility differentials were largely eradicated; fertility tended now to follow a 'U' curve, with the lower and upper classes having only a slightly higher family size than the middle classes. The 'baby boom' appeared to prove wrong the conservative argument enunciated in the 1930s that family size necessarily declined as responsibility for health, education and care of the elderly was assumed by the state. The resurgence of natality was made possible by improvements in wages during the prosperous post-war decades.

Marriage rates rose as high as they could go and the big church wedding came back into fashion. Women married earlier and had their children sooner. Many couples consciously compensated for the sacrifices they or their parents had previously made during the Depression and the war. Some were just less vigilant in their contraceptive practices.[93] Governments, fearful of the social consequences of family instability created by the war, lauded what they perceived to be a return to traditional values. Women, called by the state a year or two previously to enter munitions factories while their children were cared for in crèches, now found their jobs and childcare facilities gone. They were bombarded by pro-natalist propaganda and, for lack of any other option, appeared to have succumbed in large numbers to the appeal of domesticity and femininity subsequently dubbed the 'feminine mystique'. Even Sanger's American Birth Control League, seeking to disassociate itself from the disturbing notion of individual women's rights and to exploit familial sentiment, was rechristened the Planned Parenthood Federation of America.[94]

The domestic 'baby boom' was welcomed by the western governments; the accompanying rapid population growth of the Third World, brought about by a decline in mortality, they regarded as a threat to the global social order. The Rockefellers, financial supporters of the Population Council, were only the best-known corporate leaders concerned that Asia, Africa and South America, impoverished through over-population, would fall to the Communists. Eugenic preoccupations also reemerged in the 1950s in studies warning that the white nations could be submerged by the yellow and the black. Social conservatives began to present the small family as evidence of 'responsible' parenting. New Malthusians declared that there was a population 'problem', which could only be solved by the provision of a cheap, fool-proof contraceptive. Once fertility was seen as posing 'real' dangers, doctors and bureaucrats could finally rationalize turning their full energies to tackling the problem.[95]

Margaret Sanger, although she had largely abandoned the public spotlight in the late 1930s, continued to pursue the search for such a fool-proof contraceptive that, like vaccination, would pre-emptively protect a patient's health. Her motive was the desire to make life simpler for women, to distance the sex act as much as possible from the process of contraception and to lower efficiently the fertility of the 'unfit'. She had faith in medical science's ultimately providing such a breakthrough. Early hormonal research was carried out in Austria by Dr Haberlandt, thanks to Rockefeller money, which proved that ovulation in animals could be prevented by injections of oestrogen.[96] Experimental work on steroid interference was also pursued by Dr B. P. Wiesner at Edinburgh in the 1920s, similarly supported by American funds.[97] In the United States itself, Gregory Pincus began work in the late 1930s on synthetic hormones, at the Worcester Foundation for Experimental Biology. He discovered that, since the hypothalamus and the hypophysis controlled ovulation, the process could be blocked if these organs' activities were simulated by a drug. The original intent of such investigations, however, was not to produce a better contraceptive.

Margaret Sanger, to whom Pincus was introduced in 1950, recognized the practical possibilities of his work. She in turn recruited Katharine McCormick, a wealthy, active feminist and long-time birth-control supporter, as financial angel of his studies. By 1951, Pincus proved that progesterone inhibited ovulation, and began a search for synthetic hormones. John Rock was asked to test the new drug on women in Boston; extensive clinical trials were undertaken in Puerto Rico in 1956. Rock, a devout Catholic and Harvard gynaecologist who had earlier opposed contraception but was now alarmed by the threat of over-population, declared that the pill was a 'natural' contraceptive that Catholics could in good conscience employ. In 1960, the Food and Drug Administration accepted a Searle synthetic anovulent as an oral contraceptive pill; other drug companies soon produced similar products. By 1969, when the church categorically condemned the pill, Catholics, reassured by Rock and accustomed to its use, were not won to the pope's views.[98]

Neither Rock nor Sanger intended to launch a moral revolution. They were conservatives, preoccupied by the need to preserve stable family values and world order. They believed that the oral contraceptive could help ensure such stability. It was the appearance of the contraceptive pill – not a conversion to feminist, neo-Malthusian or eugenic arguments – that brought the medical profession to favour birth control. Biochemical and hormonal contraception appealed to doctors' idea of 'real' medical science and complemented their view of the necessity of scientific experts' managing births. Medical scientists' desire to sanitize reproduction was made clear in their embryology texts; the metaphors employed to describe conception and development had customarily been drawn from common, earthy domestic activities (sowing, baking and fermenting), but now doctors spurned such lowly associations and drew their metaphors from the science of engineering. They appeared to be more comfortable – given their references to 'pelvic floors', 'follicle walls', 'cervical canals', 'storage and transport of ovum' – when regarding the uterus as a construction site rather than as a human organ. Similarly, doctors who were still embarrassed to fiddle with a messy cream or floppy rubber contraption were happy to distribute a pill, a product of scientific research, a 'preventive medicine' that was simply prescribed.[99]

Although women employing the pill experienced a variety of disturbing side-effects, most were delighted with a contraceptive that was apparently completely effective and free of what were now regarded as the depressingly unromantic preparations of earlier methods. Men were naturally pleased to be relieved once and for all of any responsibility for birth control. Both doctors and patients embraced the idea of the pill as a panacea. In point of fact, it was not all that superior to barrier methods of protection that were methodically employed. Like any other contraceptive it could be forgotten or misused. 'Effectiveness' still depended on conscientious employment.

The faith in a 'pharmaceutical fix' to produce simple, effective control of procreation was short lived. The pill was no sooner in mass circulation than the tragic rash of deformities in the early 1960s caused by thalidomide (a sedative employed by pregnant women) sparked public fears about the side-effects of all biochemicals. But the thalidomide disaster also provided ammunition for reformers advancing the 'quality of life' argument to justify abortion. A groundswell of support in favour of reform of the abortion law had already been growing. Doctors expressed their concern that, although the numbers were far smaller than they had been in the 1930s, women continued to die as a result of back-street abortions. Lawyers complained that the vast number of criminal operations made a mockery of the law. Abortion lobbying groups protested that the existing law ignored the World Health Organization's definition of 'health', which included 'physical, mental and social well-being'. Abortion laws were accordingly reformed across the western world in the late 1960s and early 1970s. In 1973, the United States Supreme Court defended the woman's 'right of privacy' to over-ride existing state laws against early abortion. The relaxing of the law led to a decline in maternal mortality and morbidity associated with criminal abortion.[100]

But if abortion was liberalized, the control of the process was kept firmly in the hands of the medical profession, whose freedom and discretion in implementing policy was confirmed. A woman's 'right' to control her body was not recognized. Abortions continued to be treated as services requiring the close policing and surveillance of doctors; the women who sought them (in North America, increasingly younger, unmarried women) did not cease being stigmatized and demeaned.

Although the mass distribution of the pill and the coil and the liberalization of abortion did not take place until the late 1960s, journalists and scholars chose to hold the new technologies responsible for the beginning of another rapid drop in fertility that began in 1964–5. By 1975 the English birth rate was down to 12.2 per 1000, below the lowest point previously reached in 1933.[101] The media bewailed the increased numbers of 'childless women', ignoring the facts that although family size had declined the percentage of women bearing children had actually increased. In America, 20 per cent of women born in the 1901–10 cohort were childless, whereas only 7.3 per cent of the 1931–5 cohort were so. In Britain in 1921, 83 per cent of women married by age 45; 96 per cent in the 1960s.[102] In short, the twentieth century witnessed a transition from a world in which it was common for some people to have large families while others never married or reproduced, to a world in which almost everyone married and had a small family. Indeed, the continual barrage of propaganda launched by sexologists, doctors and educators in favour of efficient sexuality, motherhood and childrearing, begun in the early 1900s and still showing no signs of letting up, had successfully implanted the notion that a woman who did not reproduce was somehow incomplete. Sanger and Stopes would have been pleased to see that birth control, in place of undermining the ideology of motherhood, had become its essential prop.

Birth control was both a cause and an effect of a number of dramatic changes which took place in a little over a century in the average woman's life cycle. Completed family size dropped from about five children in the mid-nineteenth century to about two since the 1920s. A mother traditionally continued having her children right on into her late thirties and even into her forties. In the modern world they were clustered together, so that by twenty-eight she was free of childbearing. With longer life expectancy, this meant that the average woman would live for another fifty or so years after her last delivery, whereas her nineteenth-century counterpart spent most of her life bearing or nursing offspring.

Most women after World War II accordingly expected both to marry and to have a career. In Britain, only 10 per cent of mothers were employed in 1900, as opposed to 50 per cent in 1976. Marriages that once lasted less than thirty years now could last at least forty-five years. With longer life expectancy it became normal to see all of one's grandchildren born. Only in the 1970s did divorce 'compensate' for the decline in spousal deaths as a cause of family break-up.[103] In the nineteenth-century, the single-parent family was due to widowhood; in the twentieth, it was due to divorce.

Those who bemoaned the 'decline of the family' forgot that children in previous centuries had been sent out early in life into domestic service or apprenticeships and married late in life. In the post-war world, they stayed in school and lived at home until their late teens and married in their early twenties. Fears of a 'generation gap' and 'juvenile delinquency' became staple topics for magazine writers, but a longer experience of dependency could only be expected to result in the emergence of new and occasionally disturbing forms of youth culture. Generations once succeeded each other; now they overlapped. The pursuit of 'love' was one way in which young people could achieve emotional independence from their parents. Increased premarital sexual activity, plotted by Kinsey and others and permitted in part by a rise in contraceptive use, usually led on to marriage. It could hardly be called an 'emancipation'.[104]

Social scientists in the 1970s hailed the rise of the 'symmetrical family', as the last remnants of working-class traditions of separate sexual cultures appeared to be eradicated.[105] Class and ethnic demographic differentials did not disappear, but a general pattern of early marriage and small family size became true of all groups. The old joke that the family was reduced in size to fit Ford's four-seater car seemed not that far off the mark. Perhaps the most dramatic symbol of this 'homogenization of experience'[106] was the control of menstruation that resulted from the taking of oral contraceptives. Every user now had strict twenty-eight-day cycles.

From the 1960s on, the mass production of cheap clothing and foodstuffs undermined the rationale of full-time housework. Not only married women, but in the late 1970s something like a half of the women with children, surged into the work force. It was the demand that such numbers made for control of their reproduction that assured the liberalization of abortion and the provision of oral contraceptives. These in turn provided women with a greater freedom to pursue career and educational opportunities. Many embraced the feminist cause, which soon turned its critical gaze on medicine.

Women, it was realized, had gained more effective methods of birth control only at the price of assuming full responsibility for the inconveniences and risks involved. No one wanted to have to rely again on coitus interruptus, but the argument could be made that, as unsatisfactory as it might have been, it at least required a high level of male involvement. Moreover, the increased sophistication of contraceptives did not lessen the fear of unwanted pregnancy. An unexpected pregnancy was, for those whose hopes of a perfect regulation of reproduction had been raised by doctors, made all the more frightening. The medical profession had, of course, not been particularly interested in sparing women undesired pregnancies, and had only been forced to respond to the arrival of the contraceptive pill and the liberalization of the law on abortion. Since it could not stop either, the profession simply sought to control them. Medical responsibility, not women's autonomy, was the profession's key concern. The new wave of feminists were in effect asking the question – which Stopes and Sanger, had they been alive, might well have regarded as some perverse throwback to the Victorian age – whether it was possible that women in being given better contraceptives were in fact losing control of their own bodies.[107]

Notes

1 Jane Schneider and Peter Schneider, 'Demographic Transitions in a Sicilian Town', *Journal of Family History*, 9 (1984), p. 258. Fertility in northern Italy fell rapidly between the wars; in the south, only after World War II. Massimo Livi-Bacci, *A History of Italian Fertility During the Last Two Centuries* (Princeton University Press, Princeton, NJ, 1977).

2 Marie-Monique Huss, 'Pronatalism in the Inter-War Period in France', *Journal of Contemporary History*, (1990), p. 52; Colin Dyer, *Population and Society in Twentieth Century France* (Hodder and Stoughton, London, 1978), pp. 78–81.

3 Margaret Sanger, *An Autobiography* (Norton, New York, 1938).

4 Mary Ware Dennett, *Birth Control Laws: Shall We Keep Them, Change Them or Abolish Them?* (Hitchcock, New York, 1926).

5 Ruth Hall, *Passionate Crusader: The Life of Marie Stopes* (Harcourt Brace Jovanovich, New York, 1977); Ellen Holtzman, 'The Pursuit of Married Love: Women's Attitudes Towards Sexuality and Marriage in Great Britain, 1918–1939', *Journal of Social History*, 16 (1982), pp. 39–52.

6 Marie Stopes, *'The First Five Thousand', Being the First Report of the First Birth Control Clinic in the British Empire* (John Bale, London, 1925).

7 Havelock Ellis, *The Task of Social Hygiene* (Constable, London, 1912).

8 C. P. Blacker, *Birth Control and the State: A Plea and Forecast* (Kegan Paul, London, 1926), p. 34; *The Practitioner*, 111 (July 1923), p. 24.

9 Eugenic concerns led to the funding of the first serious sex research, thanks to John D. Rockefeller, who established in 1913 the American Social Hygiene Association and its research arm, the Bureau of Social Hygiene. Little work was done on 'normal' human sexuality, however, until Alfred Kinsey's investigations in the 1940s. Vern L. Bullough, 'The Rockefellers and Sex Research', *The Journal of Sex Research*, 21 (1985), pp. 113–25.

10 Margaret Sanger, *The Pivot of Civilization* (Brentano, New York, 1922), pp. 86ff.

11 Marie Stopes, *Radiant Motherhood* (Putnam's, London, 1928), p. 207.

12 Sanger, *The Pivot of Civilization*, p. 254.

13 Marie Stopes, *Contraception (Birth Control): Its Theory, History and Practice* (Putnam's, London, 1923), p. 37.

14 Marie Stopes, *Marriage in My Time* (Rich and Cowan, London, 1935), p. 116.

15 Stopes, *Radiant Motherhood*, p. 116.

16 Marie Stopes, *Married Love* (Fifield, London, 1918), p. xi.

17 Stopes, *Married Love*, pp. 43–4; Stopes, *Marriage*, p. 64; Marie Stopes, *Enduring Passion* (Hogarth, London, 1928), p. 90; Stopes, *Radiant Motherhood*, p. 3.

18 Dorothy Dunbar Bromley, *Birth Control: Its Use and Misuse* (Harper, New York, 1934), p. xiv.

19 R.H. Higonnet, J. Jenson, S. Michel and M. C. Weitz (eds), *Behind the Lines: Gender and the Two World Wars* (Yale University Press, New Haven, 1987).

20 Havelock Ellis, *Studies in the Psychology of Sex* (Random House, New York, 1936 [first edition 1906]), vol. II, ch. 12; Paul Robinson, *The Modernization of Sex* (Harper and Row, New York, 1976).

21 Theodore H. van de Velde, *Ideal Marriage: Its Physiology and Technique*, tr. Stella Browne (Random House, New York, 1926). Recent studies arguing that women were 'conscripted' into hetero-

246 THE TRIUMPH OF FAMILY PLANNING

sexuality have curiously slighted the importance of the birth control advocates. See Margaret Jackson, 'Sexual Liberation or Social Control', *Women's Studies International Forum*, 6 (1983), pp. 1–18; Sheila Jeffreys, *The Spinster and Her Enemies: Feminism and Sexuality, 1880–1930* (Pandora, London, 1985).

22 Jackson, 'Sexual Liberation or Social Control', pp. 1–18; Robert A. Nye, 'Sex Difference and Male Homosexuality in French Medical Discourse', *Bulletin of the History of Medicine*, 63 (1989), pp. 32–51.

23 Jane Lewis, *The Politics of Motherhood* (Croom Helm, London, 1980), pp. 96–8; Luc Boltanski, *Prime éducation et morale de classe* (Mouton, Paris, 1969), pp. 57–70.

24 V. A. Zelizer, *Pricing the Priceless Child: The Changing Social Value of Children* (Basic Books, New York, 1985), p. 90.

25 Margaret Leonora Eyles, *The Woman in the Little House* (Grant Richards, London, 1922), p. 129.

26 Stopes, *Enduring Passion*, p. 28. See also Elizabeth Roberts, 'Working Wives and Their Families', in *Population and Society in Britain, 1850–1980*, ed. Theo Baker and Michael Drake (Batsford, London, 1982), pp. 154–5.

27 Linda Gordon, *Woman's Body, Woman's Right: A Social History of Birth Control in America* (Grossman, New York, 1976), p. 324.

28 Lesley A. Hall, '"Somehow Very Distasteful": Doctors, Men, and Sexual Problems Between the Wars', *Journal of Contemporary History*, 20 (1985), pp. 553–74.

29 Diana Gittens, *Fair Sex: Family Size and Structure, 1900–1939* (Hutchinson, London, 1982).

30 Margery Spring Rice, *Working-Class Wives: Their Health and Conditions* (Penguin, London, 1939).

31 Edward Bernstein, 'Decline in the Birth-Rate, Nationality, and Civilization', in *Population and Birth Control*, eds Eden and Cedar Paul (Critic and Guide, New York, 1917), p. 164.

32 The Woman's Cooperative Guild declared itself in support of birth control in 1923, and in 1924 a Worker's Birth Control Group was formed after the Labour Party resolved at its annual conference that welfare clinics should provide mothers with contraceptive information. Stopes was dismayed that most feminists avoided the issue through the 1920s. In North America as well, only the Depression drove leaders of the women's movement into open support of family limitation. Lewis, *The Politics of Motherhood*, pp. 197–8; Brian Harrison, *Prudent Revolutionaries: Portraits of Feminists Between the Wars* (Clarendon, Oxford, 1987), pp. 63, 78, 110, 282.

33 Marie Stopes, *A Letter to Working Mothers* (Mothers' Clinic, London, 1923), p. 6.

34 Margaret Sanger, *Motherhood in Bondage* (Brentano, New York, 1928), p. 294.

35 Stopes, *Married Love*, p. 71.

36 Stopes, *Contraception*, p. 70.
37 Sanger, *Motherhood in Bondage*, p. 302
38 Sanger, *An Autobiography*, p. 87.
39 Stopes, convinced that she knew more about contraception than any doctor, did employ physicians, but trained nurses and midwives to staff her clinic and was not as vigorous as Sanger in wooing the medical profession. Sanger had, moreover, to compete for leadership of the American birth-control movement with Mary Ware Dennett, who was opposed to the medical monopoly. American Birth Control League Papers, 110.2, Houghton Library, Harvard University.
40 Sanger, *Motherhood in Bondage*, pp. 294–7.
41 An American described withdrawal as follows: the husband's job was to keep his head; the wife's job was to lose hers. H.W. Long, *Sane Sex and Sane Sex Living* (Eugenics Publishing Company, New York, 1919), pp. 117–22.
42 Sanger, *Motherhood in Bondage*, p. 410.
43 Alice Jenkins, *Law for the Rich* (Skilton, London, 1960), p. 21.
44 James Woycke, *Birth Control in Germany, 1871–1933* (Routledge, London, 1988), pp. 68–76.
45 W. G. Crosbie, 'Syphilis in Relation to Abortion, Stillbirths, and Infant Mortality', *American Journal of Obstetrics and Gynaecology*, (1922), pp. 42–4.
46 Janet Campbell, *Maternal Mortality* (HMSO, London, 1924); Janet Campbell, *Protection of Motherhood* (HMSO, London, 1927); Barbara Brookes, *Abortion in England, 1900–1967* (Croom Helm, London, 1988), p. 43.
47 Madeleine Simms and Keith Hindell, *Abortion Law Reformed* (Owen, London, 1971), p. 67.
48 John Peel and Malcolm Potts, *Textbook of Contraceptive Practice* (Cambridge University Press, Cambridge, 1969), p. 173.
49 *Canadian Medical Association Journal*, 29 (1933), p. 445.
50 Frederick J. Taussig, *Abortion: Spontaneous and Induced: Medical and Social Aspects* (Mosby, St Louis, 1936), p. 368.
51 Ellis, *Studies in the Psychology of Sex*, pp. 601–10; Madeleine Simms, 'Midwives and Abortion in the 1930s', *Midwife and Health Visitor*, 10 (1974), pp. 114–16.
52 Moya Woodside, 'Attitude of Women Abortionists', *The Howard Journal*, 11 (1963), pp. 93–112.
53 Madeleine Kerr, *The People of Ship Street* (Routledge, London, 1958), pp. 137, 174.
54 Helmut Gruber, 'Sexuality in "Red Vienna": Socialist Party Conceptions and Programs and Working-Class Life, 1920–1934', *International Labor and Working-Class History*, 31 (1987), pp. 37–68.
55 Bromley, *Birth Control: Its Use and Misuse*, pp. 3–4.
56 F. W. Stella Browne, 'Women and Birth Control', in Paul and Paul, *Population*, p. 254.

57 Alice Jenkins, *Conscript Parenthood: The Problem of Secret Abortions* (Standring, London, 1940); Brookes, *Abortion*, pp. 79–104.
58 John Keown, *Abortion, Doctors and the Law: Some Aspects of the Legal Regulation of Abortion in England from 1803 to 1982* (Cambridge University Press, Cambridge, 1988), pp. 49–108.
59 *Birth Control News*, August 1923, p. 4.
60 Stopes, *A Letter to Working Mothers*, pp. 5, 6, 8.
61 American Birth Control League Papers, 110.5, Houghton Library, Harvard University; Sanger, *An Autobiography*, pp. 88–92, 216, 285, 449; David M. Kennedy, *Birth Control in America: The Career of Margaret Sanger* (Yale University Press, New Haven, 1970), pp. 16–17.
62 *Birth Control News*, June 1926, p. 2; October 1923, p. 2; May 1924, p. 2; September 1925, p. 1; February 1927, p. 2; May 1928, p. 2.
63 Over three-quarters of the clients of both the US and UK clinics were already employing, with a good deal of success, the traditional methods of contraception – withdrawal, condom and douche. A study of 10,000 American case histories of clients revealed that in only 4 per cent was the diaphragm used. The author noted that half the women claimed never to have aborted; the other half reported having had on average two abortions each. Marie E. Kopp, *Birth Control in Practice: Analysis of Ten Thousand Case Histories of the Birth Control Clinical Research Bureau* (McBride, New York, 1934), pp. 55, 109–10, 121–6.
64 Steven Mintz and Susan Kellogg, *Domestic Revolutions: A Social History of American Family Life* (Free Press, New York, 1988), pp. 111–15.
65 R. A. Soloway, *Birth Control and the Population Question in England, 1877–1930* (University of North Carolina Press, Chapel Hill, 1982), p. 277. In the Depression Stopes did describe a simple contraceptive of an oil-soaked sponge; see Marie Stopes, *Preliminary Notes . . . From 10,000 Cases Attending the Pioneer Mothers' Clinic* (Mothers' Clinic for Constructive Birth Control, London, 1930), pp. 12–13.
66 Stopes, *Preliminary Notes*, pp. 20–1.
67 Lewis, *The Politics of Motherhood*, p. 126; Margarete Sandelowski, *Pain, Pleasure, and American Childbirth: From the Twilight Sleep to the Read Method, 1924–1960* (Greenwood Press, Westport, Conn., 1984).
68 Sir James Marchant, ed., *Medical Views on Birth Control* (Hopkinson, London, 1926), pp. x, 63, 94–5.
69 F. H. Rodin to Anna Kennedy, 29 April 1923, American Birth Control League Papers, Houghton Library, Harvard University.
70 Jo Manton, *Elizabeth Garrett Anderson* (Methuen, London, 1965), p. 284.
71 John Peel, 'Contraception and the Medical Profession', *Population Studies*, 18 (1964), p. 144.

72 The Schlesinger–Rockefeller Family Planning Oral History Project, directed by James Reed and deposited at Radcliffe College, provides a fascinating account of the development on the margins of respectable medicine from the 1930s onwards, of a network of activists such as Alan Guttmacher, Alfred Kinsey, Robert Dickinson and Mary Calderone, involved in maternal health, contraception, marriage counselling and sex research.

73 Brookes, *Abortion in England*, p. 2.

74 Robert H. to Marie Stopes, 1 July 1921; Winnifred R. to Marie Stopes, 20 March 1923; Mary W. to Marie Stopes, 25 September 1924; A. C. M. to Marie Stopes, 19 January 1933; Stopes Papers, British Library.

75 Leo J. Latz, *The Rhythm of Sterility and Fertility in Women* (Latz Foundation, Chicago, 1932), pp. 60–1.

76 Angus McLaren and Arlene Tigar McLaren, *The Bedroom and the State: The Changing Practices and Politics of Contraception and Abortion in Canada, 1880–1980* (McClelland and Stewart, Toronto, 1986), pp. 116–20.

77 James Reed, *From Private Vice to Public Virtue: The Birth Control Movement and American Society Since 1830* (Basic Books, New York, 1978), p. 121.

78 Enid Charles, *The Twilight of Parenthood* (Norton, New York, 1934); Joseph J. Spengler, *France Faces Depopulation* (Duke University Press, Durham, NC, 1938); D. V. Glass, *The Struggle for Population* (Clarendon, Oxford, 1936), p. 87; Michael S. Teitelbaum and Jay M. Winter, *The Fear of Population Decline* (Academic Press, New York, 1985), pp. 45–62.

79 Lewis, *The Politics of Motherhood*, p. 199.

80 Nancy Cott, *The Grounding of Modern Feminism* (Basic Books, New York, 1987), p. 165.

81 E. Lewis-Faning, *Report on an Inquiry into Family Limitation and Its Influence on Human Fertility During the Past Fifty Years* (HMSO, London, 1949), pp. 8–11; Gittens, *Fair Sex*, p. 162.

82 Griselda Rowntree and Rachel M. Pierce, 'Birth Control in Britain', *Population Studies*, 15 (1961), p. 128.

83 A classic depiction of the white-coated doctor lecturing her patient on the use of the diaphragm was provided in Mary McCarthy's novel *The Group* (Harcourt Brace, New York, 1954), pp. 66–9.

84 Margaret Sanger and Hannah M. Stone (eds), *The Practice of Contraception* (Baillière, London, 1931), pp. 17, 29. In her first pamphlet, *Family Limitation* (1914), written in her radical phase, Sanger had likewise provided recipes for simple astringent douches and cocoa-butter pessaries, and praised the sponge and condom. In her pursuit of medical legitimation she later swung her support to the diaphragm.

85 McLaren and McLaren, *The Bedroom and the State*, pp. 92–115.

86 An uncritical account of his life is provided by Doone Williams and

Greer Williams, *Every Child a Wanted Child: Clarence James Gamble, M. D., and His Work in the Birth Control Movement* (Countway Library, Boston, 1978); more useful is Reed, *From Private Vice*, pp. 225–77.

87 The new generation of plastic IUDs produced in the 1960s, though more effective than any other contraceptive, were ultimately found to produce the same sorts of infection.

88 Reed, *From Private Vice*, p. 239.

89 Barbara Brookes, 'Women and Reproduction', in Jane Lewis (ed.), *Labour and Love: Women's Experience of Home and Family, 1850–1940* (Blackwell, Oxford, 1986), p. 165.

90 Janet Evans, 'The Communist Party of the Soviet Union and the Woman's Question: The Case of the 1936 Decree "In Defense of Mother and Child"', *Journal of Contemporary History*, 16 (1981), pp. 758–62; Denise Detragiache, 'Un aspect de la politique démographique de l'Italie fasciste: la répression de l'avortement', *Mélanges de l'école française de Rome*, 92 (1980), pp. 691–735.

91 D. V. Glass, *Population: Policies and Movements in Europe* (Cass, London, 1967); R. Bridenthal, A. Grossman and Marion Kaplan (eds), *When Biology Became Destiny* (Monthly Review Press, New York, 1984); on Vichy France see C. Watson, 'Birth Control and Abortion in France Since 1939', *Population Studies*, 5 (1951–2), pp. 261–86; Roger H. Guerrand, *La libre maternité, 1869–1969* (Casterman, Paris, 1971); Francis Ronsin, *La grève des ventres: propagande néo-malthusienne et baisse de la natalité en France, 19e–20e siècles* (Aubier Montaigne, Paris, 1980), pp. 193–232.

92 The Second World War provided many male conscripts with an unexpected education in contraception, inasmuch as millions of condoms were distributed for protection from venereal disease. But the assertion of the manufacturers of Blanchard's Apiol, a popular abortifacient, that their product was dispensed to the Women's Armies was undoubtedly bogus. See Wellcome Institute, Contemporary Medical History Archives, MCS/B 23.

93 Surveys found that a third of the babies born in France between 1959 and 1962 had been undesired. Dyer, *Population and Society*, p. 143.

94 J. M. Winter, 'The Demographic Consequences of the War', in *War and Social Change*, ed. Harold L. Smith (Manchester University Press, Manchester, 1986), pp. 156–70; Gordon, *Woman's Body, Woman's Right*, pp. 341–91. On the first expressions of post-war American feminist unease caused by the glorification of the housewife, see Betty Friedan, *The Feminine Mystique* (Norton, New York, 1963), and Wini Breinis, 'Domineering Mothers in the 1950s: Image and Reality', *Women's Studies International Forum*, 8 (1985), pp. 604–8.

95 In the United States, contraception became a key concern of the Millbank Memorial Fund, the Scripps Foundation and the Rockefeller

Foundation; see James Reed, 'Public Policy on Human Reproduction', *Journal of Social History*, 18 (1985), pp. 392–5.

96 Hans Simmer, 'On The History of Hormonal Contraception', *Contraception*, 1 (1970), pp. 3–27; 3 (1971), pp. 1–19.

97 B. P. Wiesner, 'The Hormones and Their Control of the Reproductive System', *Eugenics Review*, 22 (1930), pp. 19–26; Peel, 'Contraception', p. 142; Merriley Borell, 'Organotherapy and the Emergence of Reproductive Endocrinology', *Journal of the History of Biology*, 18 (1985), pp. 1–30.

98 R. Christian Johnson, 'Feminism, Philanthropy and Science in the Development of the Oral Contraceptive Pill', *Pharmacy in History*, 19 (1977), pp. 63–77; Reed, *From Private Vice*, pp. 317–66.

99 Reed, *From Private Vice*, pp. 352–3; J. B. Thomas, *Introduction to Human Embryology* (Lea and Febiger, Philadelphia, 1968), pp. 45–6.

100 Simms and Hindell, *Abortion Law Reformed*. Eastern bloc nations, with the apparent desire of having a more direct power to enforce population policy, tended to permit abortion, but restrict access to contraception.

101 Harold Silver and Judith Ryder, *Modern English Society* (Methuen, London, 1985), p. 149.

102 Mary-Jo Bane, *Here to Stay: American Families in the Twentieth Century* (Basic Books, New York, 1976); Silver and Ryder, *Modern English Society*, p. 297.

103 Michael Anderson, 'The Emergence of the Modern Life Cycle in Britain', *Social History*, 10 (1985), pp. 69–88.

104 Martine Segalen, *Historical Anthropology of the Family* (Cambridge University Press, Cambridge, 1986), pp. 139–50; Ellene K. Rothman, *Hands and Hearts: A History of Courtship in America* (Basic Books, New York, 1984).

105 Michael Young and Peter Willmott, *The Symmetrical Family: A Study of Work and Leisure in the London Region* (Routledge, London, 1973).

106 Anderson, 'The Emergence of the Modern Life Cycle'.

107 US Senate Subcommittee hearings on the safety of the pill took place in 1970. On popular fears see Barbara Seaman, *The Doctors' Case Against the Pill* (Wyden, New York, 1969).

Conclusion

By the 1980s, something like 90 per cent of married couples in most western countries were employing contraceptives. An international survey of contraceptive users found that 33 per cent had been sterilized, 20 per cent employed the oral contraceptive, 15 per cent the IUD and 10 per cent the condom. It needs to be stressed, however, how recent this shift to modern fertility-limitation methods is. In countries like France and Czechoslovakia, for example, withdrawal was still, until the arrival of the pill in the 1970s, the most widely employed means of birth control.[1] Yet in North America the oral contraceptive was, by the mid–1970s, already viewed with increased wariness by the married, associated as it was with increased incidences of cancer and blood clotting. Young women continued to find its effectiveness and convenience irresistible. Some, worried by reports of its side-effects, turned in the 1970s to IUDs, which finally seemed safe thanks to the development of inert plastics and antibiotics that could control accompanying local infections. In fact IUDs, because they were not drugs, were neither initially investigated nor regulated by the United States Food and Drug Administration. The distribution of four million Dalkon Shield IUDs between 1971 and 1975, which resulted in a world-wide rash of pelvic infections, miscarriages, congenital birth defects and maternal deaths, cast a shadow over all high-tech contraceptives.[2] In North America, where the pill and IUD were first employed, a swing back to such barrier methods as the condom and diaphragm occurred in the late 1970s. The protection which sheaths offered against transmission of the AIDS virus dramatically increased their popularity amongst the single.

Today the married, once they have achieved a desired family size, increasingly accept sterilization as the simplest and safest way to avoid pregnancy. Over a third of North American males eventually have a vasectomy. The percentage of couples who rely on sterilization for fertility control is, however, not really comparable to that using other methods which can be employed and abandoned; sterilization reversals have a 50 to 75 per cent success rate, but entail expensive medical procedures. Sterilization has other drawbacks, including its culturally perceived threat to virility. The fact that the vasectomy is a far safer and simpler operation than tubal ligation, but that in most countries the latter operation is more common, suggests women pay a high price for fertility control.[3] Even in North America, evidence has been produced that sterilizations have been forced on those women whose fertility health officials regard as a social danger. Such operations were first compulsorily carried out on asylum inmates in the early twentieth century for the eugenic purpose of limiting the reproduction of the 'unfit'. Similar concerns obviously motivated the doctors who, in the 1970s, forced sterilizations on poor women from ethnic minority groups seeking abortion or needing Caesarian sections.[4] Similar reports surfaced in Australia in the 1980s that Aboriginal girls were, without their knowledge and consent, being injected with the contraceptive drug Depo-Provera by government health agencies for the purpose of restricting the black birth rate.[5]

Similarly coercive methods were employed in India and China, but it is increasingly recognized by family planners that effective fertility control has to be socially grounded. When fertility rates began to fall in the Third World in the 1970s, it was not simply due to the Third World countries' adoption of modern contraceptives. Such devices had been delivered to them from the 1950s on with little visible result. What made the difference was when use of contraception was combined with a shift to later ages of marriage. Coale has noted that in countries like South Korea, Taiwan and Sri Lanka, the raising of women's age of marriage in the course of the twentieth century from about 17 to 24 played a more significant role than birth control in the reduction of fertility.[6] The adoption of a family system in which large numbers of children are no longer culturally expected to provide wealth and social status had to precede the acceptance of modern contraception.[7] Contraceptives can, in short, be most confidently predicted to work in a society where fertility rates are already dropping.[8] But they can also undermine whatever success has already been gained by traditional fertility-control measures. For example, extended breastfeeding, which in the developing world is responsible for the avoidance of more pregnancies than any other birth-control method, can be threatened by hormonal contraceptives.[9]

Many of the activities of family planners deserve applause. But the idea that progressive changes in attitudes towards procreation have to come from outside the community in the form of 'education' is increasingly questioned. The success of the family planners in 'colonizing' the procreative culture of the masses has been limited. The slow advance of modern contraceptive practices is best understood as a complicated process of acceptance, resistance and accommodation. All family planners do not, of course, share the same views. As birth-control services have become increasingly professionalized and bureaucratized, their leadership has become ever more concerned with maintenance of social control. But their field and clinic workers, attracted to their calling by feminist or political concerns, often have a distinctly different view from that of management regarding their relationship to clients.[10]

The early birth controllers argued that the spread of contraception would lead to the elimination of abortion. Turning the argument around, one might argue that the failure of the abortion rates to decline provided evidence that many women could not employ 'rational' contraceptive strategies, but had to go on 'taking chances' with abortion.[11] America has one of the highest rates of abortion, approaching 40 per cent of births; the rate is closer to 20 per cent in most other western nations. In North America and Britain, the majority of women seeking abortions are now under nineteen and 50–75 per cent are unmarried; in eastern bloc nations, the majority are over twenty and only 13–37 per cent are unmarried.[12]

Teenage pregnancies have become a particular worry in the United States, which has a higher rate than most industrialized countries. By age eighteen, 25 per cent of black American women and 10 per cent of white are mothers; 90 per cent of the children born to black teenagers and 40 per cent of those born to white are illegitimate.[13] Despite the obvious rise of sexual activity, the overall rate of teenage pregnancies is down from the peak established in the 1950s, due to the wider availability of contraception and abortion. The New Right, which expresses its shock at high rates of bastardy, is at the same time opposed to the sex education and family planning programmes that play a key role in limiting such births. The Reagan administration, in order to prevent teenagers from having access to oral contraceptives, purposely exaggerated their associated health dangers.[14]

Women are often blamed by conservatives for high abortion rates. The truth is that women do not 'want' abortions; they need them.[15] Recourse to induction of miscarriage has increased, but the service is still firmly in the hands of doctors. Abortion is available 'on request', never 'on demand'. The creation of abortion pills, such as the French product RU 486 or Mifepristone, does raise the possibility of women's freeing themselves from reliance on clinics and hospitals. The public protests in France and elsewhere that news of the abortion pill's distribution elicited in 1989 served as a reminder, however, that politics will necessarily play a major role in the success of such products.

Teenage births posed problems in the 1980s; so too did the rising numbers of first births to older women. Those intent on launching a working career had to put off thoughts of having children. By the 1970s, one-quarter of married women in their late twenties were still childless.[16] The demand for reproductive technologies was fueled at least in part by increased numbers of such women postponing childbirth until their thirties. Those who did get pregnant accepted the need for ultrasound and amniocentesis to check for fetal deformities, such as Down's syndrome (trisomy 21), associated with late childbearing. Those who found that they were infertile and chose not to adopt (which was made more difficult as the supply of babies was restricted by teenage mothers either aborting or keeping their infants) turned to infertility clinics for assistance.

The purported ease with which both teenagers and career women could call upon medical assistance to relieve them of their childbearing problems aroused the ire of conservatives. In Europe and North America, the New Right launched a moral revolution in the mid–1970s against 'easy access' to contraception and abortion. Some conservatives lauded 'natural' methods of contraception. In Quebec, for example, the 'sympto-thermal' rhythm method was popularized by Catholic couples hoping to limit family size while remaining true to the Church's teachings.[17] American fundamentalists also declared themselves willing to sacrifice effectiveness to 'naturalness'.[18]

Because contraceptives are so widely accepted – Catholics proving to be as likely to employ them as Protestants – the Right has focused its attack on abortion. But as this study has argued, and as legal scholars now recognize, it is difficult in practice to draw a sharp line between fertility-control strategies. If abortion were outlawed, the IUD and the low-dose pill, which prevent the fertilized ovum from lodging in the uterus wall, logically would also have to be criminalized.[19] In any event, the Romanian experience suggests that though abortion can be banned, it cannot be prevented. The Romanian government, shocked by statistics that revealed that there were four times as many abortions as live births, outlawed abortion in 1966. The fertility rate momentarily surged upward, but within a few years it returned to its declining trajectory as women found ways round the law.

The real importance of the popular campaigns being waged against reproductive choice in North America and Europe is that they focus attention on what society regards as women's appropriate social roles. As Kristin Luker has pointed out, much of the hostility to abortion comes from those who believe it is a method by which middle-class, professional women violate traditional gender norms. Although Catholic priests and fundamentalist ministers provide the leadership of the 'pro-life' movement, full-time housewives who do not work outside the home and feel that their procreative labours are devalued by a society which blurs sex roles provide much of the campaign's grass-roots support. There is a logic in such women's thinking. Their family structure is based on a bargain between a husband who provides financial support and a wife who in return provides sex and child care. Easily accessible abortion and contraception, they fear, undercut the argument that a woman can only risk providing sexual favours if guaranteed the protection of a traditional marriage.[20]

The opponents of contraception and abortion have long argued that birth-control methods actually serve to incite promiscuity. Women will only remain chaste, they assert, if they have a good reason to fear becoming pregnant. There is little evidence to support such claims.[21] Certainly the defenders of both birth control and abortion traditionally came from those elements in society dedicated to shoring up rather than undermining the traditional family. Nevertheless, conservatives are no doubt correct in sensing that modern forms of fertility control do provide options and allow individuals to make choices. What the New Right fails to explain is why, as free enterprisers who zealously defend free economic decision making, they do not accept the morality of reproductive choice. But the most vehement are only too happy to accept such contradictions; they want the state out of the boardrooms but back in the bedrooms. Women's freedoms, they admit, simply have to be limited.[22] But interestingly enough, the religious fundamentalists' belief that women should return to more 'natural' methods of childbearing are shared by some feminists.

The second wave of feminism took some time to respond to the post-1960s contraceptive revolution. Nineteenth-century maternal feminists had been suspicious that birth control might deprive women of the identity and status that they enjoyed as mothers. In the inter-war period, the women's movement slowly swung round to the notion advanced by Stopes and Sanger that women had to be freed from unwanted pregnancies. Although feminists were thin on the ground until the 1960s, it was in this light that the oral contraceptive and the IUD were welcomed. Simone de Beauvoir, Sherry Ortner and Betty Friedan all stressed the idea that maternity had been used to keep women down.[23] Shulamith Firestone went so far as to welcome the prospect of 'artificial wombs', which would finally liberate women from subservience to reproduction. Firestone's book was badly timed; it appeared in 1970, just as the first concerns regarding the oral contraceptive were voiced.[24]

In the late 1970s a new generation of feminists, inspired by an ecological sensitivity that exalted natural processes and in response to the increased medicalization of childbirth and the reports of the hidden dangers of new contraceptives, swung back to the position that reproduction was something which empowered women, not something from which they had to be freed. Numerous self-help health groups, the most famous being the Boston Women's Health Collective, emerged, in which women sought to liberate themselves from dependency on doctors.[25] 'Natural childbirth' was lauded, in contrast to medicalized deliveries associated with the rising rates of induction, episiotomies and Caesarian sections which rendered the mother little more than a passive observer of her own delivery.[26]

The desire to reclaim motherhood from medical surveillance and return to 'natural' childbearing was testified to in demands in

North America for the reestablishment and legitimation of midwifery, in the success of the La Leche league with its stress on breastfeeding on demand, and in the emergence of the 'Family Bed' movement with its desire to break down the barriers between parents and children.[27] Such campaigns did not go unopposed; in 1972 a Los Angeles woman who fitted diaphragms was charged with practising medicine without a licence, and midwives were continually harrassed by the medical profession.[28] The irony is that this return to 'natural' methods found much of its support in the ranks of the urban middle class, who could bear the expenditures of time and energy that others regarded as unaffordable. It would be a mistake, however, to dismiss the critique of the medicalization of childbirth as no more than a 'consumers' rebellion'.

In the spring of 1989 a Rockford, Illinois, prosecutor sought to have a woman indicted for causing the death of her newborn baby by using cocaine while pregnant.[29] Until recently it was generally assumed that we had escaped the policing of reproduction which in the traditional world was carried out by the church, family and community. The medicalization and professionalization of fertility control have raised some doubts. Feminists particularly worry that the new medical technologies are shifting the attention of doctors from the mother to the fetus as patient. This process can be traced back at least to the 1920s, when hospitalization of births was increasingly undertaken to produce 'pink, brisk babies'.[30] From the 1930s Caesarian sections began to be carried out, not for the benefit of the mother, but for that of the child. More recently, court orders have been sought by governments and individuals to intervene on behalf of the fetus against the mother in everything from attempts to block abortions to charges filed against mothers for injuries suffered in the womb.[31] What such actions signify is the desire to abstract reproduction, to isolate the mother and suggest her fertility choices are not a product of her social, cultural and sexual needs.

The idea that procreation would be simplified if the mother's interest could be ignored is not new. Hippolytus complained, 'If only we could have children without the help of women!' Two thousand years after this extraordinary lament, Drs Patrick Steptoe and Robert Edwards could congratulate themselves on dramatically advancing such a possibility. In 1978 they announced to the world that they had managed the birth of Elizabeth Brown, the first 'test-tube' baby. Having begun this study with a depiction of the way the Greeks sought both to enhance and to restrict fertility, it seems only appropriate to bring the story full circle in concluding with an examination of the linkage of contemporary reproductive technologies with modern methods of fertility control.

Ironically, it is but a small step to move from Stopes's and Sanger's heartbreaking depictions of women in the 1920s who could not stop having children to doctors' heartbreaking depictions of women in the 1980s who cannot have them. Both issues posed similar sorts of problems and often attracted the same researchers. Medical scientists like Pincus and Rock, though best known for their pioneering work on the oral contraceptive pill, began their research with the goal of employing hormones to cure infertility. Some things did, of course, change between the 1920s and 1980s. The medical profession was publicly opposed to birth control throughout the nineteenth and most of the twentieth century; today its attitude towards embryonic research is more 'liberal' than the general public's. Fertility control was once a non-medical procedure for which medical help was only occasionally requested. As such its provision threatened to reduce aspiring professionals to the level of tradesmen; today both fertility control and artificial reproduction are medicalized processes that serve to demonstrate in the most dramatic fashion doctors' power over life and death.

The medicalization of procreation has clearly changed the nature of childbearing. But to what extent? Some fear that now doctors play a more important role in procreative decision making than parents. Barbara Katz Rothman has outlined one aspect of this concern in her discussion of the emergence of what she calls the 'tentative pregnancy'.[32] Thanks to amniocentesis, ultrasound scanning and other methods of detecting fetal abnormalities, women are today in the position of deciding on the basis of medical advice whether a pregnancy should be interrupted or brought to term. Such technologies have enormous potential value, but raise troubling issues. They allow, on the one hand, parents to choose early therapeutic abortions and so spare themselves the tragic births of severely handicapped children. Potential offspring are not forced to endure years of needless suffering. On the other hand, the question is raised of whether women's decisions to terminate or continue such pregnancies are 'freely' made. Do genetic counsellors simply provide the 'facts', or do they influence the decision? The marvellous new methods of observing fetal life are wielded by doctors and at the very least undermine the significance of women's testimony and experience of pregnancy.[33] The possibility of having only 'perfect' babies makes the mother who decides to go through with a pregnancy knowing that the fetus is handicapped seem somehow perverse. The congenitally disabled risk further stigmatization when the question is raised why they should have ever been born. The 'eliminative approach' threatens to undercut even the current research and therapy programmes devoted to their needs.[34] Despite protestations to the contrary, medical scientists have raised the spectre of a return to eugenic thinking.

Pre-natal diagnoses are used, in addition to detecting abnormalities, to determine the fetus' sex. Such investigations are pursued out of more than mere curiosity. Suggested applications of such findings include the limiting of the births of males with sex-linked diseases such as haemophilia and Duchesne muscular dystrophy. Some have suggested that sex determination could possibly also lead to a lowering of overall fertility rates in those Third World countries where persistent attempts to have at least one son lead to repeated pregnancies. But feminists have voiced the alarm that just as girl babies were traditionally more likely to be the victims of infanticide, so too female fetuses will be over-represented amongst the aborted if sex selection is allowed.[35]

When one turns to the more advanced reproductive technologies, similar problems are confronted. It is simplistic to suggest that such scientific breakthroughs are inevitably harmful to women, that they have been designed to undermine women's procreative power.[36] Many women might benefit from such treatments. But it is equally simplistic to argue that these technologies are somehow value free. The 'demand' for cures for infertility is in part elicited by the technologies themselves. Infertile women are informed that they have an 'illness' that medicine can 'cure'. Childless women who feel a need to conform to our society's normative maternal role are in effect forced to have recourse to such treatments. Western culture is strongly pro-natalist. Although fertility rates have declined, the percentage of women bearing children has increased. In the 1920s, over 20 per cent of white United States women were childless at age forty; by the 1980s, the figure was down to 10 per cent.[37] It may be no longer expected that a woman will have a large number of children, but an enormous amount of normative pressure is exerted by governments, churches and the popular culture on women to 'fulfil' themselves by having at least one child. Prior to the advent of the reproductive technologies, the childless simply accepted their fate inasmuch as they could do little more than stoically put up with it. Now they feel driven to pursue the new options opened to them.[38] The reproductive technologies in fact rarely 'cure' infertility; at best they circumvent the problem. Helping the infertile reproduce may have the perverse result – at least for those who pass on genetically related complaints – of actually raising the incidence of infertility.

This is not the place to enter into a full discussion of the reproductive technologies, which range from simple artificial insemination (in which semen is injected with something as simple as a turkey baster), to embryo transfer (in which the egg is flushed out, fertilized and returned to the mother), to 'surrogate' mother-hood, the curiously misleading term employed to describe the situation in which a woman carries to term a child for another woman, her own egg having been inseminated by the other woman's partner, or having received the other woman's fertilized egg by embryo transfer.[39] For the purposes of this study, what has to be noted is that many of the moral issues these sophisticated techniques raise have a much longer heritage than most participants in the current discussions realize.

Women traditionally gained a good deal of status from childbearing. Infertility was, as we noted in previous chapters, almost always regarded as a problem and women everywhere attempted in a variety of ways to elicit conceptions, determine the sex of their child and protect themselves from miscarriages. If they could not have their own children they turned to those of others. Surrogacy arrangements have a long history. Cicero's lending his wife to Cato was a famous case in point. Evidence suggests that it was not rare for women to bear children for infertile sisters. Moreover, in previous societies it was far more common for children to be 'exchanged', so that households burdened with too many children sent their offspring to homes with too few. Such arrangements rarely occasioned much comment. Formal adoptions were practised in the ancient world, disappeared in the Christian west and resurfaced in the last century. No matter how children were obtained, what is significant is that in the past the importance of social parenting was taken far more seriously than the physiological act of childbearing. The irony is that as the twentieth-century world appears to grow more 'mechanical', a compensating concern to exalt the primacy of the biological has emerged. This evolution in mentality helps explain the desperation of the infertile to become parents.[40]

Physicians, of course, have always counselled the infertile, but a qualitative change occurred when doctors began to step in to act as intermediaries in the birth process. Their direct intervention goes back to at least the eighteenth century. In 1776 the Scottish surgeon John Hunter oversaw the first successful attempt at human artificial insemination, when he instructed a linen-draper who suffered from hypospadias on how to use a warm syringe to impregnate his wife.[41] The medical surveillance of the fetus began in 1818 when a surgeon pressing his ear against a woman's corset first heard the fetal heartbeat.[42] The probability of human artificial reproduction was signalled when, in 1890, the first successful embryo transfer was carried out on rabbits by the Cambridge scientist and antifeminist Walter Heape.

The reproductive technologies which subsequently emerged have both liberating and coercive potentials. Doctors intent on 'medicalizing' the problem of infertility naturally focus on individual problems and ignore social and environmental factors. They are particularly loath to admit that much infertility, in the form of pelvic infections caused by IUDs, Caesarian sections and other forms of intervention, is in fact caused by medicine itself. Although the poor are more likely than the well-off to suffer from infertility, the latter are the main beneficiaries of the new therapies. Third World babies are sold to customers in the industrialized west. Men become fathers, but women are the ones experimented on in the often painful and humiliating processes that have as yet incredibly low success rates.[43] And as much as one sympathizes with the infertile, it would appear that the concern of many is not to help children (because adoption or fostering would offer an obvious outlet), but to help themselves.[44]

Most doctors claim, and probably believe, that their technology is socially neutral. But numerous critics have sensibly pointed out that the reproductive technologies clearly serve a social purpose in buttressing existing gender roles. In vitro fertilization and surrogacy arrangements are only offered to heterosexual couples in male-headed households; they are not made available to the poor, to racial minorities, to gays and lesbians. But if the new techniques are employed to shore up traditional family structures, they still are only symptoms, not causes, of existing social and sexual power relationships. Feminist scholars who are alive to the dangers of being labelled scientific Luddites concede that the new techniques cannot be obliterated; they argue that the challenge is to understand how they could be best turned to the purposes of addressing women's real needs. In the late nineteenth century, it might be remembered, some feminist opponents of birth control argued that contraceptives would reduce respectable women who only married in order to have children to the level of sex slaves. Similarly dire warnings have been expressed about the inevitably harmful effects of the reproductive technologies.[45] But women are no more or no less the victims of the new reproductive technologies than they were of the old.[46] It is a question of what they make of them. Artificial insemination has allowed lesbians to conceive without the direct involvement of men.[47] Women who devoted their twenties and thirties to careers and then turned their minds to childbearing only to find themselves infertile now have the option of seeking medical assistance.

The ancients explicitly linked reproduction to the needs of the household and the economy. It could be argued that the Victorian world was anomalous in attempting to privatize sexuality and cloak it in taboos. Today we once more live in a world in which conceptions, miscarriages, abortions and births are legitimate topics of public discussion. This is not altogether a bad thing. It is an idle wish to think that one could ever return to some simpler age when either fertility control or reproduction was 'natural'; they have always been the sites of political struggle.

The investigation of the issues raised by the new reproductive technologies brings us back to the argument advanced in the book's introduction. One could write a history of fertility control simply by chronicling the progressive advances made in contraceptive theory and practice. But to do so would require turning a blind eye to the ways in which the meanings of such activities were continually reshaped by concerns of class, culture and gender. An investigator of gender differences has noted,

> Although there is a widespread belief that the desire for children is either an inborn or an early acquired trait, the community and the state rarely leave to individuals the right to decide whether to procreate or not – in the same way that the society does not leave gender distinctions or the division of labour to chance.[48]

The issue of fertility control cannot be isolated from marriage and the relationship of the sexes. Children were never simply stoically accepted. Their value was always a question of debate. The question of family size was a topic over which spouses continually bargained and negotiated.

Fertility control was rarely 'unthinkable'; there were always some groups at some times that believed such controls were possible. This is not to suggest that deaths from starvation and infectious diseases were uncommon in the pre-industrial world or that fertility control by itself was responsible for the maintenance of a balance between population and resources. Nor would one deny that there was a major shift from the nineteenth century onwards, with the mass employment of contraception and abortion for the dramatic limitation of family size. But this 'fertility transition' was carried out by the use of traditional methods of fertility control. And even as national fertility rates fell, marked differences in attitudes and practices linked to class and gender concerns continued to be met.

The significance given to fertility control differed according to context. It has always been a means rather than an end. But though fertility control is primarily a product, not the cause of changing social and cultural relationships, it cannot be denied that a feedback effect does take place. The modern family structure has created a demand for highly effective forms of contraception; such contraceptives and the reproductive technologies to which they are linked serve present needs, but also create future options. Future family forms and gender roles will reflect their influence.

Notes

1 D. J. van de Kaa, 'Europe's Second Demographic Transition', *Population Bulletin*, 42 (1987), pp. 3–57; Alena Heitlinger, *Reproduc-*

tion, Medicine and the State (Macmillan, London, 1987), pp. 136–7.

2 Morton Mintz, *At Any Cost: Corporate Greed, Women, and the Dalkon Shield* (Pantheon, New York, 1985); Kathleen McDonnell, *Adverse Effects: Women and the Pharmaceutical Industry* (Women's Press, Toronto, 1986).

3 Philip M. Alderman and Ellen M. Gee, 'Sterilization: Canadian Choices', *Canadian Medical Association Journal*, 140 (1989), pp. 645–9.

4 Thomas M. Shapiro, *Population Control Politics: Women, Sterilization and Reproductive Choice* (Temple University Press, Philadelphia, 1985); Jeanne M. Simonelli, *Two Boys, a Girl, and Enough! Reproductive and Economic Decisionmaking on the Mexican Periphery* (Westview, Boulder, 1986), p. 163.

5 *The Guardian*, 2 September 1987, p. 7. The injected, long-term hormonal contraceptive Depo-Provera, though banned in North America because of its painful side-effects, was distributed by aid agencies in Third World countries. See also Stephen Trombley, *The Right to Reproduce* (Weidenfeld and Nicolson, London, 1988).

6 Alan Macfarlane, *Marriage and Love in England: Modes of Reproduction, 1300–1840* (Blackwell, Oxford, 1986), p. 43.

7 John Caldwell, 'Toward a Restatement of Demographic Transition Theory', *Population and Development Review*, 2 (1976), pp. 321–66. For a more up-to-date account see John E. Knodel, Apichet Chamratrithirong and Nibhon Debavalya, *Thailand's Reproductive Revolution* (University of Wisconsin Press, Madison, 1987).

8 Malcolm Potts and Pouru Bhiwandiwala (eds), *Birth Control; An International Assessment* (MTP, Lancaster, 1979).

9 Malcolm Potts, Shyam Thapa and M. A. Herbertson, *Breast Feeding and Fertility, Journal of Biosocial Science Supplement No. 9* (Galton Foundation, Cambridge, 1985).

10 Carol Joffe, *The Regulation of Sexuality: Experiences of Family Planning Workers* (Temple University Press, Philadelphia, 1986).

11 Kristin Luker, *Taking Chances: Abortion and the Decision Not to Contracept* (University of California Press, Berkeley, Cal., 1975).

12 Heitlinger, *Reproduction*, pp. 154–5.

13 Kristin Moore, Margaret C. Simms and Charles L. Betsey, *Choice and Circumstance: Racial Differences in Adolescent Sexuality and Fertility* (Transaction, Oxford, 1986), p. 127; Cheryl D. Hayes, *Risking the Future: Adolescent Sexuality, Pregnancy and Childbearing* (National Academy Press, New York, 1987); Maris A. Vinovskis, *An 'Epidemic' of Adolescent Pregnancy? Some Historical and Policy Considerations* (Oxford University Press, Oxford, 1988).

14 Vinovskis, *An 'Epidemic' of Adolescent Pregnancy?*.

15 Caroline Whitebeck, 'The Moral Implications of Regarding Women as People: New Perspectives on Pregnancy and Personhood', in *Abortion and the Status of the Fetus*, eds William Bondeson and H. Tristram Engelhardt (D. Reidel, Dordrecht, 1983), pp. 247–72.

16 John D'Emilio and Estelle B. Freedman, *Intimate Matters: A History of Sexuality in America* (Harper and Row, New York, 1988), p. 331.

17 Benjamin Schlesinger (ed.), *Family Planning in Canada* (University of Toronto Press, Toronto, 1974), pp. 150–5.

18 Luker, *Abortion*, pp. 168–70.

19 Ronald Dworkin, 'The Great Abortion Case', *New York Review of Books*, 36, 11 (29 June 1989), pp. 49–53.

20 Kristin Luker, *Abortion and the Politics of Motherhood* (University of California Press, Berkeley, Cal., 1984).

21 Kajsa Sundstrom-Feigenberg, 'Reproductive Health and Reproductive Freedom: Maternal Health Care and Family Planning in the Swedish Health System', *Women and Health*, 13 (1988), pp. 45–8.

22 Daniel Maguire, *The New Subversives: Anti-Americanism of the Religious Right* (Continuum, New York, 1982).

23 Simone de Beauvoir, *The Second Sex*, [1949] tr. M. Parshley (Vintage, New York, 1974); Betty Friedan, *The Feminine Mystique* (Norton, New York, 1963); Sherry Ortner, 'Is Female to Male as Nature is to Culture?', in *Woman, Culture and Society*, eds Michelle Rosaldo and L. Lamphere (Stanford University Press, Stanford, 1974).

24 Shulamith Firestone, *The Dialectic of Sex: The Case for Feminist Revolution* (Morrow, New York, 1970), pp. 224–7. See also N. Birdsall and L.A. Chester, 'Contraception and the Status of Women: What is the Link?', *Family Planning Perspectives*, 19 (1987), pp. 14–18.

25 Boston Women's Health Book Collective, *Our Bodies, Ourselves* (Simon and Schuster, New York, 1973); Nancy Kleiber and Linda Light, *Caring for Ourselves: An Alternative Structure for Health Care* (University of British Columbia School of Nursing, Vancouver, 1978); Claudia Dreifus, *Seizing Our Bodies: The Politics of Women's Health* (Vintage, New York, 1978).

26 Ann Oakley, *Women Confined: Toward a Sociology of Childbirth* (Martin Robertson, Oxford, 1980); Barbara Katz Rothman, *In Labor: Women and Power in the Birthplace* (Norton, New York, 1982).

27 On the La Leche League see Rima D. Apple, *Mothers and Medicine: A Social History of Infant Feeding, 1890–1950* (University of Wisconsin Press, Madison, 1987), pp. 177–9.

28 Sheryl Burt Ruzek, *The Woman's Health Movement: Feminist Alternatives to Medical Control* (Praeger, New York, 1978), p. 57.

29 *New York Times*, 27 May 1989, p. 10.

30 Edward Shorter, *A History of Women's Bodies* (Basic Books, New York, 1982), p. 140.

31 Barbara Katz Rothman, *Recreating Motherhood: Ideology and Technology in a Patriarchal Society* (Norton, New York, 1988), pp. 159–68.

32 Barbara Katz Rothman, *The Tentative Pregnancy: Prenatal Diagnosis and the Future of Motherhood* (Viking, New York, 1986).

33 On women's sense of being separated from their bodies see Emily

Martin, *The Woman in the Body: A Cultural Analysis of Reproduction* (Beacon, Boston, 1987), p. 84.

34 E. Peter Volpe, *Patient in the Womb* (Mercer, Macon, 1984), p. 7.

35 Sex selection can be achieved prior to conception by separating the spermatozoa and inseminating artificially. Mary Anne Warren, *Gendercide: The Implications of Sex Selection* (Rowman and Allanhold, Totawa, NJ, 1985), pp. 11, 160–6.

36 Gena Corea, *The Mother Machine: Reproductive Technologies from Artificial Insemination to Artificial Wombs* (Harper and Row, New York, 1979).

37 Ronald R. Rindfuss, S. Philip Morgan and Gray Swicegood, *First Births in America: Changes in the Timing of Parenthood* (University of California Press, Berkeley, Cal., 1988), p. 62.

38 Rona Achilles, 'New Age Procreation', *Healthsharing*, (Fall, 1985), pp. 10–14; Michelle Stanworth, ed., *Reproductive Technologies: Gender, Motherhood, and Medicine* (University of Minnesota Press, Minneapolis, 1987).

39 See the special issue devoted to 'Embryos, Ethics, and Women's Rights: Exploring the New Reproductive Technologies', of *Women and Health*, 13 (1987).

40 A further irony is that the twentieth-century exaltation of the joys of maternity which has so clearly captivated the infertile was advanced by the birth control advocates as a way of defending the need for family limitation. The Catholic church was alarmed by both artificial reproduction and contraception.

41 F. N. L. Poynter, 'Hunter, Spallanzani, and the History of Artificial Insemination', in *Medicine, Science and Culture: Historical Essays in Honor of Oswei Temkin*, eds L. G. Stevenson and R. P. Multhauf (Johns Hopkins University Press, Baltimore, 1968).

42 Ann Oakley, *The Captured Womb: A History of the Medical Care of Pregnant Women* (Blackwell, Oxford, 1984), p. 25.

43 Gregory Pincus noted that little work was done on male sex problems because few men ever volunteered to be studied. Those who did were concerned by infertility; never by the problem of being too fertile. Pincus, *The Control of Fertility* (Academic Press, New York, 1965), p. 194.

44 R. Snowden, G. D. Mitchell and E. M. Snowden, *Artificial Reproduction: A Social Investigation* (Allen and Unwin, Boston, 1983), pp. 68ff.

45 Patricia Spallone, *Beyond Conception: The New Politics of Reproduction* (Macmillan, London, 1989).

46 A similar debate has focused on the use of anesthesia. In the 1920s women demanded 'twilight sleep'; in the 1970s they swung back to 'natural childbirth'.

47 Hilary Homans (ed.), *The Sexual Politics of Reproduction* (Gower, London, 1985), p. 11.

48 Cynthia Fuchs Epstein, *Deceptive Distinctions: Sex, Gender and the*

Social Order (Yale University Press, New Haven, Conn., 1988), p. 201; and see also Kathleen Gerson, *Hard Choices: How Women Decide About Work, Career, and Motherhood* (University of California Press, Berkeley, Cal., 1985).

Index

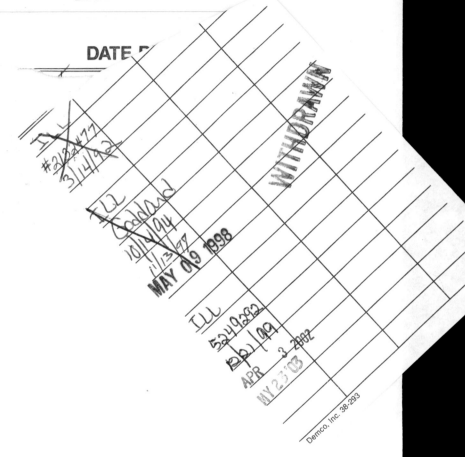